Ch
Development

Joan Gomez was born in Suffolk, but has lived most of her life in London. She was Senior Scholar at St Paul's Girls' School and studied medicine at King's College, London. After she married George Gomez, a London GP, and was bringing up their large family, she began writing. She also ran a nursery school and a club for the elderly. Later, when the children were older, she specialised in Psychiatry and became a consultant at Westminster Hospital. Now she divides her time between patients and writing.

Dr Joan Gomez

Childhood Development

From conception to 12 years old

VERMILION
LONDON

1 3 5 7 9 10 8 6 4 2

Copyright © Joan Gomez

Joan Gomez has asserted her moral right to be identified as the author of this work in accordance with the Copyright, Design and Patents Act, 1988.

All rights reserved. No part of this publication may be reproduced, stored in a retrieval system, or transmitted in any form or by any means, electronic, mechanical, photocopying or otherwise, without the prior permission of the copyright owner.

First published in the United Kingdom in 1997 by Vermilion, an imprint of Ebury Press
Random House UK Ltd
Random House, 20 Vauxhall Bridge Road, SW1V 2SA

Random House Australia (Pty) Limited
20 Alfred Street, Milsons Point, Sydney,
New South Wales 2061, Australia

Random House New Zealand Limited
18 Poland Road, Glanfield
Auckland 10, New Zealand

Random House South Africa (Pty) Limited
Endulini, 5a Jubilee Road,
Park Town 2193, South Africa

Random House UK Limited Reg No 954009

A CIP catalogue record for this title is available
from the British Library

ISBN: 0 74 932273 X

Typeset by Avon Dataset Ltd, Bidford on Avon, Warks
Printed and bound in Great Britain
by Cox & Wyman Ltd, Reading, Berkshire

Papers used by Vermilion are natural, recyclable products made from wood grown in sustainable forests.

To my dear children

Francesca
Lavinia
Vivienne
Peter
Paul
Anthea
George
Matthew
Coralie
and Helena

– who have taught me so much.

Contents

	Introduction	1
1	Laying the Foundations: conception to birth	5
2	Brand-New: the first six weeks	37
3	Becoming A Person: six weeks to six months	68
4	Miracle Months: six to twelve months	83
5	Toddlers: one to three years	107
6	Three–Four–Five Child Alive: the pre-school years	130
7	Love, Life and Laughter: taking stock	153
8	School-time: five to ten years	170
9	The Threshold: eleven to twelve years	197
10	Brothers and Sisters	213
11	Hiccups in Development	219
12	What They Were Like: famous people as children	235
	APPENDICES	
i	Toys and Play	246
ii	Books and Reading	254
iii	Route Plan Chart	263
iv	Puberty Chart	269
v	Tooth Chart	271
vi	Sleep Chart	273
vii	Immunisation Schedule	276
viii	Growth Chart: Boys	279
ix	Growth Chart: Girls	281
x	Useful Addresses (UK, Australia and USA)	285
	Index	291

Introduction

The world has no such flowers in any land,
And no such pearl in any gulf the sea,
As any babe on any mother's knee.
　　　　　　　　　Swinburne: 'Pelagius'

So – you are joining the greatest and best-loved fellowship in the world: the mothers. We are the miracle-workers who hold the next generation and through them, all the generations to come, in our arms. It is we who set off, with an act of love, the marvel of making a living, breathing, feeling, unique individual from a morsel of tissue no bigger than a full-stop.

From the first pricking of your breasts, after the period that didn't come, you know that you are on the threshold of something very important. Nothing else you ever do in your life comes up to this. It's exciting, a touch scary and certainly strange. And you have much more than a ringside seat from which to experience your child's development. You are part of it.

To start with, what happens is a secret, safe inside your body, and hidden even from you. Later on the new person makes him- or herself felt, stirring and stretching and making you big. Then comes the magical moment when at last you meet. In that instant you are a different being. You find that you have feelings you never knew you were capable of: a mix of aching

Childhood Development

tenderness and fierce protectiveness. Your little one is so vulnerable, and innocent.

This sounds seriously sentimental stuff – but you have an awakening in store. Your baby's personality soon begins to emerge, and you are in for shocks and surprises, battles of will – and a liberal sprinkling of fun. Seeing how your child changes and grows and learns about life is the most fascinating, amazing drama. But of course you won't have the leisure to sit back and observe: you'll be busier and more tired than you could imagine.

That is the reason I want the privilege of going with you on this momentous journey into new territory, and sharing with you all I have found out – as a doctor, a psychiatrist and proudest claim of all, a mother. I want you to be able to enjoy it all to the full, and not to miss or misunderstand the subtler details of what happens. For example, if you are not sure what to expect, you may be worried about something that is perfectly normal, or overlook a tiny, but significant, step forward.

You will want to know what you can do to help your child's development at each stage. Children change so fast that sometimes, just when you think you have the situation taped, a new twist or turn can catch you out. Like when young Joanna learned – overnight – to unfasten the cot-sides. One factor to keep in mind is that your child is unique. There never has been and never will be another human being exactly the same – even identical twins aren't. You shouldn't look for your child to be sitting up, talking or dry all night at the same age as the baby next door, or what knowledgeable friends tell you is right. My son Paul learned to tie his shoe-laces long before he went to school, but Peter, his twin, went around with his laces draggling on the pavement when he was eight.

For sure, your child's progress will take the same direction as that of other children, but the pace and

Introduction

the precise order of events is up to her or him, and not very relevant. When your friend's child is prattling away and your little one only seems to know two words, and one of them is 'No', remember that Einstein didn't talk until he was four. The twins are grown-up now and Peter is doing just as well as Paul in his career.

Your child's development is not like a trip down the motorway, with speed the be-all and end-all. It is more a matter of exploring with your youngster a winding path that ends up at the same destination of adulthood. As with any child on a walk, there'll be times when she wants to stop and pick a dandelion, or he is fascinated by some men working in the road. Other times he or she will be skipping ahead. Let's set out . . .

1

Laying the Foundations:
conception to birth

The most wonderful things will be happening over the next nine or ten months – and you won't even know it has all started until you miss a period, or perhaps have an oddly scanty one. Of course you know that you have made love, but not whether one of the millions of sperms from your partner has met and united with the single, vital ovum, or egg-cell, from you.

The meeting takes place in one of the Fallopian tubes. These tubes run from the ovaries, one on each side, where the egg-cells are stored and released at the rate of (usually) one a month. The ovum is wafted gently along the tube, taking two or three days for the journey, and finally reaching the womb. This is designed as a secure resting place, with a soft, warm, velvety lining: somewhere where a baby can grow and develop and all his or her needs are supplied, deep inside his mother's body.

The miracle of conception is the convergence of a male and a female germ cell. They instantly recognise that they were made for each other and one, the ovum, embraces the other and they become united. In that magic moment three people's futures are irrevocably changed. The woman becomes pregnant with all that implies; the man is a father-to-be; and the microscopically tiny entity that is part of them both starts on its life as a new, unique individual.

Already the coiled strands of DNA (deoxyribonucleic

acid) within each embryonic cell carry the complete blueprint for the infant's development. It programmes not only such ordinary human attributes as having five fingers on each hand and a brain that outstrips the most complex computer, but very personal characteristics. Eye and hair colour, and of course sex, are determined in the instant of conception, plus the more subtle legacies such as the potential talent for maths or music, science or art.

Apart from the secret life of the baby-to-be, hidden away out of sight, you are also changing. Your figure will gradually alter, but you will have time to adjust – and to buy a new outfit; your breasts will feel as though they are coming to life; and as your whole metabolism revs up you will feel glowingly warm whatever the weather. With the bodily changes there comes a roller-coaster of emotions: from heady exhilaration to deepest doubt, from happy anticipation to a feeling of being trapped. Whatever else, it won't be dull.

Twinkle-in-the-eye stage

You may have picked up this book when you have got no further than thinking about having a baby, and wondering what you might be letting yourself in for. If so, this is an ideal situation, because if you do decide to go ahead with the great adventure, you have the opportunity to plan ahead.

Pre-pregnancy Preparation

This is somewhere between going into training for an expedition up Everest and rehearsing for the star role in a West End play. Gillian and Jack were planners, and

Laying the Foundations

they took their family planning seriously. This is the common sense scheme they followed:

Contraception

Gillian stopped the Pill and she and Jack used condoms for a three-months' run-up before they started trying for a baby. This would not have been necessary with the other, non-hormonal methods of contraception. (Two months is probably long enough if you are impatient to get going.)

General health

It makes sense for both partners to be as fit as possible when they take the important step of making a baby. If Gillian in particular had been seriously overweight or more than ten per cent below the average weight for her height, she would have tried to put that right well in advance of the actual pregnancy. What is unwise is to plunge into a slimming jag just before becoming pregnant. It didn't matter that Gillian was a few pounds over the odds.

She and Jack gave their lifestyle an overhaul, to include regular doses of fresh air, exercise and sleep, and avoiding stress where that was possible.

Risks

You will not know for certain whether you are pregnant until a few weeks after conception, yet in those very early days, when your baby is at the embryo stage, his or her life is fragile. Development can be put off course in major ways. So it is prudent to side-step the avoidable snags from the moment you begin trying to become pregnant.

Smoking. Gillian and Jack both enjoyed a smoke. She

Childhood Development

went in for low-tar cigarettes with filters an inch and a half long; he preferred a pipe. Ought they both to give up? Yes, and in good time, since it takes several weeks for the toxic effects of tobacco to get out of the system. Smoking can impair a man's sperm, but the most damning aspect is its effect on the unborn baby if the mother smokes or is exposed to a smoky atmosphere often.

Smoking reduces the supply of oxygen to the developing baby; this effects his or her growth, specifically that of the brain. The children of smokers are slightly smaller than they would have been at birth, but more importantly, they are, on average, slower in learning to read than children whose mothers did not smoke during the pregnancy. Gillian and Jack had a hard struggle to give up what is becoming an out-dated habit.

Alcohol. Everyone knows that too much alcohol, especially in the occasional binge, can seriously damage a baby-in-the-making. As with smoking, the baby is likely to be undersized and he may develop the Foetal Alcohol Syndrome. This can involve characteristic abnormalities of the face, heart and limbs as well as reducing intellectual ability. Of course, all this is the worst scenario: the effects may be far less severe.

Jack and Gillian drank socially, but not heavily. The difficulty was to know how much alcohol would be too much from the baby's angle. Unfortunately, while the guidelines for how much is 'safe' for adults, especially those over forty-five, were revised upwards in 1995, there is still no certainty about the effects on the unborn baby. It appears that what most people would regard as moderate drinking can sometimes be harmful. Gillian decided to be on the safe side and cut alcohol out altogether before trying to conceive. Besides, with either alcohol or tobacco, there is an increased risk of miscarriage.

Laying the Foundations

It was different for Jack. Although three or four pints of beer a day could be enough to reduce the quality of his sperm, he wouldn't have the responsibility of sharing his bloodstream with the foetus during the pregnancy. In the event he compromised by cutting out booze with Gillian – apart from an occasional night out with the boys.

Other drugs. Heroin, as you'd expect, is disastrous to a developing baby, and there is definite evidence against cannabis. Not enough is known to be sure of the effects of other social drugs, but they are all likely to be risky. Gillian did not use any of them, nor did she take any medication, or over-the-counter preparations, including herbal types, without asking the doctor if they would be suitable if she became pregnant.

X-rays. These can be damaging from the moment the pregnancy begins, so it is essential to mention the position if an X-ray is suggested.

Infections. Gillian – or you – could ride through most infections without an unborn baby coming to any harm, but there are a few exceptions:

German measles (rubella): a mild feverish illness with a rash. You would take hardly any notice of it in the ordinary way but if you catch it in the first three months of pregnancy it can leave your baby blind, deaf and physically or mentally crippled. Gillian wasn't sure if she had ever had it or whether she had been vaccinated against it. This latter would have happened around the time she started her secondary school, between ten and fourteen. Nowadays rubella is included in the MMR vaccination (measles, mumps, rubella) given to babies at fifteen months. The MR (measles and rubella) campaign of 1994 meant that ninety-two per cent of schoolchildren in England are immune to rubella, so they can't pass it on to you or anyone else.

It only needed a simple blood test to check if Gillian was immune to rubella. It is done routinely in most

Childhood Development

ante-natal clinics, but ideally you need to know before you are pregnant. Gillian wasn't immune so her doctor vaccinated her right away. The only snag was that it meant a three months' wait before she could safely – for the baby – start a pregnancy.

Toxoplasmosis: a rare disease, but it can be harmful in pregnancy. It is caused by a parasite which is harboured in undercooked meat – the French are most often affected – and cats can also be infected. Gillian liked her food well-cooked anyway, and there was no need to part with her cat, Raffles, but she would not have taken on the job of cleaning out his litter tray if he had used one.

Two other infections that matter come from food:

Listeria: a type of food-poisoning that attacks pregnant women in particular. It can lead to septicaemia (blood-poisoning) or meningitis. It is conveyed by poultry and soft cheeses, especially the delicious French ones, and also blue cheeses, like Stilton. Gillian stuck to boring old Cheddar and made sure to cook chicken thoroughly.

Salmonella: the commonest cause of food poisoning, and, like listeria, it can be more serious in pregnancy than at other times. The infection can get into the blood-stream and so affect the baby-to-be. Eggs and poultry are the main sources, so Gillian made sure to boil her egg for ten minutes, even if it did not taste so nice. She avoided home-made mayonnaise, with egg yolk, and similarly, mousse and ice-cream.

STD (sexually-transmitted diseases): if there is the slightest chance that you could have been in contact with herpes, gonorrhoea or HIV, you need a check before you embark on a pregnancy. They can all harm your baby seriously unless you receive the appropriate treatment in due time, yet the symptoms can sometimes be so slight that you may not realise the germ has sneaked into your system.

Laying the Foundations

Saunas. An ordinary warm bath is fine but an extra-hot, extra-long one or a sauna can upset an unborn baby's brain development.

Massage and aromatherapy. Mention that you are pregnant, especially in the early stages when no one would guess. There should be nothing too vigorous. Energetic aerobics and step exercises are unwise in the first three months and awkward later.

Diet

Gillian and Jack thought it would be a good idea to get into the habit of eating the right foods in advance of a future pregnancy. In particular, as well as eating enough of the main foods, Gillian wanted to make sure that her reserves of the necessary minerals and vitamins were adequate for the demands a growing foetus would make. It was a matter of good housekeeping, especially as many women feel nauseous and are unable to eat properly during the early weeks of pregnancy.

Minerals. The greatest drain will be on stores of iron and calcium, so iron tablets are often prescribed during pregnancy. In the pre-pregnancy stage Gillian only needed to make sure of eating the foods which would provide the minerals for her own needs.

For iron this meant:
- sardines
- spinach
- All-bran
- egg yolk
- beef
- Marmite
- wholemeal bread
- dark chocolate – a perfect excuse for a small treat

For calcium the best sources were dairy products, especially:
- Cheddar Leicester or Double Gloucester cheese

sesame seeds
tinned sardines
broccoli
nuts

Vitamins. There is no need to rush out and buy vitamin pills. A normal, mixed diet is by far the healthiest way of getting your supplies, and for some vitamins it can be definitely harmful to have too much. Megadoses of vitamin A and D should be avoided, and it is not even advisable to eat liver if you might be pregnant, because it contains so much vitamin A. Too much vitamin C can also disturb the baby's metabolism, so that after he or she is born the baby reacts to taking much less from the milk he or she lives on then.

The vitamins that matter most in pregnancy are both in the B group: B9 (folic acid) and B12 (cobalamin). They act together and are essential for the perfect development of the nervous system and to avoid such disasters as spina bifida. They are also necessary for making blood. Here is where you find them:

Folic acid:
  green leafy vegetables and salads
  (preferably raw, steamed or microwaved)
  lentils
  soya
  wholemeal bread

Cobalamin:
  all the animal foods – beef, lamb, pork
  fish, especially mackerel
  a little in eggs and Cheddar cheese
  Alcohol
  and the type of Pill that contains an oestrogen interfere with the absorption of this vitamin.

Gillian was a vegetarian, which complicated matters for vitamin B12 (cobalamin). She decided to stretch a point and include dairy foods, including eggs, and some fish in her diet. These would be just as necessary all

Laying the Foundations

through the pregnancy. Had Gillian been a strict vegetarian or vegan it would have been vital for her to consult with a dietician: her GP would know where to send her. Apart from the cobalamin, vegetarians also have to make great efforts to provide enough protein for making a baby. Nuts and beans and soya are needed in generous quantities.

The Basic Diet. While you are waiting to become pregnant and afterwards also, the keynotes of a good diet are mixture and balance. That means having something from each of the five main food groups every day:
- milk and milk products
- meat, fish, cheese and eggs and other high protein foods, such as soya
- bread, cereals, potatoes, rice and pasta
- fruit and vegetables, preferably fresh rather than pre-packed and processed
- fats and oils

This is not the time for a lot of sweet and sugary or junk foods. You are too important to be filled with rubbish.

When pregnancy comes as a surprise

Unlike Gillian and Jack, far from having planned and prepared for your pregnancy, it may come as a complete surprise – even a shock. There are 101 ways this can happen, from a split condom to taking a risk 'just this once'. Don't panic. You will have plenty of time to re-jig your life to accommodate a small newcomer.

By the time you realise the situation you are likely to be a few weeks into the pregnancy. Should you worry on the baby's behalf? If the problem was a failure of one of the barrier methods of contraception – condom or diaphragm – this will have had no effect on the baby.

Secondly, it is not all that uncommon for a pregnancy to start up even when you have a coil in place. It is usually best to have it removed since it may set off a miscarriage, but there is also a small risk of this in having it extracted. If it is not removed the coil will finally come out with the baby, and won't have done any harm meanwhile.

The contraceptive pill almost never fails, unless you forget to take it one night, you have a gastrointestinal upset with vomiting and diarrhoea, or you are taking an antibiotic. Naturally enough, before you knew you were pregnant you would have gone on taking the Pill. Fortunately this situation does not appear to affect the early development of the foetus and there have been several research studies to show this. There is not so much certainty about the possible effects of the morning-after pill if that hasn't worked, but there has not been enough experience with this, to date. Its main snag is the high failure rate – up to forty-four per cent.

How do you know you are pregnant?

Whether you have been anxiously waiting and hoping, or your pregnancy catches you by surprise, there are signs and symptoms that will tell you the news and tests to confirm it.

Missing a period. Other causes could be over-enthusiastic slimming or exercising, an emotional upset or having just come off the Pill – or if you are in your forties, an early menopause. Sometimes very light periods can continue for a month or two into the pregnancy.

Breast sensations. You may feel tingling or pricking or your breasts may ache a little even sooner than you miss a period, but it is quite common for these feelings

Laying the Foundations

only to become noticeable from about the third month. Later on, your breasts get a little bigger and feel heavier: a supporting bra is comfortable.

Sickness and nausea. Not everyone has this problem, and most people don't actually vomit with it, but it is very common to feel nauseous, especially when your stomach is empty, like first thing in the morning, or when you are tired. This symptom can plague the early months of your pregnancy – just when you would otherwise be extra happy and excited. Nearly always it gets better by about the twelfth week, but meanwhile, small, frequent snacks are a help and a supply of plain, dry biscuits like Maries or Rich Tea.

Spending pennies. It is commonplace to have to pass water more often than usual in the early weeks. This improves in mid-pregnancy and doesn't come back until nearly the end, when the baby isn't leaving much room for your bladder.

Feeling funny. Unexpected faintness, unusual fatigue or just feeling 'different' can be a sign of a baby beginning.

Tests

You can buy a DIY kit over the counter at the chemist and try it out on a sample of your urine passed first thing in the morning, as soon as your period is overdue, but it is more accurate if you wait for two weeks or more after the missed period should have begun. The test picks up a hormone (HCG) which is produced within two days of the fertilised egg – now an embryo – settling into the womb. No test is right every time but the pregnancy test is ninety per cent reliable, done at the right time. It is rather more likely to give a false positive than a false negative result.

You can also get a test done – on blood or urine – by

Childhood Development

your family doctor, at a family planning clinic or by some chemists.

Ultrasound scans: this method provides a picture of your womb by transforming an echo into something visible. From about six weeks into a pregnancy an expert can just make out the presence of a developing baby by this method. Unlike X-rays, ultrasound is perfectly harmless.

Hearing the baby's heart: although it starts beating long before, it is not until the sixteenth week that the midwife or doctor is able to hear your baby's heart.

Once you know that you are truly part of a living miracle, you have a lot to think about and plan. To start with you need to discuss with your partner and your doctor where you will have your baby. The back-up of all the hospital facilities and expertise makes this the best and safest choice with a first baby, but if you are an old stager you may prefer a home delivery with a community midwife whom you will get to know in advance.

Ante-natal care is essential

You are likely to begin by going to the ante-natal clinic at the hospital, but there are also clinics in health centres or the GP's surgery. When you clock in for the first time you will be weighed and measured and your blood pressure taken. Tests on your water and your blood will confirm the pregnancy and cover such items as your blood group, whether you are immune to German measles and to various other illnesses you may have had, and whether you are anaemic. As well as the common type you get with heavy periods or other reasons for being short of iron, there are two unusual hereditary forms of anaemia which will be checked out: sickle cell and thalassaemia.

Laying the Foundations

A doctor will examine your heart and lungs and breasts and general physical status, and may do an internal examination: this gives information on the stage of pregnancy. There will also be lots of questions, especially about your periods and any illnesses you have had or that run in the family.

If everything seems straightforward at this point, it will be the community midwife or your family doctor who will monitor your progress on a monthly basis. At the twenty-eighth week you will go back to the hospital clinic, attending every week for the final month.

Between the sixteenth and eighteenth weeks you will be sent to the hospital for an ultrasound scan. This confirms the length of the pregnancy, identifies twins, may reveal the sex of the baby (if you want to know), and provides useful information about his or her position in the womb and that of the placenta: the source of all his supplies for living.

Journey into life

Ellie and Bill and *Sarah and Dominic* had each magicked their baby into beginning. Ellie and Bill were twenty-three and twenty-eight respectively, and had been together for nearly a year. Sarah and Dom were thirty-one and forty-one and got married with the full works four years before. Sarah had become aware of the tick-tick of her biological clock. Ellie and Sarah were both working girls. Ellie was PA to a business tycoon with a dodgy temper, while Sarah made videos and often had to travel to outlandish places.

Neither of them could rely on regular, easy hours, but there was nothing in either job that was specifically harmful to foetal development. If they had worked with chemicals or been involved, even indirectly, with anaesthetics, they would have had to think twice about continuing during their pregnancies.

The journey had started: 266 days to go from conception to birth.

First month

Babies. They were already making spectacular progress, from within hours of the merging of ovum and sperm. As a tiny ball of cells, each of the new beings travelled gently down the Fallopian tube and within a week had arrived in its mother's womb, to nestle snugly in the soft, thick lining. Each drew strength and nourishment directly from the enveloping tissue.

Dramatic developments were going on at amazing speed. A protective water jacket formed around each baby-to-be, to save him or her from bumps and jarring, and already three different layers of cells could be distinguished. One would grow to form skin and nails and hair, and also the brain and nerves; another would become liver, kidneys, stomach – all the internal organs except the heart; and the third layer would provide the material to make muscle, blood and bone.

A most important, special muscle is the heart.

This would start developing in the early weeks, together with a rope of blood vessels linking mother and baby. They would be the lifeline bringing food and oxygen from the mother, and ultimately forming the umbilical cord. From the third week, the placenta appeared as a special organ in one part of the womb, which was adapted to provide for the baby's needs. The ancient Egyptians, in 3000BC, called the placenta 'the bundle of life'. At the same time as the heart and essential blood vessels, the brain and liver were also beginning to be recognisable.

At the end of this first wonderful month both babies, now called embryos, were the size of a pea and very much alike. Over the next weeks and months, however,

Laying the Foundations

each would follow his or her own developmental destiny, according to an individual DNA programme.
Mothers. Ellie and Sarah knew nothing of these exciting events until around three weeks after conception, when they had all begun. Ellie's period was late – in fact it didn't come at all. She told Bill and he was as pleased as Punch, taking all the credit. Sarah, who had been anxious to start a pregnancy, had a light, two-day period and hoped. Her doctor said he would do a test in three weeks if nothing had happened by then.
The tests. Both were positive, Ellie's done at home and Sarah's by the GP. Now they were both plunged into the world of ante-natal care, examinations and testing. Everything was normal, so they had the go-ahead to start re-planning their lives.

Six weeks

Babies. The embryos, apart from their surrounding membranes, were now about ¼ inch (6 mm) long. They had little curved bodies with a definite head at one end and tiny buds on each side which would grow into arms and legs. Most miraculous of all, their minute, rudimentary hearts were already trying to beat.
Mothers. Ellie's breasts were pricking, a little like the way they felt before a period, but she felt well. Rather than feeling sick she was extra hungry. Sarah wasn't so lucky: she battled with waves of nausea and wondered why anyone ever had a baby. Dom was concerned, and made her cups of tea. The plus point was that mothers who have morning sickness seem less likely to suffer from post-natal depression later. This wasn't much consolation to Sarah when she was feeling queasy.

Two months

Babies. Now they were beginning to look like real

Childhood Development

human beings, with their facial features forming. Their eyes were covered by skin but this would develop into eyelids, and they would be able to open them in about three weeks. They could also turn their heads a little. Meanwhile the limb buds had been growing, with hands and feet and recognisable fingers and toes forming.

By their ninth week the embryos graduated to be called foetuses, the correct term right up to birth for a baby-in-the-making. Life-supplies all came through the vessels of the umbilical cord now.

Mothers. Ellie still felt fine, apart from the mild irritation of having to pass water more often than usual, even waking up some nights. It took her – and Bill – by surprise when she fainted without warning when they were queuing for seats at Wimbledon. She soon recovered and the doctor said that it didn't mean anything – only that standing for a long time was a bad idea now that her blood pressure was more reactive than normally.

Sarah was still feeling nausea uncomfortably often and began to worry that she wasn't able to eat enough for the foetus. She need not have been concerned. Except in severe, prolonged starvation, the foetus has priority and takes all it needs. Besides, someone who is less than an inch (2 cm) long doesn't need much nourishment.

Ten weeks

Babies. They looked like two doll-size professors, with heads disproportionately big for their bodies, to be expected at this stage. Their eyes were now open and they could open and close their tiny mouths. Their arms and legs had come on apace, and now they could close their fists as though to grasp something.

Mothers. Ellie and Sarah had their second ante-natal

check. Ellie had put on half a stone (3.5kg) and looked blooming. You will wouldn't have guessed that Sarah was pregnant from her slim figure, but she was putting on weight gradually. This did not mean that her baby wasn't growing as well as Ellie's. In fact, it turned out that he (or she) was probably growing a little faster of the two. In general boy foetuses are ahead of the girls.

By now both women had invented pet names for the babies they were carrying. They had begun to think of them as little people and sometimes had private conversations with them. Ellie's was called Lumpy and Sarah's Junior. Of course the mothers and fathers and grandparents-to-be were already mulling over real names for the babies, when they were born. There were shoals of suggestions.

Twelve to thirteen weeks

Babies. Lumpy and Junior now had all the essential parts and organs. Their finger- and toe-nails were beginning to grow, and they already had the tooth-buds in their gums for their twenty milk teeth, while the one who was to be a baby boy showed signs of sexual development. At this stage they were around 2¾ ins (7 cm) from head to bottom: their little legs were folded up in front of them and would have been difficult to measure. Their main progress now would be in growing bigger, and in making myriad finishing touches.

Their eyes, which had been open, now closed and would not open again until the refinements of eyelashes and eyebrows were in place, at about six months. In the last month the babies' eyes would be tight shut again, not in sleep, but to be ready for the momentous four-inch journey down the vagina into life. Because feeding would be so vital for their existence in the outside world, the two were learning to swallow and

Childhood Development

use their lips and tongues, with the amniotic fluid surrounding them to practise with.

Mothers. This was a good period. Ellie found she didn't need to go to the loo so often and Sarah stopped feeling sick, but she had a nasty fright. She noticed a brownish stain on her pants and then a little bright blood. Sarah was horrified. It could be the start of a miscarriage – she knew they were slightly commoner if you were over thirty. Her doctor was reassuring. He told Sarah to rest in bed for a couple of days and then take it easy for a week or two. Leave the housework to Dominic, he said.

The bleeding stopped and the risk period for miscarriage passed as Sarah went into the thirteenth and fourteenth weeks of her pregnancy.

From this time on the womb escapes upwards from the close confines of the pelvis, bounded by bones on all sides, into the roomier, stretchy abdomen. Accompanying this there is often a sense of relief and growing contentment in the mother's mind. Sarah, especially, felt this.

Sixteen to eighteen weeks

Babies. Lumpy and Junior could now move their arms and legs and heads and straighten their backs. They did so – vigorously – and often interspersed their exercise periods with little rests, perhaps a snooze: rather like us. They were growing fast and at the same time changing their bodily proportions to be more like real, post-birth babies.

Although their hearts had been beating steadily for many weeks, now the midwife or doctor could hear the reassuring tick-tick through the abdominal wall.

Mothers. Ellie was wondering if this odd sensation in her tummy was wind or indigestion, then the penny dropped. It was nothing to do with what she'd eaten: it

Laying the Foundations

was Lumpy kicking and stretching. Sarah had been longing to feel her baby 'coming to life' and was on the alert. She kept getting excited – far too early – over a passing collywobble, but finally there was no mistaking Junior's jerky movements. They were most noticeable when she was lying in bed. Being slim, she could feel them if she rested her hand on her abdomen. A lovely warm feeling of importance and optimism swept through her.

This was the time for the routine ultrasound examination. This involved drinking a lot of water beforehand but not going to the loo until after the test, a manoeuvre that lifts the womb up out of the pelvis so that the pelvic bones don't get in the way of the picture. The mothers' tummies were smeared with oil or jelly, so that the transducer (the pick-up head) could slide over the skin easily.

Both Ellie and Sarah were given fuzzy, black-and-white stills from the moving ultrasound pictures of their babies. Only the eye of faith – or expert interpretation – could make these pictures seem anything like a baby, but the mothers treasured them. The value of the examination was that they now knew that they did not have twins, that their babies had grown to approximately the right size for their age, calculated from the date of the last normal period, and that they had no major abnormality such as spina bifida. It was useful to know that the placenta (the afterbirth) was not so low down that it might block the baby's exit through the cervix (neck of the womb). Neither Ellie nor Sarah wanted to know the sex of her baby at this stage, although it might have been possible to tell.

At about this time both Ellie and Sarah had a maternal serum screening test. This is a blood test which was introduced towards the end of the 1980s to detect an increased risk of Down's syndrome, a common type of mental handicap. In nine out of ten women the test gives a negative result. Ellie was one of the nine, Sarah the tenth. It didn't mean that she was definitely carrying a Down's baby, but that the chances were more than 1:250.

Sarah felt that she could not ignore this. It was sensible to make sure of the position: by an amniocentesis. This involves taking a sample of the fluid surrounding the baby through a very fine needle, guided by ultrasound. Sarah felt an odd sensation but it did not hurt at all. After the procedure she had an anxious wait for four weeks for the result. The time seemed endless, but at the end she knew for certain that her baby would not have Down's syndrome. She breathed again. There are two other fairly recent tests for Down's. CVS – chorionic villus sampling – is done between eight and eleven weeks, but involves more risk to the baby than amniocentesis; and the use of ultrasound, perfectly safe, at around the fourteenth to sixteenth week. This may show up an extra broad head or thickened tissue at the back of the neck (the nuchal fold), but is too unreliable to be really useful.

Twenty to twenty-two weeks

Babies. Lumpy and Junior were growing at record speed and also learning a great deal. They were practising sucking and breathing movements, using the amniotic fluid in place of milk and air. They were also learning the muscle movements for crying, but until they had real air they could make no sound. Another preparation for the great moment of taking their first breath was the production of surfactant, a lubricant to prevent the inside surfaces of the lungs from sticking together.

The babies could open and close their eyes now, but all they could see was the velvety blackness inside the womb. Hearing was a different matter. They could hear

Laying the Foundations

and be reassured by their mother's regular heartbeats and also hear her voice when she spoke, and music played close up. You could tell by the way they quietened their kicking and moving – to listen. The sound which seemed to soothe them best was their own mother's voice: so it wasn't silly of Sarah and Ellie to talk to their unborn babes.

Mothers. Ellie and Sarah were feeling calm and happy and definitely pregnant, but not yet unwieldy. Around week twenty-four they had a routine test for diabetes: there is a type that crops up at about this time in pregnancy. They both had the all clear. The fact that babies were on the way was no secret and friends and relatives who had the skill started knitting and sewing tiny garments. It was also time for serious shopping. Vests and one-piece stretch suits were the basis, with knitted cardigans to go on top, and a shawl or cellular blanket to snuggle into. Bootees, woolly hats and absurdly small mitts are pretty and delightfully quick to knit, but they hardly ever stay on.

Super-essential were disposable nappies: they save a lot of work; but it is useful to have, say, a dozen terry towelling ones in case you run out. In any case they may be better at night when you don't want to change them so often. Plastic pants, say half a dozen pairs, to use over the top are especially useful in social situations and also save wet bedding. However, with any type of nappy they make a rash more likely if they are used as an excuse not to change Baby often enough.

The bigger items: carry-cot or Moses basket; transporter/buggy, stroller or a Rolls Royce big pram are often grandparental gifts, and that is how it was for Ellie and Sarah. Two extras were a baby sling, which is handy in the early days and feels natural, and one of those rear-facing car-seats which can be carried indoors without disturbing the occupant.

Childhood Development

Twenty-eight weeks to seven months

Babies. From this age a baby-to-be is said to be viable. That means that if he or she were to be born any time from now there would be a better than seventy-five per cent chance of survival. Of course, babies as young as twenty-three weeks have made it, with extra special care. By this stage Lumpy and Junior could blink like us if they were startled by a sudden noise. They could also have hiccups, which the mother may be able to notice. And at this stage they still have plenty of room to move and can kick and jump and turn somersaults. Mother's voice, singing or talking, gentle music with a regular beat, and the rocking rhythm of their mother strolling along all seem to settle a lively babe – temporarily.

Mothers. Sarah and Ellie were by turns excited and apprehensive as B-day – the birth day – drew nearer. At the visit to the hospital ante-natal clinic they were taught to do the Cardiff Count. This involved keeping a count of how often the babies moved, starting at nine in the morning and stopping when the number reached ten: noting the time. This was a daily check on the babies' well-being. Their heartbeats were monitored regularly, the midwife using a so-called foetal stethoscope, like a small trumpet. The more sophisticated CTG (cardiotography) can be applied in hospital, if there is a special reason to check the baby's heart – more likely later or during labour.

Thirty-two weeks

Babies. Lumpy and Junior hadn't much room to move now and at this stage most foetuses fit into the womb most comfortably upside down – that is, with their head towards the cervix, or exit. Lumpy was already in this position, but Junior still preferred to be head-

Laying the Foundations

uppermost. Both babies were covered in vernix caseosa, a kind of self-made skin cream. This acted as a protection from being immersed in liquid all the time. Think what it does to your skin if you soak in the bath too long.

Mothers. Ellie and Sarah, like their babies, were putting on weight fast. The average weight gain during a whole pregnancy is between twenty-two and 28lbs (10,000–12,500g). The baby usually accounts for six to 8½lbs (2700–3860g). The rest is made up of the womb and placenta, the baby's water cushion, bigger breasts (about 2lbs), extra body fluid and a little extra fat. Ellie and Sarah could look forward to getting a stone lighter from the moment their babies were born.

Thirty-six to forty weeks

Babies. A month ago they each weighed about 3lbs, now, at thirty-six weeks, this had gone up to 4½lbs, and would rocket up to around 7lbs by the great day: their birth day. The advance in size was impressive, but the really important achievement of these last few weeks was the enormous number of finishing touches. These were needed to make it a matter of all systems go, so that Lumpy and Junior could hold their own when their current lifeline, the umbilical cord, was severed.

Even so, some parts are not quite ready by the deadline: for instance the nervous system, the kidneys and liver. In fact the nerves are not finished to perfection for nearly a year after birth, and some babies are jaundiced when they are born because their livers are immature (this can be put right by bathing the baby in ultraviolet light). It is because of all the important developments in these last weeks in the safety of the womb that it is a good thing for the baby not to be born much before the due date.

Childhood Development

Since Junior still lay in the breach position – bottom down – which is not the ideal way to be born, the clinic doctor eased him (or her) around by gentle manipulation from the outside. Fortunately he decided to stay that way: it was a better fit. A few weeks before their EDDs (expected dates of delivery) Lumpy and Junior shifted position. Their heads became 'engaged', that is they slipped down between the pelvic bones and were held in the best possible position for birth. Around the same time the babies closed their eyes, as though they were asleep, another part of getting ready for the momentous four-inch journey into life.

Mothers. Ellie and Sarah found these last weeks tiring and tedious – all the worse when the weather was warm. Sarah had stopped working in the last month, but Ellie stuck it out for another fortnight, in spite of her backache and the awkwardness of bending down. Sarah's worst time was in the night. Junior seemed to have made that his exercise period. What with this and the fact that she could find no comfortable position to lie in, Sarah lost a lot of sleep. She felt worn out, while Ellie, by contrast had that odd burst of energy which grips some women near the end of pregnancy.

She decided to redecorate the tiny box-room that was to be Lumpy's nursery in the end. The trigger for Ellie's activity was waking up one morning feeling more comfortable in her abdomen: this was when Lumpy's head had moved down, taking the pressure off. Sarah also experienced the 'lightening' but had no wish to start spring-cleaning or the like.

Both mothers-in-waiting had packed their cases for hospital ages before. In fact Ellie had to keep opening hers to get things out, for instance the new range of cosmetics she had bought specially. There were ordinary things like nighties, toiletries, STs, slippers, dressing gown and a bedjacket. Ellie went for those short nighties like a man's shirt, buttoning all the way

Laying the Foundations

down, but Sarah had gone for glamour, and hers did not need a front opening since she was not planning to breast-feed.

The hospital, in each case, gave a list of what was needed for the baby, and then there were the luxurious extras. Ellie packed her bear, Walkman and a couple of novels. Sarah took a pack of notelets and stamps, and a tapestry picture to make, which would incorporate the baby's name. On top, in both cases was a list of names and telephone numbers.

Another set of clothes – clothes for two – was left ready to take to the hospital when mother and baby were to come home. Sarah worried whether her figure would be back to anything like presentable, but both she and Ellie had the tenderest delight in putting out a tiny vest, number 0-size stretch suit (white or primrose) and a shawl, as soft and warm as a hug.

Last day – first day

Babies. It was Lumpy and Junior, the babies in the case, who set off the process of labour and birth. They did it by releasing increasing amounts of a hormone called oxytocin, which made the womb muscles begin contracting. A hormone is a chemical messenger, made by the body, which travels in the bloodstream. Mother and foetus share their bloodstream, via the placenta, so the hormone from the foetus could affect his or her mother.

For their personal preparation for birth, the babies each closed their eyes and folded themselves into a neat aerodynamic shape – to make their progress as easy and fast as possible when the rhythmic pressure from the muscles of the womb was pushing them towards the cold, bright, big world.

Mothers. On and off for several months, Ellie and Sarah had felt their uterine muscles limbering up for

Childhood Development

the great task ahead, by tightening and relaxing. Sarah was surprised the first time it happened and her tummy felt hard, but she knew this wasn't the sort of contraction that meant action stations, labour beginning. When the real pains started, at first she thought that the curry she'd had for supper hadn't agreed with her, but when they kept fading away and then coming back some time later, she realised that these were labour pains.

Ellie's labour started differently, with 'the waters breaking', an escape of the fluid surrounding Lumpy. She had been quite energetic that day, and it had included a bumpy bus ride. She didn't have any pains when she felt the water running down her legs, but Bill was sure that he should get her to the hospital.

This was it: for Ellie and Sarah, the beginning of what they had been waiting for, for nine months; for the babies, the beginning of their lives.

Helping your baby's development during the pregnancy

It is a wonderful, true story: how your baby develops from almost nothing to a living, breathing personality with a great deal to give you, the mother. You, with her (or his) father have made it all possible, but that is not all. There is a lot for you to do to help, all through these hidden months before you meet.

Practicalities

Most of these have already been dealt with in the section on pre-pregnancy preparation (pp 6–13). They include general health, the risks to avoid, from smoking to saunas, and most fundamental of all: what to eat.
Diet. The basic guide-lines are laid out on pp 11–13, but when you know for certain that the pregnancy is under way, you need to review the position. To start

Laying the Foundations

with, forget the old wives' tale about eating for two. It doesn't apply in adult terms, but you will use about 200 extra calories a day throughout. That's the equivalent of a glass of full-cream milk, a chicken leg, a ladle of casserole, a small sultana scone or four apples. In fact, most mothers don't have to think about it at all – they just naturally take slightly bigger helpings.

Pregnancy seemed to make Ellie especially hungry, and if anything she would have eaten more than necessary. Sarah's appetite turned capricious, so that she didn't enjoy what had been her favourite foods; also, she wanted to keep slim. In her case it made sense to check that she was allowing herself enough. Now that they were definitely in the baby-building business, they were both prescribed iron and folic acid tablets, but no other supplements.

The ideal diet to provide for a precious new person doesn't have to be expensive, only full of variety. The blessings it can confer on your baby will last all her life: affecting her adult height and proportions, how well she does at school, and as a very long-term protection against such nasties as high blood pressure, stroke and heart disease.

Thinking and feeling

The foetus is not just a machine for turning food into flesh. As early as three weeks after conception he or she already has a brain. True it is a simple affair compared with what it will become, but it is the little creature's centre for learning and feeling. We know about the physical skills a baby learns before he is born: breathing, sucking, swallowing and moving his arms and legs. Some even discover the knack of sucking a thumb.

What is just as important and even more fascinating is the emotional learning. You can teach your baby-in-

Childhood Development

the-making to appreciate music, a delight to last a lifetime, from about the sixteenth week. Why not be like Sarah and set aside a period when you rest and listen to music with your baby? The source of the sound must be close to your bulge, and you will know if your little person is enjoying it if he quietens down his kicking to listen. Most unborn babies of about twenty-two weeks show a preference for Mozart over Beethoven, Country and Western compared with rock.

Another way to give your unborn baby pleasure is by combining music and movement: by dancing – but gently. Of course, the most beautiful sound in the world to your baby is your voice, singing or talking. He or she hears your voice, as you do, not only from the outside but through your body. Although she will like other human voices – they will be able to soothe her later, when she is out in the big world – it is only yours that she can share in this intimate way.

Your talking is a fundamental learning experience for your baby, and we all know how important communication is in life. Words will come later, but already your tone of voice and the cadences of your speech will be picked up by your baby. After he is born, his earliest 'talking', apart from crying, will include a quiet, wordless murmuring, often by himself. This will reflect your intonations, the balance of your sentences.

Conversations with your unborn baby are a vital part of education. These are some of the subjects you can talk about, aloud:
– your day, and what you are doing
– how you love him or her, whichever it is
– his father, granny and other people he will meet
– happy times you've had during the pregnancy
– happy times to look forward to as he grows up
– the great adventure of being born, shared with you

It is not only from the tone of your voice that your baby can tell how you are feeling. When you are upset

Laying the Foundations

the stress hormones in your blood get through to her, too. That is why it's better to sidestep awkward situations and confrontations at present and go for peace. Mothers who feel chronically stressed out tend to have restless babies – the last thing they need – so it makes good sense to consider your own happiness and well-being as a priority. A supportive partner is pure gold during pregnancy, and, failing that, a really good friend – or even your mother.

What about love? Most mothers fall in love with their babies at first sight, that first moment of wonder. But you can practise exchanging love with your baby long before this by the conversation method. Your feelings towards him will be conveyed in your tone, while the words will reinforce in you the growing feelings. When you finally meet you will already have a warm, understanding relationship.

It is tempting, but better not to try too hard to visualise what your baby will be like, especially in personality. If you expect a sweet, dainty little girl, like a doll to dress, you may be thrown if your baby turns out to be always hungry, always on the move, loudly demanding and the other sex. Or the lively hero-son you thought you were carrying is really a solemn-eyed daughter. Your first loving has to be blind: all you know for sure is that half his or her make-up comes from your genes, the other half from the father, and the particular mix has never been made before.

You may, like my friend Alice, feel definitely fed up at being pregnant, even if you went along with the idea in the beginning. It is not unusual, and certainly not a crime, to feel resentful towards the person growing inside you, who threatens to turn your life upside-down. That's sad for you. Alice felt guilty that her baby would be – and feel – unloved after she was born. In fact such an outcome is a rarity. There is a switch which operates just after the mother and baby

Childhood Development

have come through the pain and struggle of the birth together – and meet. Having a child may not be what you wanted, but when you see the person whom you have made with your own body and blood, helpless and weak and depending on you, your heart melts, willy-nilly.

Ante-natal classes

One way of helping yourself to relax and feel confident about pregnancy and the birth is to go to classes: if your partner goes with you, that is good, but by no means essential.

Hospital or community ante-natal classes

These are part of the NHS, free, and likely to gear you up for a birth in your local hospital. They comprise information about childbirth and parentcraft, and breathing and relaxation exercises. They are better in some areas than others.

National Childbirth Trust (NCT) classes

NCT classes are good quality but there is a small fee. The NCT also provides post-natal and breast-feeding advice which is free: you don't have to have attended the ante-natal classes.

Active Birth classes

These teach the idea of different positions during labour: most of them are included in the NCT classes. Active Birth and NCT classes promote 'natural childbirth' without artificial pain relief: an ideal that only some of us can achieve.

Laying the Foundations

Yoga specifically for pregnant women

These are available in some places and suit some people better than standard ante-natal classes.

A big advantage with any of these classes is the social side: making friends and discussing problems with others in a similar situation. Husbands and partners are welcome in all the classes, and the 'New Man' may enjoy being involved. Others, more trad, could not bear it: it does not mean they are lacking in love.

If you can't get along to regular classes, don't worry. If you take a reasonable amount of exercise your muscles will stay in good trim, and at the time of the actual birth you will be told what to do, step by step. Anyway, in the excitement of the real thing it is easy to forget what you have been taught in the classes.

Father's role

Because they don't have any of the physical changes of pregnancy, fathers' preparation for parenthood must be all in the mind. It is difficult for a man to envisage what his baby will be like: they seem only able to think of big children whom they can play with. It is up to us, the mothers, to bring fathers in and help them to have as much of the joy as possible. They need to feel that their part is important: much more than a single act of love. It is especially important for the father-to-be to have a sense of worth, and to know that he will be loved doubly when he is a dad.

Men need to understand how precious their support can be to the mother throughout this joint project, and that the unborn baby can already learn to recognise his father's voice as different and better than that of other men. This is a side benefit when a couple talk in bed, when the noise and bustle of the day is over. The more a man can be helped to share the pregnancy, the more at ease he will feel with the baby.

Grandparents' corner

Grandparents, they say, have all the fun and none of the responsibility. In fact, their role is often an essential one, particularly in the later stages of the pregnancy, and of course a grandmother is likely to be a vital cog in the family machinery during the first weeks of her grandchild's existence. Grandparents, especially grandmothers-to-be, are expected to be delighted from the moment they hear the news, and indeed many of them positively look forward to their new status.

Not all, however. These days when a woman of forty-five or fifty-five seems young, and may be a dynamic business woman, or a man around his fifties is particularly keen to come across as full of new, youthful ideas, the terms granny and granddad simply don't fit. If you are pregnant and your parents or in-laws come into this category, don't be hurt, be understanding. They all come round in the end.

From the grandparents' point of view, you have a tricky path to follow. Your age and experience are of undoubted value, but the absurd pride of some young couples can make it difficult to be gracious about it. The grandparents' role is to be available on the sidelines, ready to advise or help, but doing nothing which could be seen as 'taking over'. There is an affinity between the grandparents' generation and the youngest to look forward to over future years. It is cement for the family in an uncertain world.

2

Brand-New:
the first six weeks

It's exciting, awesome and there is no turning back for either of you – the one giving birth, the other being born. Your baby, finding himself uncomfortably cramped in the womb – hardly room to move – had set off the whole process with a hormone that stimulated your uterine muscles (see p 29). After that, all the effort was left to you, a stint of many hours' muscular exertion.

Giving birth

In fact you are giving life: the greatest benefit anyone can bestow. You can feel proud.

Labour

The practical aspect of helping your baby to enter the real world involves hard physical work that may go on for twelve hours non-stop.

Starting signals. Any of these may be the first intimation that it has begun:
- a show: this means a bloodstain on your pants for a day or two, or the escape of a small quantity of blood-stained, jelly-like mucus from your vagina all at once. This had been acting as a kind of seal in the cervix, the neck of the womb through which the baby will emerge.

Childhood Development

- increasingly frequent and long-lasting twinges of discomfort or stomach-ache, sometimes accompanied by a pain or ache in the back. This means that the womb muscles are getting into gear for the task ahead.
- a liquid starts trickling, then running, out of the vagina in a way that you can't control: part of the amniotic fluid surrounding the baby.

Stages of labour

First stage: this consists of increasingly strong and frequent contractions, as the muscles tighten up round the baby, pressing her head against the cervix, at first gently then with more force. Little by little the cervix stretches and relaxes, rather like what happens when you push your foot down into your tights. The contractions may feel like bad period pains or cramps, but the one good thing about them is that they ease off at intervals. You may also get a backache, but this may not go on all the time.

When the contractions are few and far between, at the beginning of this stage, have a light snack of something easy to digest like breakfast cereal or toast, because you won't be able to eat or drink when labour gets properly under way. Walking around probably helps the labour along, but do lie down when you feel like it. With a first baby, your body is experiencing something tremendous which has never happened before and this stage may last twelve hours. It will be less with any other babies you have, when your body knows the ropes.

Just as you are beginning to find the griping sensations difficult to bear – they have settled low down in your abdomen by now – they change in character. You move into the next stage.

Second stage: this is the home run, which is much shorter and ends up with the baby in your arms. At some point in the first stage, often towards the end, although, as in Ellie's case (see p 30) it can be at the very beginning, 'the waters break' – this is the escape of the bulk of the baby's cushion of amniotic fluid which protected him all through pregnancy. What breaks is the thin membrane which had held the fluid in while it was needed, and there is no discomfort to you when it gives way, only the unexpected sensation of wetness.

Once the fluid has gone your muscles can get to grips with pushing the baby directly. Progress revs up. In fact one way of starting labour off deliberately (induction), or of speeding it up, is to make a nick in the membrane, releasing the liquid. In the second stage, instead of being like period pains only worse, the contractions feel purposeful and powerful. You are carried along by an urge to push to your maximum and the midwife – or doctor – is encouraging you. Then, when the urge is at its strongest, and you really want to push, the midwife tells you not to.

This is excellent news. It means that the baby's head, the most difficult part, is beginning to emerge, and it will come through most easily if the midwife can guide it. She turns the baby's body a little so that it, too, slithers out smoothly. It is better for this skilled and delicate manoeuvre to happen without any rush, which is why you need to hold back from pushing at this crucial point. It also helps to avoid a tear in the perineum, the skin and tissues round the entrance of the vagina. These have to stretch to allow the baby's head through – better done slowly and gently than as the result of a hard shove.

At this stage, you will not have much feeling in the perineal tissues, and it is common for them to develop a small slit without your noticing. If the perineum seems tough and at risk of tearing badly, a little cut may be made in it (which you won't feel) to allow the baby's head to slip through comfortably. This is called an episiotomy.

Childhood Development

Now is the climax and the reward for the long months of waiting and the long hours of labour: your baby is born. She may lie against your skin for your body heat to help her keep warm for a brief moment, the umbilical cord is cut, and you are likely to hear her first, miraculous cry towards independence – her heart-catching, lamb-like cry. The midwife will tell you that you have 'a beautiful little daughter – or son'. But labour isn't quite over yet.

Third stage: this is the passing out of the placenta, or afterbirth, its great task of nourishing the foetus during the past nine months completed. It usually follows soon after the birth, certainly within twenty minutes. The womb muscle makes one final effort and the midwife helps by pulling gently on the cord. But you will have more exciting things to think about and may hardly notice what is going on.

Now is the time for tidying you up and making you comfortable, but first, while the parts are still numb from being stretched, any stitches that are needed after an episiotomy or perineal tear are done. You also have an injection of local anaesthetic. Then you are washed and helped into a fresh, clean nightie, and your baby, snugly wrapped, is by your side. You are a mother, proving your womanhood as nothing else can.

Pain relief

Both the Active Birth and NCT classes aim at so-called 'natural childbirth' – without drugs or other artificial ploys to deal with any pain. The idea is to distract your mind from messages about pain by teaching you to concentrate on different breathing techniques at every stage of labour. The ordinary hospital or community ante-natal classes also include helpful advice on methods of breathing at each stage, but without such

Brand-New

high expectations. Of course, it is splendid if you can sail through the whole business of giving birth without feeling anything worse than mild discomfort. Don't feel a failure if you find, like most of us, that you need some help.

Non-drug methods. There are a few non-drug methods which work for some people: for instance, hypnosis, for which you must practise beforehand, acupuncture or the TENS apparatus. This is a method of stimulating the nerves electrically so that they are too busy to convey pain sensations: you get a tingling instead – if it is effective for you. There's no guarantee with any of these methods.

Pain relief involving medication comes in several types:

Pethidine. Pethidine, given by injection early in labour, dulls the discomfort and makes you feel a little strange. It tends to make the baby drowsy if you have the injection within three hours of the birth.

Gas and air (usually Entonox). This is what both Ellie and Sarah plumped for. This is a mild anaesthetic which you breathe in from a mask which you hold in place yourself. It doesn't affect the baby and you can't do yourself any harm; you use it as and when you need it and you are in control. The trick is to take a few good breaths at the beginning of each contraction. Sarah and Ellie were expert at the technique by the time the pains were unpleasantly griping, towards the end of the first stage.

Epidural anaesthesia. An epidural blots out pain almost completely but doesn't put you to sleep. It is particularly useful with a complicated birth, for instance twins or when the baby is in an awkward position. It is also often used for a Caesarean birth, and some mothers prefer to have an epidural for a perfectly ordinary birth – to be sure of not feeling too much. All that is involved is an injection in the back which interrupts sensation in the lower half of the body. **Full anaesthetic**. This is always available at the crunch, but this is only likely when the birth has to be assisted in some way.

Water births

These sound 'green' and were very fashionable a few years ago. The advantages were thought to be a more comfortable labour for the mother, with less need for pain relief, and the birth less of a shock to the baby. After all, he or she had been surrounded by fluid in the womb. The snags have shown up in a national survey, published in December 1995. There are increased dangers for the baby of breathing problems, infections and hypothermia, with more likelihood of landing up in the intensive care unit (ICU) for survival. There is also an increased risk of complications for the mother.

Fathers and the birth

They, too, may reduce the mother's pain. New men, and those who profess to be, are usually dead keen to be present at the birth of their child. Ellie's Bill was one such. In fact he felt himself to be something of an expert in these matters, on the strength of the two classes he'd been to with Ellie. He was around from the last part of the first stage, and tried to ease the contractions by rubbing Ellie's back. He wasn't a wonderful masseur, but where Ellie did find him a strength and a comfort was in the second stage. He held her hand and talked to her all through. For this he remained at the head end, partly because he felt oddly guilty about what was going on at the baby's end. He shared Ellie's delirious first sight of their daughter.

Sarah's Dom was different. He said he didn't want to be involved, but waited, a nervous wreck, outside.

Sarah wasn't hurt. She was certain of Dom's love, but knew that he wouldn't be able to cope with his own powerful emotions if he were present for the physical part. For him, birth was even more of a miracle than it was for Bill: he thought Sarah the most wonderful woman in the world when he saw their son. Sarah felt a great affinity with her own mother – all mothers.

Dom felt an unaccustomed sense of unity with his father from the time of the birth; so indeed did Bill with his father, although they had not always hit it off.

Being Born: the baby's angle

While labour is hard work for mothers, for the babies it is a long ordeal of being squeezed and pushed helplessly towards the unknown. With each contraction the baby's heart-rate speeds up temporarily. It is already much faster than an adult's, at 120 to 160 beats a minute compared with ours at sixty to eighty.

The baby's heartbeat gives an indication of how well he is standing up to the stresses of being born. It is taken as a sign of distress or at least discomfort, if the rate is too fast or too slow. The baby may need help to be born more quickly. It is to check the baby's heart that the midwife listens with a trumpet stethoscope or an electronic monitor over the mother's abdomen increasingly often as labour progresses. There are also receivers which can be strapped in place to give a continuous record of the baby's heartbeats and the mother's contractions on a computer screen.

In most cases there is no cause to 'rescue' the infant. He or she comes through the birth process as normally as Ellie's and Sarah's babies did.

Childhood Development

First breath

The baby looks an alarming leaden blue or white while he or she is actually coming out of the vagina, but after her first indignant cry the intake of oxygen brings the reassuring pink or dusky red colour of the newborn. Cutting the cord literally cuts off the supplies of food and oxygen. Now the infant has to fend for himself – well, almost.

Ellie's daughter began to cry almost before she was out of the vagina, but Sarah's son was quieter. He began breathing regularly as soon as his face and body had been wiped dry.

The Apgar test

When he is one minute old and again at five minutes the new baby has to pass an exam, with marks out of ten. This is the Apgar test, named after a female American children's doctor. It is an assessment based on heart-rate, breathing, muscle tone, reflexes and colour. The top score is ten, but anything from seven upwards is fine. Less than five indicates a need for extra oxygen: this may just be a matter of clearing the baby's airways with a mucus extractor, or blowing oxygen lightly over his face. Of course there are more thorough-going methods available if necessary.

Apgar Criteria

Heart-rate	over 100	2
	below 100	1
	absent	0
Breathing	regular, crying	2
	slow, irregular	1
	absent	0

Brand-New

Muscle tone	moving actively	2
	moving limbs only	1
	limp, floppy	0
Reflexes	cough or sneeze	2
(to a tickle up the nose)	pulls a face	1
	nothing	0
Colour	pink	2
	body pink, hands and feet blue	1
	blue, pale	0

The other measurements which are made are weight, head size by the circumference, and length. The first and last of these are often included in the birth announcement cards proud parents send out, but it is the first two which are of interest to the doctors. If either of these measurements is much smaller or much bigger than the average they may want to do some extra tests.

Low birthweight means less than 5½lbs (2500g) or for babies of Asian origin 5lbs (2300g).

Extra heavy means more than 9½lbs (4300g).

Head circumference for a 7½-pound baby (3300g) is – on average – 14ins (35cm) and more or less in proportion to size.

Length for a 7½lb baby averages 20ins (50cm).

Vital Statistics for Ellie's and Sarah's babies

	Ellie's daughter	*Sarah's son*
Weight	7¼lbs (3300g)	6½lbs (2900g)
Length	20ins (50cm)	18ins (46cm)

Sarah had made friends with another mother at the ante-natal classes. Her name was Shireen and she and her husband came from India originally. Their baby was just as sturdy and perfect, although slightly smaller: 5¾lbs (2600g).

The impact of birth

It's a shock after the security of the womb. The baby suddenly experiences a 14° C drop in temperature. Imagine an instant switch from sunbathing weather on a Mediterranean beach to a winter's afternoon in Scotland, and you've got nothing on and your skin is wet and clammy: that's what it's like. At the same time there's an urgent necessity to breathe, now that the oxygen supply from the placenta has been permanently disconnected. To make it more difficult, the air passages are full of fluid: that was all the foetus could practise with in the womb. If he has arrived very early, it may be difficult for him to expand his lungs properly, because of a shortage of surfactant, the lubricant for preventing the inside surfaces sticking together (see p 24). Help is at hand if needed.

The dazzling brightness of the big world is a shocker after the velvety blackness which is all he has experienced until now. So is the cacophony of sounds, unmuffled by the mother's body and clothing. And almost as soon as he – or she – has got the hang of breathing in a steady rhythm, he's aware of another urgent need. The constant flow of nourishment is no longer being piped in and his reserves will only last a few hours. This has set off a powerful urge to suck – to see if that helps. With any luck he will very soon be allowed to try his skill on his mother's nipple and get some of the special high-protein colostrum. This is available before the milk supply is established, and most babies benefit from having a chance of this within their first hour.

Just as it was the baby who started off her or his mother's labour by releasing the hormone, oxytocin, so it is the baby, through her sucking, who stimulates her mother's breasts into action: the sooner, the more effective. Babies, like Sarah's, whose mothers are not going to breast-feed, don't miss out. They get a small thirst-quencher from a bottle.

From Jesus' day right up to now, very young babies feel safest wrapped up like a cocoon, if not actually swaddled. This is the nearest equivalent to the tight all-over pressure of the womb in the last weeks of pregnancy. Of course, after a fortnight or so, your baby will want to move his arms and legs around freely and doesn't need to feel constricted. Sarah's baby was particularly keen to be freed from the confines of the lovely shawl his grandmother had knitted.

The second-day medical

When they are two days old, babies receive a full medical examination, including heart, lungs, tummy, back passage, genitals and checks for hernia in the groin or at the navel, and also for congenital dislocation of the hip. Sarah's and Ellie's babies came through with flying colours, like the great majority, but the part their mothers noticed most was their skin and hair.

Ellie's little girl, whom they had decided to call Jessica, had what her granny called 'stork marks' at the back of her neck. These purply-red V-shaped stains are common in new babies, and usually fade; anyway they will be under the hair later. So far Jessica's hair consisted of a fine goldish down.

Sarah's baby son's skin looked mottled and red for a few days while his circulation adjusted to the new arrangements, now he was doing his own breathing. After that it began peeling slightly, rather as it does when you are recovering from mild sunburn. All of this was normal. Unlike Jessica, he had plenty of hair, dark and some of it 2 inches long. His name was to be Jack.

Milia, or 'milk-spots'

These are the little white spots you often see on a very young baby's nose. They are nothing to do with milk, but are tiny lubricating glands. They are normal, and disappear in a few weeks.

Jaundice

As many as one in five babies develop a yellowish tinge to their skin after the first day or two. This is due to a pigment called bilirubin, a waste product from old red blood cells which are being replaced. It is the job of the liver to dispose of bilirubin, but sometimes a new baby's liver cannot do it quickly enough. It is a matter of maturity. Luckily there is an easy way of helping the baby through this temporary difficulty – sunshine.

Ultraviolet light deals with the bilirubin if the baby's skin is exposed to it. Phototherapy – light treatment – as it is called, employs artificial light for convenience. The baby sunbathes wearing just a nappy, with pads over his eyes to protect them. He can have the treatment right next to his mother, for company. Baby jaundice is not a long-term problem.

The fontanelles and funny-shaped heads

Mothers – Ellie and Sarah were no exceptions – often feel uneasy about the diamond-shaped 'soft spots' towards the front of their babies' heads, where the bones haven't joined up yet. These are the fontanelles. You can sometimes see the baby's pulse-beat under the skin. This is perfectly normal but may make you think that the fontanelle is a very delicate area, so that you are chary of washing that part of the baby's head or

Brand-New

brushing her fluff of hair. There is no need to worry: there is a strong, tough membrane between the bones and they themselves are flexible.

This apparently unfinished arrangement is no mistake. It means that there is enough 'give' for the baby's head to adjust to the shape of the birth canal as it comes through. It also allows for the fantastically rapid growth of his brain just before and just after he is born. Because of the moulding process during transit, your baby's head may look an odd shape at first: this is a temporary matter.

The flexibility of a new baby's head is a safety factor, not a weakness. Think how much more breakable a hard china cup is than a bungey rubber ball.

Bow-legs

All babies are bow-legged, to enable them to fit comfortably into the womb. The bones straighten out from the time the baby begins to walk, and are usually quite straight when he is two. A big wodge of nappy between the legs tends to exaggerate the bow-legged tendency, but modern disposables are no problem.

Who does the baby take after?

While Ellie and Sarah each knew that their baby was the most beautiful and lovable in the world, and were fascinated by every tiny detail, everyone else was playing the delicious game of 'Spot the Likeness'. Grannies and grandfathers, aunts both honorary and blood-related, plus the friends who had come to pay homage – all scanned the tiny mites' features for points of resemblance to various family members.

This isn't silly. The curious fact was established in 1995 that babies of under a year, of either sex, resemble

Childhood Development

their fathers to a recognisable degree. Observers, who did not know the families concerned, were able to pair up photographs of babies with those of their dads correctly far more often than with pictures of their mothers or other relatives. The theory is that this helps fathers to accept as theirs, and take responsibility for, their offspring.

What your baby can do from day one

Feeling and enjoying the sensation of touch on his skin

From feather-light stroking to a firm hug. It must feel interesting and exciting, since until now the baby's water cushion has prevented any direct contact.

Hearing

Your baby can hear almost as well as you can, including a whisper, as soon as the surplus fluid had drained out of his ears. Right from the start he will find your voice, above all, reassuring in his bewilderment: but any loud noise will frighten him.

Seeing

As yet he can only focus at a range of 6 to 10 inches, the distance from your face when you are nursing him. Your baby is likely to keep his eyes open for much of his very first hour – and it is you he wants to see. He won't be able to appreciate colours at this stage, but that will come over the months – and his first preference is likely to be pink. He won't like bright lights any more than loud noises – both are so harshly unfamiliar to him.

Tasting and smelling

These two senses work together, as they do for us, and what a baby finds incomparably attractive is the subtle, sweet smell and taste of his own mother's milk. Touch comes in, too. If your baby's cheek comes in contact with your breast, he will locate the nipple with the help of the other two senses. This is called the 'rooting reflex'.

A bad smell or a bitter taste will make your baby pull a face, but he – or she – enjoys something sweet on his tongue. Vanilla and strawberry flavours are both popular with the newborn. Perhaps it is no accident that vanilla and strawberry are favourites in ice-cream. The baby preference for sweetness also comes into more serious matters, the naming ceremonies of the Muslim, Sikh and Hindu religions. Something sweetened with honey or sugar is put onto the baby's tongue, while among the Jews he is given a minuscule sip of sweet wine – all more likely to keep the infant quiet and contented than a splash of water on the forehead during a christening.

Sucking and swallowing

Brand-new babies know a lot about these – they have been practising in the womb for months (see p 24). Sucking – actually getting a mouthful of milk – seems quite easy, but what is tricky is synchronising this with swallowing. Newborns sometimes even swallow in reverse, so that as much runs out of the mouth as went in, and choking and spluttering are common during a feed. It takes several weeks for a baby to master the neat co-ordination of sucking and swallowing.

Childhood Development

Crying

This is first-class exercise. Your baby puts everything into it – arms, legs, chest and body and his face may go beetroot-red with the effort. The lungs are expanded to the full and any residual fluid is cleared out. Then there is the sound, so designed that it is impossible to ignore it. Ellie and Bill, Sarah and Dom, became thoroughly weary of their babies' crying, especially in the night, when they had just put him or her down – again.

A mother (and, unexpectedly, also a grandmother on the mother's side) can distinguish her own baby's crying in a nurseryful of others, and it can be guaranteed to wake her from sleep. This is because her baby has learned something individual, from hearing her voice during his sojourn in the womb. It is something they share, because, as we have seen, the baby recognises and responds to her voice as to no other.

Baby's crying is an essential for survival. How else can he or she tell you that she is hungry, cold, wet or just lonesome, when you are in another room? Some people believe that they can diagnose the problem from the way the baby is crying, but most of us can't do much more than distinguish full-throated crying from whimpering, or the bleating wail of the newborn from the more mature crying that supersedes it. A very sick baby cries weakly, so however wearing to your nerves, loud crying can be reassuring.

Ellie, looking at Jessica, noticed that although her baby was crying hard, her face bent up with the effort, there wasn't a single tear to be seen. Her friend, who had no children, said this showed that it was just temper, not sadness or suffering making Jessica cry. She was wrong. Young babies simply can't manufacture enough tears to overflow, like those of more mature people. On this occasion Jessica just wanted, urgently, the reassurance of her mother's touch. She wasn't wet or worse, but she settled down peacefully after Ellie had been through the ritual of picking her up and checking.

Sneezing, coughing, hiccuping and yawning

These are all to do with breathing and at the beginning help to clear the airways. Yawning, especially, looks absurdly adult in someone so tiny.

Sleeping

Babies sleep sixteen to eighteen hours of the twenty-four, leaving six to eight hours when they are awake. That would be wonderful if it meant a long, unbroken stretch of peace at night and a largely wakeful day. But it never does. In his first six weeks it is physically impossible for your baby to last more than three to five hours without a feed. His vital glucose reserves are only enough for a few hours. Matters will improve, but you should not expect your baby regularly to sleep through the night until he is at least four months old. Dutch babies sleep for longer than others in the Western culture, while in Kenya it is the norm for babies to wake several times a night through most of the first year. It's all a matter of training. In Holland parents value their own night's sleep highly, and tend to be unsentimental. In Kenya mother and baby sleep in close contact, and the baby can snack on and off all night without really disturbing the mother. Dad may not be around.

Sleep is an essential, since this is when the production of growth hormone peaks and the baby does his growing.

It seems that even tiny babies, including premature ones, dream. They have a larger proportion of what

Childhood Development

would be dream sleep in adults, and their expression can change when they are asleep.

Sarah was touched to see Jack busy making sucking movements with his mouth when he was sleeping.

Sleep patterns are an individual matter largely inborn, not just a matter of mother management. Ellie's baby, for instance, was easy. She slept or, rather, dozed most of the time between feeds although she would complain vociferously enough when she felt that she was being starved. Sarah's Jack was a complete contrast. He was either asleep, but never for very long, or thoroughly awake and restless. They say such babies grow into particularly interesting, thoughtful children, but meanwhile Jack's parents were worn out. They did all the 'right' things and some zany ones, but there was no magic formula. Time would help – a little.

Reflexes

These are automatic responses over which the baby has no control. We have some too, such as blinking at an apparent threat, or 'jumping' when a door bangs. Babies have many more, all to do with primitive manoeuvres for survival. They include:
- the grasp reflex: your baby's tiny hand will grip your finger tightly if you put it in his palm
- the sucking reflex: you can feel the action if you put the tip of your little finger to Baby's lips
- the startle reflex – the same as our 'jumping' but involving legs and body and arms, not just the shoulders
- blinking occurs in response to a sudden noise as well as to a dazzling light
- the Moro reflex (Ernst Moro was a German doctor): it is like a big startle reflex but the little one cries with fright. It means that he or she is afraid that she is falling. This is such a distressing feeling that you

Brand-New

want to make sure that your baby is firmly supported, head and body, all the time.

Progress in the first few weeks

First week

Babies normally lose up to ten per cent of their birth-weight during the first week. Ten per cent comes to more with a big baby than a smaller one:
    Jessica lost 190g of her 3300g
    Jack lost 170g of his 2900g
    Most of the loss is due to off-loading surplus fluid, and absolutely nothing to worry about.

Second week

On the seventh day the stump of Jack's umbilical cord came away, while it wasn't until day eleven that Jessica's separated, leaving a small raw spot. Ellie kept this clean and dry until it healed completely. Some babies have a protruding navel: this usually goes flat by itself, so don't worry about it for at least the first two years!

Both babies got back to their original weight during this week. From then on the trend was upwards, not steadily but in steps and stops, like a staircase. It averaged out at somewhere between 5 and 6oz (140–170g) a week, but so long as there was no slipping backwards a lower rate of increase in a lively baby need cause no worry.

Two to three weeks

Every day, at this stage, your baby is stronger and more knowing. He or she is learning all the time. At two weeks old Jessica showed that she recognised Ravel's

'Bolero', a tune that Ellie had shared with her before she was born. She gave a wriggle of pleasure and then lay quiet, seeming to be listening. Most young children find the music they had heard pre-birth comfortably familiar.

Sarah was delighted to see Jack making a wobbly smile in his sleep. Such smiling is practice for the smile muscles, but at this stage it is only an involuntary reflection of a feeling of security and contentment. It usually occurs first during sleep – sweet dreams, perhaps – but soon begins to happen at any time, sleeping or waking.

Colic. There was one troublesome development for Jack at about this time, which was probably worse for Sarah and Dom. When he was three weeks old, Jack started to have colic: it is a spasmodic gut pain rather like irritable colon in adults, but adults don't cry. It came on mainly in the evenings – that's usual – and Jack would cry incessantly for an hour or more while his parents walked up and down with him and tried everything they could think of. It often came on after a feed, so it wasn't hunger, but sometimes a few drops of sweetened water on his tongue or a dummy to suck would help. The doctor said that there weren't any effective medicines, and it wasn't caused by wind.

Colicky babies, although they cry so bitterly, put on weight normally and are perfectly healthy. The only consolation for parents like Sarah and Dom is that babies always grow out of their colic within three months. In fact it is called three-months colic. Meanwhile the chief essential is a reliable baby-sitter, to give the parents a break and reduce their stress.

One month

It's not exactly a birthday, but a good time to take stock. Your baby has come a long way. Now, when you pick

Brand-New

him or her up, he feels firm and compact compared with the fragile little bundle of four weeks ago. The ordinary rhythms of life – breathing, heartbeat and circulation – are securely established. Sucking and swallowing are better co-ordinated, although even with his improved feeding technique, he will still gulp in air and need burping.

Ellie and Sarah knew that the correct way to put a young baby down to sleep is on his or her back, for the minimum risk of cot-death. Now, however, Jack and Jessica had ideas of their own and didn't stay that way. The favourite position for both was lying towards the right, head turned that way, and the right arm stretched out straight. The other arm was crooked up.

It wasn't a babyish quirk or a coincidence that these two babies chose the same attitude. It was a sign of normal development in progress. They were working towards the co-ordination of hand movements and eye, and they were likely to be right-handed, from the side they favoured.

It was about now that Ellie found that if she dangled a toy in Jessica's line of vision, she would follow it with her head and eyes for a moment or two. Jack could do the same, and both babies would turn their heads towards an interesting sound, and follow their mothers' movements. Jack's little face looked alert and attentive when he was listening or watching.

Another clever thing that a one-month-old can do is to lift her head up for a few dizzy moments, if she is put down on her tummy. All the muscles are stronger and although the arm and leg movements are jerky, the baby obviously enjoys them. Jack who had been suspicious of his bath initially, now found it a wonderful opportunity for kicking. Jessica had always luxuriated in the all-over warmth and freedom of her tub.

Both babies began 'talking' to themselves: little throaty murmurs which Bill said was grumbling. Jessica

Childhood Development

always stopped when Ellie talked to her. This was the beginning of something important.

Six weeks

For you, the mother, this is the end of the puerperium, the physical recovery period following the birth. It is marked by an important post-natal medical examination, to check that your body is back to normal inside.

For the baby, too, six weeks is a watershed. Until now your baby's relationship with you has been all one-way. You give care, she receives it: bathing, feeding, carrying, changing, talking. All she or he contributes is her or his touching weakness and dependence. Now it is different and the big differences are social:

Your baby can smile – a wavering, toothless, endearing effort, with eye contact so that you know that it is meant, and meant for you. It tells you that your baby recognises you for sure, and that she understands about love. She can feel that you (and her father and perhaps granny) love her and she loves you back.

Communication: another great stride on the social front is the precursor of talking. You can have a delightful conversation with your baby now: she coos, squeaks, gurgles and goes 'Ooo' for you. As well as making these interesting sounds in an interaction with you, she enjoys them so much that she will often run through her repertoire when she's on her own.

Body language: this depends on muscle power and control. Your baby's limb movements are smoother and stronger, but the exciting bit is that you can see him trying to reach out for things – but his arm won't go where he tells it. His little tight ball of a fist will open now to grasp your finger if you touch it, and often he will open it just because he can. The tiny fingers uncurling put me in mind of a flower opening.

Head control is now almost a doddle. Your baby can

Brand-New

hold his head up from the tummy position for much longer, and even for a little while when he is in the upright burping position against your shoulder. Turning his head to either side is no problem.

You will often see your baby looking at you intently. He is learning to imitate your facial expressions. When Dom puts his tongue out, playing with Jack, Jack responds by nearly sticking the pink tip of his tongue out, too.

Personality: this is beginning to show clearly now. You can get an idea of what sort of person – child or grown-up – your baby is likely to become. On that score, Ellie's little Jessica seems bound to be an easy-going, sunny character, full of fun and something of a chatterbox. Jack, by contrast, looks to become a restless, questing individual, interested in everything but preferring to weigh things up before plunging into action. Perhaps he'll be a leading scientist . . .

Adopted baby. Six weeks is a red letter day for those mothers and fathers whose babies arrive by adoption, since this is the time which is generally chosen for them to join the family. It is a wonderfully well-chosen time.

Up till now your baby has been in what is called the 'pre-attachment phase', when he or she is not certain who his mother is and is only just beginning to recognise different people. Mothers' bonding to their babies is like love at first sight – and you can expect that with your adopted baby, too. For babies, attachment or bonding is a gradual affair, not reaching fruition before he is six to eight months old. Solid bonding develops between eight months and two years, when separation from the mother he loves is heart-rendingly distressing.

As we have seen, it isn't until six weeks that personality develops to any extent and imitation of his parents' expressions and voices. Everyone used to say about my adopted son, Georgie: 'You can see whose

Childhood Development

boy he is!' By the time he was two he had acquired a number of my husband's individual characteristics, which he had started learning at six weeks.

You have only missed a few of the least important weeks of your adopted baby's life, because it is only now that he is old enough to learn to love and trust. How splendid that you are there to teach him at just this crucial period. The best part lies ahead.

Helping your new baby's development

There are three important areas where you can help:
– caring
– feeding
– playing

Caring

From the very beginning this tiny, bewildered new being needs reassuring. We instinctively hug someone we love, and put our arms round someone who is frightened or upset. It makes them feel loved and safe. Your baby needs holding close to you, his head, body, all encircled and supported by your arms, while you tell him, however little he is, how good and sweet he is. When he isn't in your arms he will – for the first two or three weeks – feel more secure with a shawl or blanket wrapped right round him.

It reminds him of your soft, warm all-enveloping womb. Like Jessica, he may take to his bath like a duck to water: after all, he was bathed in amniotic fluid while he was with you. Jack, on the other hand, was scared of the bath and the unaccustomed freedom. How can a fellow feel sure that it is safe?

Another big comfort for newcomers is rhythm. It is especially effective when it is linked with movement:

when you rock him in your arms, walk around, carrying him, or push him in his pram. Babies are first-class travellers. Most of them are soothed by a car trip and take to the air or the sea equally contentedly. When Sarah was exhausted by Jack's crying in his colicky phase, Dom would strap the carry-cot in the back of the car and drive round for half an hour.

Rhythm also comes with sound. Speech has its patterns, and the lullabies like Rock a bye, that are passed down from generation to generation, have a gently repetitious flow. We automatically repeat words and phrases when we are trying to comfort a baby or child. 'There, there,' we say, 'never mind, never mind.' Touch has its rhythms, too – when you pat your baby's back, stroke his head or play with his feet. And the rhythm your baby supplies for himself is the rhythm of sucking.

Feeding

Your baby's feeds are the high spot of his or her social life, a chance for you to commune together, and precious.
Breast or bottle. The sixty-four-dollar question is: breast or bottle? Your baby can thrive either way, but it is worthwhile to consider the pros and cons:
Breast-feeding: The good things about breast-feeding are:
– correct amounts of protein, fat and carbohydrate, minerals and vitamins for a human baby
– easiest food to digest
– least chance of an infection causing a tummy upset
– increased immunity to such illnesses as measles, diphtheria and polio (but not whooping cough) to add to the temporary immunity derived through the placenta
– for you: it speeds up the return of the womb to its normal neat size

Childhood Development

Bottle-feeding: The plus points of bottles are:
- you can see how much your baby has taken
- your partner can take turns with the night feeds
- easier for a weak, perhaps premature, baby to get his nourishment
- greater freedom for you
- no risk of sore nipples

The 'Formula' that babies have in their bottles is a very much modified product.

	Human Milk	Cow's Milk
Water	88.5%	87.0%
Fat	3.3%	3.5%
Lactose (sugar)	6.8%	4.8%
Casein (protein)	0.9%	2.7%
Other Protein	0.4%	0.7%
Minerals	0.2%	0.7%

Of course, if you are ill or on long-term medication, you have no choice: you can't breast-feed. Otherwise, make your decision by what you feel will be most comfortable and enjoyable for you and Baby together. A valuable compromise is to breast-feed for the first six weeks, which gives the baby a good start, and then switch to bottles, allowing two or three days for the change-over.

Whether breast or bottle, the social side of feeding is almost as important as the nourishment. Mother and baby are in a magic circle of giving love and giving life: like no other relationship in the world. It combines warmth, bodily contact, eye contact and a chance to tell your baby – everything. He can't answer, but you know that he can hear and that he likes the sound of your voice, however softly you speak.

Clock or demand? The second important question

Brand-New

about feeding. Clock or Demand? Your little one has been used to a continuous drip-feed for the last nine months. It is a shock for her or him to find that now the supply switches off as well as on – and she has to work for it. A fair compromise is to let your baby feed whenever she is hungry, for the first two weeks. Sometimes, when she wakes and cries you find she only takes a few mouthfuls and then goes back to sleep. It's like you having morning coffee or a biscuit, but not wanting a full meal – perfectly natural. Go along with it, but with a bottle you have to discard the unused part because of the danger of a tummy infection.

By the end of the second week you will probably find that your baby is sleeping for longer periods, and you can start working towards three- then four-hourly feeds.

The practical technique of feeding your baby, either by breast or bottle, like riding a bicycle, is best taught by someone on the spot: to demonstrate, explain and encourage you. It isn't difficult. The midwife will start you off and after that you'll have loads of practice. Your baby is keen to learn the ropes too, but if you do run into problems there is the midwife, the health visitor and a local advisory service to help you.

Already, from the way your baby feeds, you will get a preview of how he will tackle the problems of life. Jack always seemed to be in a panic in case his bottle was suddenly whisked away, and in his hurry he would choke and splutter, no matter what size the teat hole. He would have been the same with the breast. Jessica approached the matter differently. In general she took things as they came; she was 'laid back' as they say. The one snag was that although she started off eagerly enough and was soon sucking contentedly, she sometimes fell asleep after only five minutes. Ellie was aiming for ten minutes on each side. Many mothers are taught to use one side only at each feed.

Childhood Development

Usually babies take what they need, and they get a large proportion in the first few minutes, when the flow from the nipple is at its maximum. The weekly weigh-in is the most useful check that the baby is taking enough, that and how happy and lively she is. For these first six weeks milk is the only nourishment necessary for your baby, and for which his immature digestion is geared. Sarah and Dom, like many other parents with colicky babies, hoped that adding cereal to Jack's feeds might make him sleep more and cry less. It didn't work.

Playing

Playing with your baby helps him to learn. The term 'intellectual stimulus' might make you think of challenging concepts and learned professors, but it is exactly what a baby needs and enjoys. Everything is a challenge when you are a beginner at life – trying to make sense of what you see and hear, and finding out such things as how to turn your head and eyes towards something interesting. Then there is learning to use all your strength and will to lift your head when you are on your tummy, so that you get a better view; working at the problem of controlling what your arms and legs do; and trying to find out the trick of talking, since that is what your mother does.

When Jessica is awake Ellie takes her all round the flat in her carry-cot so that she has a range of experiences in sight and sound, as Ellie cooks or cleans or chats on the 'phone. Sarah, who went back to full-time work soon after Jack was born, goes in for definite playtimes with her son, on a rug in a warm room. He was against it at first, but soon found it could be fun to wave all four limbs and catch sight of them as they moved. Sarah and Dom tried the tickly games like Incy Wincy Spider and played with Jack's fingers and toes, since, apart from the pleasure of physical contact, it helps a baby's awareness of the parts of his own body. One of Jack's favourites was when Sarah danced to lilting music with him in her arms: he had had an ear for music since before he was born.

Talking to your baby may strike you as ridiculous, but research in the nineties has shown that long before he or she can utter a meaningful sound, he is already learning the meaning of long and difficult words. This is one reason why the adult phrases used by Beatrix Potter enhance rather than spoil such stories as *Peter Rabbit*.

Of course, when you are helping your child with language – and it is never too soon to start – you can do the same as a teacher explaining a foreign language. You demonstrate the meaning of the words 'nose' or 'mouth' by touching the part and saying the name, or 'bath', when it is time for that event. Introducing Granny or Aunty by name helps the baby to know what to say much later on when he has got the hang of talking.

It is not too soon to look out for treasures to share with your little one. He or she can't understand yet, but he will sense your feeling of pleasure at the scent of a hyacinth, the song of a bird, or the pattern of leaves moving in a tree over the pram. Babies are exquisitely sensitive to mood and atmosphere. That's why you need to avoid quarrels when you have a baby in the family, learning from you how to live. Besides, most clashes seem pointless afterwards.

Father's role

Mothers have a nine-months' start in getting to know their babies. Fathers can feel at a disadvantage. Even when they are there during the birth, as ninety per cent are these days, they are conscious that they are basically only onlookers. Afterwards, especially when the mother is breast-feeding, they can still feel – horrible word – redundant.

Ellie was concerned that Bill should not be hurt and that Jessica should have the fullest benefit from having such a nice father. Although Bill held his daughter as though she were an unexploded bomb, and Ellie could do it much better, she praised his prowess, and his confidence blossomed. Soon Bill could bathe Jessica or change her nappy to the manner born, while Ellie busied herself in another room. That way Bill could build the foundations of a relationship with Jessica which was to be a delight to them both. Ellie benefited by sharing some of the baby chores; it was a godsend when she had 'flu that Bill could take over.

With their mortgage and the uncertainty over Dom's job, Sarah was keen to get back to her job as soon as humanly possible. It meant that she was often deadly tired in the evening, especially when Jack developed three-months colic. Dom was under strain too, but the couple could take turns with Jack's night feeds and get a reasonable amount of sleep. Dom had no doubts about his importance as a father.

A masculine input is part of a child's emotional education, including during babyhood. Although babies normally recognise and smile at their mothers first, delight at the sight of their fathers comes a close second. All through childhood and adolescence the father's contribution is valuable and special – and more exciting. When a mother is on her own a grandfather or uncle may help fill in some of the gaps.

Grandparents' corner

At the nought to six weeks stage, while the grandfathers' role is mainly to admire, grandmothers are often at the forefront of the action, especially in the first fortnight. Those who are pressed into service or volunteer do a wonderful job. It may be too good, and the new mother may feel inadequate by comparison, and even resentful. Tact is needed on both sides.

Grannies are often asked for advice. This is a trap. What an inexperienced mother really wants is reassurance that what she is doing is right, and that she is managing brilliantly.

Baby-sitting, even for an odd hour in the afternoon, can take the pressure off a tired mother and revive her spirits. A grandmother is the most natural sitter, and one whom the baby will instinctively trust, but nowadays you can't take it for granted that your mother or mother-in-law has the time and energy to fit in with your needs. On the other side, if you are a granny baby-sitting your young grandchild, you have to remember that you are only a stand-in, and must do everything the way the real mother prefers. If there is consideration from both parties, the baby's life will be enriched for years to come by the marvellous sense of family.

3

Becoming A Person:
six weeks to six months

Of course your baby needs you, but from now on he or she is much more than a precious adjunct to you. She is becoming a person in her own right, with her own individual way of responding to everything she sees and hears, to her feelings, such as hunger or loneliness, and to you and other people. And she won't always react the way you expect. You can help and guide and provide, but from now on you are dealing with someone with a will of her own.

One aspect of individuality shows up more and more when you compare notes with other mothers. It is the variation in each child's development: in the rate and the details of which advance comes first. Remember that your child is a one-off, made to a special, unrepeatable design. That's half the fascination of watching from your privileged ring-side seat your baby's personal itinerary into the future.

If your baby is happy and shows an interest in the major events in his or her life – feeds, bath-time, kicking on a rug – you've nothing to worry about even if his development doesn't keep to the schedule in the books. Babies don't travel at the same rate, just the same general direction. All I shall do is outline some of the exciting advances to look out for at different ages, and see how Jack and Jessica are faring.

The most important lesson of your baby's first six months is an emotional one. Little ones have to learn

Becoming A Person

to love and trust before they can think and act and thrive. It's a matter of confidence. You can't be a fearless baby explorer without it, using first your eyes, then hands and mouth and finally moving around to discover the boundaries of the playpen, the room, the world. You need to feel safe, that you are surrounded by goodwill and grown-ups who think you are good and clever, and whose chief delight is to feed you and bath you and play with you.

It follows that during this enchanting half-year your baby regards everyone as a friend. Jessica's smile was beamed on all and sundry. Jack would jiggle his little body with pleasurable anticipation when he saw his daddy, his granny, an honorary aunt or the postman, and – top rating – his mother. The fun and exhilaration of being picked up was always on the cards if a big person came into view.

The other major development of the first half-year is your baby's amazing, fast-track growth. Most babies more than double their birthweight in the time. Imagine if your weight went up from nine to eighteen stone between January and June! They'll also have shot up, or rather, grown longer by an average of 5ins (13cm), and are into the third size of stretch suit. It's impressive.

For pure enjoyment and pride in achievement from the baby's point of view tops is learning to control his arms and legs and body. This is hard work and you can see on your baby's face the concentration and effort required. Another pleasurable advance is on the sound front. Babies of this age are constantly experimenting with the different noises they can make, apart from crying.

Events to look out for from six weeks onwards

(remember they may come earlier or later for any particular baby)

Childhood Development

Eight weeks

The big deal now is Baby's discovering his or her hands. Jack – will he be an engineer or a surgeon? – was fascinated by his, and gazed at them most earnestly, especially the backs. He knew there must be a way of moving them where he wanted, for instance towards the jingly mobile hanging by his cot or the bright-coloured ball in front of him when he was on the floor. He would make batting movements towards these intriguing objects and now and again, by chance, he would connect. Jessica did not try so hard.

Jack had also put on a whole kilogram (2lbs plus) since he was born, and being a boy this was mainly muscle. Jessica had put on a similar amount of weight, but because of her feminine genes there was a larger proportion of fat. It made her extra cuddly.

Both of them could not only lift their heads but also their chests when they were lying on their tummies. You could see that Jessica felt powerful and important doing this. Bill took several photographs of her.

Instead of the wondering look of very tiny babies, Jack and Jessica often had an expression of rapt attention nowadays, when they were looking or listening to something strange or interesting.

Jessica was 'talking' a lot. She could make several sounds like the middles of words: ah, eh, uh and oo. Jack was not so keen on conversation. He was more into muscle work, but he often gave a big sigh, as though he had a load of worry.

Ten weeks

Jessica, the sociable type, spent a lot of time looking round the room. Her eyes could focus better now and in three or four weeks she would reach our adult standard of visual acuity. It would still be too soon for full colour vision and natural wood toys were just as attractive as the gaily painted. Both Jack and Jessica enjoyed the panoramic view when they were carried round the room or burped over their mother's or father's shoulder. They liked their heads and shoulders to be raised to enlarge the vista from their carry-cots.

Twelve weeks

Three months, a quarter of a year – your baby has come a long way. One of the bonuses of being a parent is the way your baby's face lights up into a wide, gummy smile and his or her gurgles of welcome when he sees you. Both Jack and Jessica had learned these social graces, and knew how to express pleasure. Jack in particular could also convey anger, for instance when his bottle was delayed for all of two minutes by the telephone ringing, or with the terrible frustration of hand and rattle refusing to make contact, no matter how he tried.

An emotion that is notable by its absence at this age is guilt. No matter if there's another dirty nappy directly after a thorough clean-up and change. Shyness doesn't come into the three-monther's repertoire of feelings either, although they both develop later. A sense of humour does seem to operate at this stage, however, from the chuckles that greet a tickly game, or the mere sight of the family cat or a familiar figure.

You'll be charmed to hear much less crying and a lot more happy baby sounds, when your baby has a conversation with herself or with you. As well as gurgles, chuckles, grunts and the vowel sounds there is the cooing – lovely, liquid and musical. It makes me think of spring and birdsong. Jack and Jessica both amused themselves and delighted their mothers with quite long periods trying out all their interesting noises.

A welcome relief to Jack and his parents was the

Childhood Development

disappearance of his evening colic. By the fourteenth week it had stopped for good. He slept peacefully while Sarah and Dom could enjoy their evenings again. About the same time both Jessica and Jack started sleeping right through the night quite often – and their parents could catch up on their sleep too.

Jack was still struggling to get his hands to do what he wanted. He could hold his rattle for a few dizzy moments – but it always got away, and he would forget about it. Sometimes he would make a wobbly swipe at what he wanted but he couldn't quite connect yet. Jessica was also interested in her toys and what her hands could do, but she took the whole matter more lightly than Jack. Everything was a huge joke to her.

Four months

This month both Jack and Jessica got down to this hand business seriously, deliberately touching one hand with the other, which they could feel as well as see. They watched the process intently. Then they discovered an effective two-handed manoeuvre for getting to grips with a toy or any other grabbable object within range.

At this point in development anything a baby manages to get hold of, he or she tests out by sucking, biting or chewing. There's no difficulty in locating his mouth. This means you have to keep anything sharp, breakable or otherwise harmful out of reach, for instance a biscuit he could bite and choke on.

A new source of entertainment first discovered by Jack the athlete, but soon after by Jessica, was their toes. It was high sport trying to catch them, and Jessica soon found that with her short, stumpy legs when she had got hold of a foot she could easily take it to her mouth and suck a toe. Towards the end of their fourth month both babies could not only chuckle, but laugh aloud, a joyous sound. The joke could be Mummy playing Peep-Bo or Daddy 'helping' at bath-time. Jack loved to bang his hand down on the water and kick his legs for maximum splashing.

Seeing everything that was going on was Jessica's insatiable concern. She loved being propped up in a more or less sitting position. Her eyes would be wide – until she slipped down again, annoyingly soon.

Five months

By this time you know for sure that your baby can recognise the important people in his or her life – you, of course, and his daddy and anyone else he sees often, and the family pet. Jack is beginning to reserve his smiles for the people he knows and to give a straight, sober look at anyone strange.

Both babies are biting everything they can lay their hands on, they are dribbling a lot and blowing bubbles with the dribble. Their mothers put it all down to the two tiny bottom front teeth which were likely to come through about this time, but the experts say it is really to do with language. The babies were learning to use their mouths for speech later. They were practising for 'f's and 's's, and they could already manage some of the easier consonants: mm, bb, dd and gg.

Six months

With some consonants as well as vowels at their command Jessica and Jack were saying the 'words' Mumum, Dada, Baba – music to Sarah's and Dom's, Ellie's and Bill's ears. They liked to believe that their little ones were calling them by name: Mama and Dada, and by the way they responded they made this come true. Jack and Jessica had lost interest in babbling to themselves now. They wanted interaction with another person, even if they were lacking in words as

Childhood Development

yet. In emergency, they had an auxiliary method of conveying what they wanted – body language. When you go to your six-month-old baby he'll tell you plainly that he wants to be picked up by lifting his head and holding his arms up. Irresistible. And he'll complain if you look as if you are going away, with a miserable, grumbly whimper, or even a loud yell.

The best-known event of being six months old, give or take a few weeks, is the ability to sit up without being supported all round. Of course, it is tiring so your little one can't keep it up for very long at first, but it makes an enormous difference to his view of the world. Now he can see everything from the same angle as you, instead of obliquely from the horizontal position. The other great convenience is having a tray attached to his chair where he can have toys and other oddments ready to hand, instead of having to reach up for them. Everything he can handle is a plaything – a wooden spoon, a plastic egg cup, his hairbrush . . . As well to remember that they will all be tested by mouth.

It is a help to making full use of the sitting up and toy tray situation, that the babies are growing past the need to use both hands together to manipulate anything. Jack was fascinated by the way he could pass his wooden peg man from one hand to the other, and pick him up with either. Banging the peg man, a block or a spoon on the tray made a noise that was satisfying, too. Jessica's new trick was letting go of anything that came to hand, over the side of her chair, cot or pram – and watching Ellie pick it up again, and again.

Dom gave young Jack his first big present on his half-birthday: a baby-bouncer. Most babies are ready for one of these at six or seven months. It's a safe way for a baby to exercise his or her limbs, and tremendous fun – a favourite until the real first birthday. Jessica had a bouncer from her granny.

Becoming A Person

There are two very important developments in the six-week to six-months stage: the introduction of mixed feeding and the beginning of the immunisation programme.

Mixed feeding

There's no argument about breast milk or formula being all a baby needs for the first six weeks. It used to be the fashion to give one or more feeds thickened with cereal at this point, especially at night, in the hope that the baby would sleep for longer. In fact sleeping through is a matter of maturity, and a good many babies do not have a digestive system sufficiently mature to cope with solids until they are about four months old. By six months a baby definitely needs something more than milk, and in particular may run short of iron (vital for the blood) if he does not get it.

Biting and chewing, with or without teeth, are a hint that your baby is ready for mixed feeding. Biting comes into play at about four months; chewing, a more complicated matter, a couple of months later. By around four months it is time to introduce your baby to a new game: sucking food off a spoon, then the clever part – suck and swallow. Don't even think about getting much nourishment in – the first essential is for Baby to get used to this strange new technique and learn the trick of it.

Jack was wary of the tip of the spoon being slipped under his top lip – the recommended approach – but as Dom told Sarah, everybody has learned how to eat off a spoon by the time they are twenty-one. Jessica got the hang of it quite quickly. Both Ellie and Sarah resisted the temptation of putting the new food into a bottle diluted with baby formula: it is better to start with cup and spoon, so that weaning comes easily and naturally.

Childhood Development

Except that they know that they like sweet things, most babies haven't got a well-developed sense of taste at four or five months. This makes it easier to help them to get accustomed to healthy foods like vegetable purée and mashed banana. They are less likely to spit them out than when you introduce a strange flavour for the first time later.

It doesn't much matter which food you try to start with, but it is best to stick to the same one for several days running before trying a different taste. Ellie found that Jessica liked sweetened cereals best, but these have the disadvantage of tending to make the baby fat and not to train her into liking healthy foods. Vegetable and protein foods (cheese, meat preparations) are better. Jack was a meat-eater, like Dom. Up to seven months all these foods should be sieved or puréed, and beginners of five or six months often prefer their food to be runnier than the directions advise: a matter of mixing in boiled milk and water.

Some babies, and Jack was one of them, are desperate to grab hold of the spoon as early as six months, or, as in Jessica's case, dabble their fingers in the cup or dish and then suck them. Neither baby managed to get much into their mouths, but they made a terrible mess. Ellie and Sarah were good mothers and let their babies have a go at the beginning of the meal, before taking adult control. Jack and Jessica were still having the nourishment of bottle or breast to follow.

It isn't important to measure the exact amount of the new foods that a baby takes. The right amount is what he or she will take willingly, once accustomed to the taste. Ellie believed that as a mother of the twentieth to twenty-first century it was only good sense to use the scientifically prepared commercial baby foods in cans, jars and packets. Sarah, who had green tendencies, went in for fresh foods, organic if possible, made into the right consistency by the modern technology of a blender. Either method, or some of each, provides excellent nourishment.

Teething and eating go together and the first teeth may be through by the time your baby reaches six months, but the whole saga of teething comes in the next chapter, and the teething chart is on p 271. There is a disadvantage to having teeth.

Finger foods. Babies who can sit up enjoy holding something like a hard rusk in their own hand and sucking and biting it. Jessica loved to suck the outside of a chocolate finger until it was white and then bite it with her two new teeth. The chocolate was fine as an occasional treat, but the biscuit could be dangerous if she managed to bite off a hard chunk. Jessica and her age group weren't expert enough to cope with lumps of food. In fact she wouldn't have the teeth and the skill to chew her food up and swallow it safely for another two and a half years.

Meanwhile, it meant close supervision especially when she was eating from her own hand. The commercially made rusks that melt to a mush in the baby's mouth are the safest choice, but even so you have to hook out any big pieces your baby manages to bite off.

Drinking from a cup. You can start this any time from three months on, but it is worth making a serious effort to help your baby learn how when she is six months old. That leaves plenty of time for her to get used to it before gradually giving up breast or bottle feeds. Baby feeder mugs with lids and spouts save the spillage. Learning to eat and drink like a grown-up takes a long time, a lot of mess and endless cleaning up – but the learner enjoys it.

Immunisation

This is something to discuss with your health visitor, your family doctor or at the clinic. It's a life-saver, a way of protecting your child against certain potentially lethal viruses and bacteria. The ploy is to alert the body's defences to various enemy organisms so that if the child is exposed to infection he already has the antibodies to zap it.

You might think that there is no point in immunising your baby against illnesses that nobody ever seems to have nowadays, for instance diphtheria and polio. Our children don't have these horrible illnesses only because so many of them are protected by immunisation, but there is certainly a lethal epidemic of diphtheria in Russia, and in Mexico and the USA there are still deaths or paralysis from polio – among those who ducked out of being immunised.

The current immunisation programme in the UK is set out on p 276. It is constantly being updated. However, by the time your baby is six months old, he or she will already have started, with the triple vaccine, DPT. This protects your baby against *D*iphtheria, *P*ertussis (whooping cough) and *T*etanus. He will have injections of the vaccine at two months, three months and four months – although particular clinics may run to a slightly different schedule. He will also be given the polio vaccine, by mouth. Booster doses will be needed when your little one goes to school, but meanwhile he is safe.

Some babies are fretful, restless and even mildly feverish for a few days after an injection: Jack was and Jessica wasn't. Jack benefited by half a teaspoonful of Calpol. Any more serious or longer-lasting symptoms should be reported to the doctor, as they could well signal some totally unconnected problem.

Whooping cough is extra dangerous to young babies,

yet for years we didn't have a vaccine suitable for tinies. Now it has been developed and is saving a lot of babies' lives. There is a proviso, however: it is not generally suitable for babies who suffer from epilepsy (fits), so they can have only the diphtheria, tetanus and polio immunisation.

Helping your baby's development

At this stage both you and your baby have a more varied role, although, of course, there is still the ordinary routine care of bathing and dressing and airings out-of-doors which underlies everything. Areas to concentrate on now:
- unhurried feeding, including time for your little one to take a hand, and with a choice of healthy foods to train her tastes for life
- love that shows, as ever the essential ingredient for all your baby's progress: smiling, cuddling, stroking, carrying round in your arms, and murmuring all the endearments you can think of: this won't spoil your baby
- talking to him as though he were a real person: which he is. Encouraging his efforts to communicate, by showing your interest and praising his cleverness
- providing toys (fathers and grandparents are useful here): these are your child's learning materials. They can be shop-bought and more or less expensive or home-made with affection, like a tiny knitted Teddy, or household articles like cotton reels, plastic containers, wooden pegs (not the spring kind) and spoons.

Choosing toys

You can judge what your baby needs by what he or she can do.

Childhood Development

Under three months. His main talents are for looking and listening. That means mobiles and other toys that swing and tinkle, a rattle he may clutch if you put it in his hand, and the mandatory small, soft toy which is destined to become a familiar and well-loved companion. Make it small enough and light enough for your baby to handle when he's learned how: big bears and the like only impress adults.

Three to six months. She will be able to pick things up and finger them, so supply different shapes and different textures, in sizes to fit her hand. Cloth-covered foam bricks, wooden blocks of all shapes, peg people, rattles. She likes to bite and gnaw: that means rings and other toys of hard plastic, wood or synthetic rubber. She can wriggle on her tummy so give her a big, bright ball or other rolling toy to strive after. For a start to her intellectual life there are books – the cloth or board variety: they won't mean much yet, but make a good excuse for a cuddle on your lap. See p 246 for toy lists.

Toys are good on their own but most rewarding when they are part of a game with someone else. When you can't move around, a rolling toy is not much fun unless someone rolls it to you, and toys that squeak when you squash them may need demonstrating first. Playtime is invaluable.

If play is a baby's work, toys are the tools, but some play doesn't require any props:
- face games, like pulling funny faces and putting your tongue out, or trying to touch each other's noses, or popping up from behind a paper or hiding your face and head under a big hanky;
- singing and chanting and movement games, and nursery rhymes with actions: like Pat-a-cake, Incy Wincy Spider, This Little Piggy, Pop Goes the Weasel and Two Little Dickie-birds. You can improvise the actions. For example, you can transform Rockabye

Becoming A Person

Baby into something exciting. You rock your baby in your arms then swoop him down to the ground for 'Down will come Baby, cradle and all.'
– exercise: it's good for everyone, and babies have bathtimes with water play and exercise periods for kicking and rolling on a rug or on a wide bed. Something interesting nearly out of reach is a great motivator to whole body efforts which will, in the end, result in crawling, walking, running . . . And a baby-bouncer strengthens the limbs ready.

Because you are a busy person, you can't play with your baby all the time, but fathers and grandparents are experts in this field, and they have the advantage of coming fresh to the task. Don't waste their talents – put them to work.

Father's role

Especially after the first three months when mother and baby are enclosed in a magic circle of togetherness, fathers begin to come into their own. Everyone – even at less than half a year old – knows that mothers are useful but fathers are fun. Right from the start fathers are the leaders in the sports section: play and exercise. They are the action men, immensely strong, who will lift you nearly to the sky in their arms, or drive your pram or buggy like a Porsche.

Taking turns with the routine chores of changing, bathing, dressing and feeding with cup and spoon helps father and baby to build a firm relationship for the future. It is also useful from a practical viewpoint. Bill wasn't phased when Ellie had 'flu, or at any rate a rotten cold, because he could look after Jessica that weekend without a qualm. Jessica relished the novelty, most of the time.

Childhood Development

Grandparents' corner

You've always loved your grandchild, but there's much more for you to enjoy now. For starters, not only will you be the object of delightful, heart-catching smiles, but the little one will definitely recognise who you are and be pleased to see you. The happy noises and body movements tell you so.

Grandparents and toys go together, and now you will have the satisfaction of seeing your grandchild wave the rattle you brought him, clutch the little cloth elephant you made, or, when he can sit up, laugh as he pushes over the bottom-weighted policeman on his food tray.

When Jack and Jessica were very tiny, the happiest situation was when they were sleeping peacefully, looking like little angels. Their grannies' chief concern was not to wake them. From three months onwards it's different. Now grannies and other interested persons are likely to have a chance of playing with the babies. Grannies are the natural experts at talking and singing play. The good news is that these activities are just what the psychologist ordered to help along psychological, intellectual and emotional development.

Grandmothers are a comfort to their daughters and daughters-in-law, for they recognise when a baby is teething, or just over-tired, and know that it isn't a matter of serious illness – because they've been there before.

4

Miracle Months:
six to twelve months

At the beginning of the second six months your baby is still nourished mainly by breast or bottle, can only sit up in a wobbly fashion, with help, and language is a wordless babble. When he or she celebrates that momentous first birthday, with cake and candle, she will be sitting bolt upright, like a princess in her clip-on chair. She'll be holding a slice of cake to eat by herself. At ground level she will be mobile, with an individual method of crawling, but on the verge of walking without holding on. Speechwise, she'll have said her first real word, maybe more. In fact, all in all, she – or he – is not merely 'the baby' but incontrovertibly a member of the family.

Each baby runs on his personal schedule of development, without checking on a chart or time-table, but here are some of the things to look out for, so that you don't miss any delicious detail.

Seven months

Your baby is not so interested in looking at his own hands as before: he is too busy using them. No sooner does he see some manageably sized object than he gets hold of it. He feels the outside for the texture, turns it round in his hands for the shape, takes it to his mouth for further assessment, swaps it from one hand to the other – and then repeats the whole process. Thorough

Childhood Development

examination of one novel toy – it doesn't have to be an actual toy – would sometimes occupy Jack for as long as twenty minutes.

Grabbing something and leaving go are different skills. Jessica would take the plastic duck or cotton reel which Ellie offered her without any problem, but when she wanted to give it back she would hold it out but – surprise, surprise – her hand still held on to it. Of course, in the ordinary way, babies often drop things they are holding, either because the muscles get tired or they relax because of a fresh distraction.

Until now, Jessica seemed to forget all about whatever it was she had dropped, or she might look vaguely puzzled to find her hand with nothing in it. Ellie noticed that recently Jessica would look down on the floor to see where the object had fallen. This was the beginning of a fine game for Jessica which would drive her mother spare. In a few months' time Jessica would have acquired the muscle control to drop things on purpose, for Ellie to retrieve. Jessica would laugh and squeal merrily, but by the ninth time Ellie stopped seeing the joke.

Two new emotions often develop at around seven months. One of them is fear. Jack had already shown doubts about strangers. Now he showed definite fear, shrinking and crying when Sarah's smart girlfriend tried to chat him up. She went in for power-dressing in black: babies' least favourite colour. Jack was upset nowadays by anything unusual: his new, big cot and a wind-up toy that made a whirring noise.

It was part of emotional maturing, and in the long term you'd want your child to be wary of strangers. It's the flip side of being able to recognise familiar figures, who've been passed as 'safe' by mother. Memory comes into it, too. At seven months most babies can remember someone they've met up to a fortnight before.

Miracle Months

Even Jessica made it plain that she preferred people she knew, and she was delightfully sociable with them. Sometimes now, though, she began to be shy when there were strangers in the company. Adults need extra sensitivity with little ones of this age, and some babies even look askance at their fathers – transiently. The one place that banishes all doubts, all fears, is in their mothers' arms, held tight. Jack and Jessica felt safe and confident with their mothers. When your baby is insecure or frightened, however silly this may seem, he really needs the reassurance that only your arms can give. It is important that babies at this stage have plenty of opportunities of getting to know their fathers, in the ordinary routine matters of baby care. A special 'Daddy time' every day is well worth instituting, to last all through early childhood and beyond.

The other new emotion is surprise: much pleasanter than fear. It leads to endless games of hiding things and suddenly finding them under a mug or a cloth – or popping up from behind a screen – to squeals and crowing with delight. These new noises add to your baby's ways of expressing himself.

Eight months

Your baby is sitting up strongly enough to use a high chair, or, more conveniently, a clip-on type. Ellie found the latter handy when the family – she, Bill and Jessica – went to stay with the grandparents and to have a meal out at a restaurant that wasn't geared for babies.

Jessica was ahead of Jack in her interest in faces. She hadn't taken much notice of mirrors till now – any more than your cat shows any interest in TV. Now she gave a brilliant smile of recognition at her own reflection and even kissed the glass. It wasn't only her own face that fascinated her, she was discovering how interesting other people's faces were. New babies all gaze intently at their mothers' faces, but now Jessica wanted to feel Ellie's face, to touch it and stroke it, investigate her nose and eyes, get hold of a piece of flesh. Not unkindly, but in more of a scientific manner.

Other faces, so long as they were familiar, were also interesting. Jack's grandmother felt honoured when he patted both her cheeks with soft little hands.

Nine months

Jack knew his own name and Mummy and Daddy and Bing (the cat). He also had six teeth: four at the bottom and two to smile with, at the top. But the most exhilarating advance was that he could crawl. He had started by a wriggly swimming on his tummy, which unfortunately took him backwards. Then he found a way to use his hands and knees and got the hang of the forward gear. He could travel fast.

Jessica used a different method of progression. From a half-sitting position, she could hitch herself across the floor in any direction, but her favoured target was the cupboard where Ellie kept her pots and pans. Anything goes in the mobility stakes. Some babies start by rolling, and a good many do the camel walk, usually as a prelude to actual walking. This employs hands and feet with the body held well above the floor. Rolling toys come into their own now, and there's nothing to beat a big, bright ball with a bell inside.

Sight and hearing tests are carried out as a routine at about this age, since babies can now co-operate. You would already know if there was any serious problem, from your baby's behaviour, so these tests need not worry you.

Ten months

Gradually your baby's repetitive babbling – strings of

consonants and vowels without any form – changes its character. Jessica might be busy playing with her favourite toy, currently a string of wooden beads, and all the time keep up what sounded like a conversation. She had her mother's intonations off to a tee. Then came the breakthrough. She linked consonant and vowel together to make a real word: No. She had said Mummum and Dada before this but did not intend them as more than a nice noise, with no special meaning until her parents started responding. Jessica had learned the meaning of 'No' so she could use the word appropriately, for instance when she didn't want to eat her spinach purée. She also understood what 'good girl', 'Daddy's coming' and 'milk' meant. Milk was her second word.

Jack's first words, apart from Mama and Dada, were 'Bing' (the cat) and 'Bye-bye'. He said the latter when his mother had a visitor, sometimes as soon as they arrived. Both babies found that they could make a new noise. It is called 'razzing' and consists in pressing the lips together loosely, then blowing out through the saliva, producing a bubbly, dribbly, zizzing sound. It is partly a step towards learning control of the mouth and lips, but also due to the copious flow of saliva during the teething period, nine to twenty-four months. See below.

Some of the finer details in the development of your baby's nervous system are being completed now. You'll notice how much he – or she – uses his mouth and tongue and his finger tips to investigate anything new and strange. These parts have become extra sensitive, as they are in adults, and have come under more precise control. The lips are also more sensitive and better controlled, so that drinking from a cup doesn't involve quite such a spillage.

As well as increased sensitivity your baby is discovering the neat trick of holding toys or rusks with his fingers on one side and his thumb opposite, instead of all in a bunch, the baby way. This new method also enables him or her to use his thumb and one finger, the forefinger, like a pair of pincers. Sarah was fascinated to see Jack carefully and accurately picking up the tiniest crumb. She had to stop him when he got hold of a peanut – notorious for causing choking or being inhaled.

Jack also found several other uses for his index finger on its own: to poke and prod, probe and explore. Any hole or crevice acted as an invitation and Sarah had to take precautions when he began investigating an electric socket in the skirting.

With her improved finger control Jessica managed to build a tower of two bricks, and she was trying for three. She also enjoyed using her hands expressively, imitating Ellie to play Pat-a-cake, or clap to music or wave good-bye.

Over the last two months the babies have become solidly bonded to their mothers. This attachment goes on strengthening right up to the end of the second year, when it is rock-hard. Jessica wanted Ellie and Jack wanted Sarah in preference to anyone else, and near at hand if possible. Jessica would cry when she saw Ellie putting on her coat to go out without her. Jack's mouth turned down and quivered when it looked as though Sarah was going to hand him to someone else – even his granny – to hold.

Baby-sitting became a problem because the babies objected. Ellie was flummoxed. 'But she used to be perfectly happy to go to anyone . . .' she would explain as Jessica's face crumpled at the sight of the minder. The critical period is from nine months to two and a half years, and it causes a child great distress if she or he is separated from her mother for more than a few hours.

Any mother planning to return to work would be

wise to have her baby established in a regular routine with the other carer before the age of seven months, or older than two and a half. Incidentally, babies and children love mothers who go out to work just as much as those who stay at home, and are just as firmly bonded. This is confirmed statistically. It may be that if the times mother and baby can be together are limited they are precious, and made particularly warm and enjoyable. The key is quality time. Weekends should be seen as a special time for the family, not as a chance for the mother to have a break from the child. Single mothers often develop the most enduring, affectionate understanding with their children – facing the world together.

As well as those of hands and face, the larger muscles have also developed. By now your baby will be able to sit up by himself from lying down, and, by pulling himself up by the bars of his cot or playpen, he can actually stand. Jack was thrilled by the experience. His legs could now take his weight, but his balance let him down. Persistence paid off in the end. He was persistent in another way, too. Now that he could sit up and stand up, he simply wouldn't lie down – unless he was asleep. He usually fell asleep on top of the blanket, and Sarah would cover him up then.

Another muscular improvement that develops at about this time is the ability to turn and bend to either side, from a sitting position. A month ago it had been a major problem to pick up a toy that had rolled beside him.

One year

You could never have imagined so much happening in one year. Your baby isn't a baby any more but an eager little child, almost a toddler, on the threshold of life. Gone for ever are the days when you could put your baby in a pram or carry-cot and know she would still

Childhood Development

be there in five minutes. Gone, thankfully, is the niggling worry about cot-death and whether she has rolled into the wrong position.

The dramatic difference is mobility. Spurred on by that same inner spark that made man travel to the moon, your baby will crawl at surprising speed to explore to the outermost limits of his universe. Jack was a climber before he could walk. He tackled stairs upwards like a mountaineer, with no thought of how he would make the return journey. The low settee was another challenge. He clambered onto the seat and was scaling the back when Sarah caught him.

Sarah had thought that when Jack grew out of his evening crying and colic and slept through the night, she could be able to relax. But a fearless, mobile baby, fired by curiosity means non-stop vigilance for the mother, except when her adventurer is penned in. A playpen is boring, constricting and frustrating by this age, except for a brief emergency. A gate across the doorway of the room or at the bottom of the stairs may be useful precautions.

Standing up and holding on to the bars or someone's hand was a proud achievement, but just a beginning. By his first birthday Jack was cruising round the sitting room, courtesy of the furniture. Jessica, who still sat down with a bump as soon as she stood up, travelled at ground level. She was becoming an expert cracksperson. Her small fingers opened any low cupboard, and she cleared the bottom bookshelf with great satisfaction. The cupboard under the sink was no longer a suitable place for bleach and household cleaners.

Musical appreciation comes to the fore at one. Jack acted out his enjoyment by bouncing in time on the soft, low settee. I don't hold out much hope for the springs. Jessica also took an active pleasure in music. Ellie had taught her to clap hands to the rhythm.

Now that your little one is leaving baby ways behind,

although he will still take things to his mouth it no longer seems so important. His hands are taking over for routine investigation. While Jack's fingers were always busy, Jessica was the first to find the usefulness of her index finger as a pointer. It started with her pointing at something she was just going to pick up, but soon she was using her finger, imperiously, to convey what she wanted.

This is the age of the hand, and in the next few weeks your child is likely to show a preference for right or left. It used to be the practice to guide children to use their right hands regardless, but since handedness is connected with the wiring in the brain, it is better to leave your child to follow what nature tells him.

Bath-time is more riotous now that your baby can sit up strongly and disport himself with plastic ducks, little wooden boats or a beaker for filling and pouring. Dressing has become a more co-operative matter. Jessica liked holding her arms out for Ellie to slip into the sleeves, and one garment she could already put on and take off by herself. It was a hat – with a brim to hold it by: not very useful, but fun.

Jessica had long since learned to let go of things more or less when she wanted to, on most occasions. She enjoyed playing a game of dropping bricks, biscuits, toys – anything – and seeing Ellie pick them up. Now Jack became skilful at leaving go, partly because Dom had been teaching him to throw a ball. Of course it didn't always work out the way Jack intended: sometimes he relaxed his hold too soon and the ball would fly backwards. Too late and it would just dribble down to his feet.

A satisfying discovery was that he could throw anything that he could manage to pick up. This made it hazardous for Sarah's shopping or any other object within reach. Catching is much more difficult than throwing, so the ball games Jack played with his dad

Childhood Development

were all one way – Jack throwing and Dom retrieving.

With such versatile hands, a whole range of toys and other articles could be manipulated. Jessica's favourite plaything was a set of nesting boxes, and a little later some Russian dolls. They were too hard to pull apart for a one-year-old. Jack had a wooden hammer and a fat peg in a round hole. He soon began hammering other things: a saucepan upside down made a splendid noise, while a biscuit on his tray was shattered to 1000 fragments.

One-year-olds are surprisingly knowledgeable. For instance they understand the purpose of various articles and show this in their play. Jessica would apply her brush and comb to her bear's head, although he only had short bristly fur, and Jack would pretend to drink out of a dolly-sized cup. Another thing that shows how much a baby understands is the way he or she will follow your instructions – if he agrees with them. He will usually 'Wave bye-bye to Daddy' or 'Kiss Granny' or oblige if you say 'Give me that brick – or spoon or cake.'

Of course your baby knows his or her own name and will turn round when she hears it. Now he or she can say it, too. 'Jack' was easy to imitate, but 'Jessica' came out as 'Esky.' At about the same time the concept of ownership was developing. You'll find that your child will have a firm idea of what belongs to him, and it won't be long before he says: 'Mine.' Sometimes he will apply the word to articles he would like to own – your dangly earring, or a visiting baby's toy.

The national average is a vocabulary of three words at the age of one. Some babies know many more: Jessica was one such. Others seem loath to commit themselves to speech, like the English abroad. Einstein and Charles Darwin were this type. Darwin's work in explaining how human beings evolved is closely concerned with our children's development. Jack couldn't say the words but he could point to all the parts of his body, or Sarah's, when she said, for example, 'Where's your leg?' He was beginning to recognise the same parts in a picture.

It had to be tough paper and a thick crayon, but Jessica had found a new skill: writing. She would grip the crayon in her fist and do a scribble of lines going roughly the same way. It would be an advance when she changed to a round and round method. Either way she pressed very hard.

There seems no end to the discoveries your baby has made this year, and his amazing development, both physically and mentally. Emotional development has advanced, too. Now he – or she – is one, he will share more of the feelings that you and I have as adults. They are not all good: jealousy, for example. It grows from fear of being supplanted or forgotten, and any fear calls for loving reassurance. It was probably asking too much of Jessica when Ellie took eight-month-old Cathy onto her knee. Cathy and her mother had come to tea. Jessica, who was standing insecurely holding on to Ellie's jeans, bit Cathy's leg. Cathy's mother snatched up her baby, Ellie apologised, and Jessica clambered onto her lap, triumphant.

Two of the most rewarding emotions of all flower at about one: affection for other people and the ability to sympathise. Until now Jack and Jessica accepted love with pleasure but their outlook was strictly selfish. Jack started practising caring with his Teddy, stroking him kindly and wrapping him up if it seemed cold. Jessica put out her plump little hand to pat Ellie's face when she barked her shin and her eyes filled with tears. Your one-year-old's expression will reflect her concern when she is feeling sorry for a person or animal who has been injured or is sad. She used only to be able to convey pleasure or misery in her features.

As well as feeling sorry for someone in distress,

Childhood Development

babies of this specially interesting age begin to feel sorry when they've done something which will upset their mother. Earlier, Jack would have laughed when he managed to turn his dish upside down and all the junior lamb stew spilled on the floor. Aged one, he looked guilty. It is all part of recognising other people as real too, not merely puppets that feed and bath a fellow.

Babies, like us, find it particularly gratifying if they can make someone important laugh. The difference is that a one-year-old will go on doing the same thing again and again. He has no concept that what was clever and amusing the first time is likely to drive his mother spare at the ninth repeat. So be careful what you laugh at. It isn't fair to get cross when your baby is only doing something that seemed to pleased you only five minutes before. For instance, when Jack distinctly said 'Shit' over a difficulty he was having in making the red jelly stay on his spoon, everyone laughed. They would rather he didn't go on saying it . . .

It was the same for Jessica when she learned to drop things for Ellie to pick up. How could she be expected to understand why the joke she had shared with Ellie to start with inexplicably stopped being funny?

Helping your baby's development

There are four essentials at this stage:

A secure environment

The baby from six months to a year is an inveterate explorer and investigator, on a tireless quest for knowledge and new experiences. He or she will have no thought of risk. It is your responsibility to check for danger points and make them safe.

Miracle Months

Space to play

Crawling and practice for walking requires at least a whole room.

Reliable love

The great task of parenthood is to give your child the confidence to tackle whatever life throws up, in the sure and certain knowledge of your love. This has a biblical ring because now, and for some years to come, you are in the wonderful position of being able to turn the sunshine on (or off) for your child, to 'make it all better' when he is hurt, and restore his courage when he is afraid.

Interest and stimulus

For healthy development your baby's body needs a variety of nutrition. His mind, too, is hungry, and the foods it requires are novelty and new experiences. You are his chief guide and teacher at this momentous juncture, when he is on the brink of walking, talking and having grown-up meals.

Play

You can help your growing-up baby by providing toys to exercise his muscular co-ordination and his ingenuity. Most valuable of all are playtimes with you and with his dad. Playthings don't have to be shop-bought or sophisticated. A great favourite at one is a basket with an assortment of harmless articles in it, to pack and unpack. A brief, cheap delight is a sheet of greaseproof paper to crackle and tear, or a stout crayon and paper. A board book, bricks, large and small, to manipulate, a stuffed doll or animal with a simple garment to take on and off, rolling toys and balls, and, if you can bear it, a drum – all of these are grist to the mill of your baby's active body and enquiring mind. (See toy list, p 246).

Although playing with a parent or grandparent is always popular, you don't have to teach a child to play. The exploring and creative urge comes from within. At this stage your child has the gift of awareness of and delight in his world. His current play consists in finding out and doing: imaginative play will come later. Playing with you provides practice in interaction and co-operation – you push his truck towards him, he pushes it back; you put things in it, he takes them out. Or you amaze him with a toy that pops up when you press a button, until he learns the trick of it.

A sturdy wagon with a high handle acts like a supermarket trolley to the old and infirm. It is a help towards walking independently, but for most babies, just one is a little early – although the future is running to meet you, and the wagon will soon be in use. Another aspect of this is your child's need, from this age, for the company of her own generation. Ellie started by taking Jessica with her as a spectator to the local playgroup. She was wide-eyed with interest as she watched from the safety of her mother's knee.

Sarah launched Jack's social life by inviting her friend Fiona to tea: Fiona's little Kirsty was eighteen months old. She looked at Jack with curiosity, but when they were both on the floor with the toys, each played separately. Nevertheless, they were fully aware of each other's presence.

Walking

Walking gives your child a new slant on life, literally. She

Miracle Months

is eye to eye with the rest of us who can walk upright. Jessica loved holding Ellie's or Bill's hand and staggering with her wide, drunken gait round the room, in the garden or by the pond in the park. Jack was into the equivalent of free fall. He liked to lurch independently from Sarah to Dom and back – no hands except at either end.

Talking

Speech is the greatest gift of all. It sets us apart from all other animals. It allows us to exchange our thoughts, our know-how and our feelings. Professor Jean Aitchison, foremost expert in the field, showed in 1996 that, like the eruption of teeth, the acquisition of language is a matter of your child's individual genetic programme. As a mother your role is vital in facilitating this development, but you cannot make your child's brain mature enough to absorb words ahead of what nature had ordained for him.

Language is learned by imitation, and obviously if you seldom speak with your child his eager young mind will have nothing to latch onto. Nor do radio or TV voices have more than a minimal impact. Your baby isn't fooled into thinking that a flickering shape on a screen is a person who can feed him, play with him, or respond to him – any more than your dog is mad to chase a bunny on the box. The onus is on you. If you want your child to learn useful words and to string them together harmoniously, you must provide the material.

It has been calculated that a child has to hear a word 500 times before he or she knows it. It involves a lot of conversation for the learning to take place naturally. Of course, you can teach some single words, like No, Cat, Nose and Drink, but your baby also has to learn

Childhood Development

the rhythm and music of speech. That means talking to her properly, and giving due attention to her efforts to communicate in return. Colwyn Trewarthen imagines that this is what your baby would say if she could:

> 'I know how to be in a conversation, and if you will be polite and listen to me, I will talk to you and learn from you . . .'

Baby talk, concerning 'gee-gees' and the like, can be helpful in presenting the child with words that are easy to imitate, and so give him confidence. But it is also very important for your little imitator to hear ordinary sentences with a normal vocabulary. When you are learning a foreign language you don't have to master the diminutives first, yet babies are better at learning language than we are.

That's why, from one onwards, if not earlier, it makes sense to read little stories to your child. He hears the cadences and sees the pictures, from the snug comfort of your lap. The rhyme and rhythm of verse appeals to your child before he understands the nuts and bolts of language, much as many of us clever adults listen to music with benefit, although we couldn't compose.

Children's rhymes and singing games make effective learning material, but the big plus is the lasting pleasure they give. When people are very old, and their memory is full of holes, they can still repeat 'Pussy-cat, Pussy-cat . . .' and the rest, which they learned with love at their mother's knee eighty years before. Poetry has a place, too. So much of it is as simple as the nursery rhymes, but spangled with beauty. Like Wordsworth's golden daffodils and Stevenson's *Child's Garden of Verses*.

Miracle Months

Teething

The exact timing of when your baby's teeth come through is personally, genetically pre-determined. There's nothing you can do to speed it up or slow it down, and it bears no relation to the rest of his development. Occasionally a baby is born with a tooth already through, and equally it is not abnormal to reach the first birthday with none. The chances are, however, that your baby will get several teeth in his second half-year, so that by ten to fourteen months he'll have the four front incisors, top and bottom, the teeth that show, and the first molars, one each side, top and bottom, for chewing.

Teething is often blamed for any indisposition that affects a baby of this age. It doesn't cause fits, loss of appetite, diarrhoea, bronchitis or a high fever, so any of these symptoms need looking into on their own account. A mild, miserable grumbliness is the worst that can be expected, purely due to teething. Sometimes your baby may splutter, snuffle, gurgle or cough because of the extra saliva filling his mouth, and there is certain to be overflow dribbling.

You may see a little red swelling in the gum where a tooth is about to come through, but there's no call to rub it with gels or ointments, which are anyway washed away almost at once. Your baby will have an instinct to suck, bite and chew everything, as anyone who has brought up a puppy can confirm. If your baby puts his fingers or thumb in his mouth during teething, this doesn't indicate pain but the urge to press his gums onto something. Any toy to hand or the corner of his blanket will be pressed into service, and a hard teething ring to gnaw is very acceptable.

Tooth care should begin as soon as there is a tooth.

Firstly, the Don'ts: dummies dipped in something sweet are out but even worse are those miniature

Childhood Development

comforter bottles containing concentrated fruit juice for the baby to suck at leisure. Drinks of orange, rosehip or blackcurrant juice are an integral part of a baby's diet when milk no longer has the major role. When the first teeth have appeared, the habit should be established of giving your baby a few mouthfuls of water after one of these sweet drinks.

It is never too soon, either, to build up a routine of regular morning and evening tooth cleaning. To start with you simply rub over the tiny teeth and the gums with a piece of gauze or a cotton bud dipped in warm water. A hint of fluoride toothpaste can be introduced after a week or two. The first, soft, real toothbrush comes into play – the right term – around your baby's second birthday. Its use is still your responsibility.

Teeth need exercise. That means biting and chewing as soon as there are enough teeth for both operations. Mushy foods don't provide exercise but bread baked into rusks and pieces of fruit do. Calcium and vitamin D are necessary for healthy teeth. Calcium is no problem for someone whose nourishment is based on milk and dairy products, but drops of vitamins A, C and D make up any shortfall of these when your baby is in the early stages of mixed feeding. Overdosing with vitamins A and D is dangerous, so keep to the recommended quantities. More isn't better. (See teething charts p 271).

Feeds become meals

The way your baby feeds undergoes a revolution during his second six months. At the beginning, even if he can drink from a cup with your help, he or she still needs the pleasure and comfort of sucking some of the time. After the last feed at night you want your baby to sleep soundly and contentedly, well-nourished but not

Miracle Months

stimulated by a contest over who should hold the spoon – or the mug. Whether breast or bottle, this should be the last milk feed to be relinquished.

Your baby will usually indicate when she is bored with this old-fashioned method of feeding: usually at around seven to nine months. Some devoted mothers and their babies may want to go on until the first birthday. That is enough for anyone.

Although your baby may be brilliant at drinking from a cup, it doesn't mean that his metabolism is mature enough to deal with ordinary cow's milk. If there is any allergy in the family – shown by asthma or eczema – it is all the more important to delay giving it for the whole of the first year. There is a specially modified follow-up milk for babies moving on from breast or bottle, but if you do give some cow's milk dilute it with water and boil it until your baby is one. Perhaps, like Sarah, you use skimmed or semi-skimmed milk for yourself. This is not suitable for your baby until he is grown-up too: eighteen years plus.

All the time that Jack was bottle-fed, Sarah had to be meticulous about sterilising all the equipment for making feeds. Ellie didn't have this trouble. When babies move on to mixed feeding, hygiene is still important but not to the point of sterilising. Cans or jars of baby food are sterile until you open them. After that you must keep them in the fridge, and no longer than fresh food.

From six months onwards Jack and Jessica were increasingly enthusiastic about self-help. Jack was particularly fractious if Sarah tried to spoon food into his mouth when he wanted to handle it himself. He was triumphant when he managed to drag the spoon across his tray and then lick it. Jessica was more relaxed about her spooncraft. It was a delight to her to smack the spoon down flat on her puréed vegetables or jammy rice pudding.

Childhood Development

Foods to eat by finger were another fine game, but under-ones have neither the skill nor the equipment for chewing hard lumps. Fingers of cake and pieces of banana were favourites, and on her first birthday Jessica could use her thirteen teeth to eat a finger of soft buttered toast or a biscuit.

Jack had liked holding his own bottle from about six and a half months, but Sarah would never leave him with it. He always had a combined bottle and cuddle. Both babies became more and more adept at drinking from a cup, at first gently poured in by their mothers, then with their own hands steadying the cup, and finally – at one – drinking the last quarter-cupful single-handed. Jessica always put her mug down upside down at the end.

At nine or ten months most babies are ready to have three meals a day, approximately at adult times, for future convenience, and an evening nightcap of milk. This latter can be dropped as the babies sleep right through the night after their supper.

What they enjoyed. At ten months Jessica had a cereal breakfast while Jack had soft-boiled egg on bread-and-butter fingers. (Some mothers don't introduce egg until age one, for fear of allergy.) At lunch they both had a vegetable dinner with meat, fish or cheese incorporated, and supper was fruit with a rice or custard pudding. At first, milk completed every meal, but then they had fruit juice with the midday meal and an extra fruit drink – washed down with water – in the afternoon. Babies get thirsty when more of their food is solid. Until seven or eight months everything has to be sieved or puréed, and from then on it must be mashed or minced so that there are no big lumps.

At one year old Jessica and Jack could both manage lumpy food without choking, except for meat, which requires a full set of milk teeth and a good chewing technique. All the foods must be moistened with gravy or, for sweet dishes, milk, to make swallowing easier. By one, the babies could manage to eat pieces of toast, cheese and fruit by themselves – but it would not have been safe to leave them to eat alone.

After the first year, the aim is to reach a stage when the little one is having the equivalent of a pint of milk a day in one form or another, and some protein (meat, fish, egg, cheese) plus vegetables and fruit. On this mix there is no need for extra vitamins, but meanwhile the tooth and general health vitamins needed are A, C and D, conveniently available as drops.

Jessica was a 'good eater' once she had become accustomed to a new flavour. Jack was conservative. It took many tries to persuade him even to taste something new, and at best he would only eat small quantities. Sarah was worried, but Jack was as lively as a cricket. An undernourished child is quiet and expends the minimum of energy.

Jack's situation was a perfectly normal consequence of much slower growth after the fantastically fast rate in the first six months. Jessica, on the other hand, would have to watch her weight – through her mother. Cuddly baby plumpness could become definite fat. It was a matter of making sure that fruit and vegetables made a sufficient contribution to her diet. This is in line with what many of us adults need, too.

Father's role

Everyone knows that fathers are immensely strong, clever and daring. Bill proved it by swinging Jessica up onto his shoulders for a high exciting ride, her hands clamped round his forehead. Dom showed it by letting Jack put his small feet one each on Dom's large ones, and then walking along. He also played at floor level, a horse or a bear, on all fours. Jack didn't need much encouragement to clamber onto his back for a ride.

All this was good sport, but being a father involves more than playing. Sarah, like Dom, was working, so together they ran through the vital infrastructure of family life, to share out the tasks. In your family, if there are two parents and a baby, how many of these jobs are shared?

General	*Child care*
shopping	preparing food
cooking	feeding
washing-up	changing
Hoovering	bathing
dusting	dressing
washing	putting to bed
ironing	playing and talking
driving	taking for an airing
cleaning car	getting up in the night
earning money	arranging a baby-sitter

How often do you and your partner have an adults only outing? They are essential for re-charging your batteries as parents.

Grandparents' corner

Now that your grandchild is mobile, your daughter or daughter-in-law has to be on the *qui vive* every moment the cute little darling is awake. Mercifully he or she still has an afternoon nap – although in Jack's case nap was a misnomer. He accepted that he had to spend an hour in his cot after the midday meal, but his wistful, bright eyes watched Sarah as she left the room, and whenever she peeped in he would still be wide-awake. He was usually standing up, ready for the next bit of excitement.

Ellie and her mother-in-law disagreed about Jessica's rest. Ellie thought it better for her to get thoroughly tired in the day, so that she would be sure to sleep at night. Her mother-in-law felt sure that, at this age, Jessica would get over-tired without a daytime rest and be whiney and miserable by the time Bill came in. There are a host of points where an experienced grandmother is convinced that she knows best – but she isn't in the driving seat. Nobody welcomes a back-seat driver.

Although your grandchild may unexpectedly turn shy with you at this age (it is purely a matter of a stage in maturity), there has never been a time when the parents were in more need of a break. Now that he or she has graduated to mixed feeding, verging on normal meals, you can sometimes take your grandchild to your place – for instance on one of the weekend days. This is more comfortable for you, and it means the baby's mother can relax in her own home if she wishes, without any worrying baby sounds.

It is worth having nappies and a change of baby clothes, mealtime supplies and a few oddments of toys at your place, and, if you can run to it, a clip-on high chair. The stimulation of a different environment is of benefit to your grandchild: a new world to conquer and enjoy, much as you might feel on a holiday in Rome or the Costa del Sol. Your conversation will also enrich your grandchild's mind and vocabulary.

If your partner is available, that is a big bonus. Grandfathers and grandchildren have a natural affinity for each other. There is a kind of mutual respect, even at this age. But the greatest boon you as grandparents can bestow is a sense of unhurry: all the time in the world to play the same game over and over, or for trying to make a spoon work.

You are valuable as a sounding board during discussions on education – from nursery school to comprehensive or public. It is wise to keep your opinions under wraps until you know where the real parents stand, and perhaps the other grandparents. Self-restraint and tact is the name of the game.

However much or little you have been able to see your grandchild during his or her first year, you will have helped to build a sense of security, trust in his environment and a hopeful outlook for the future. If you have not been able to do as much as you would have liked, don't have regrets. Too much help, or anxiety in case he hurts himself, can blunt your grandchild's motivation to experiment and practise new skills.

5

Toddlers:
one to three years

The toddler is a bundle of delights and surprises. For a parent it's like April: the sunshine of seeing your baby of eighteen months toddling gaily towards you, arms outstretched like a tightrope walker; the storm of a two-year-old's tantrum, when communication isn't equal to the emotions he's feeling.

And in between, the uneven advance towards better weather. There will be great achievements in the two years from one to three:
– walking
– talking
– toileting

Progress will be in fits and starts and stops, and when there are forward strides in one area, there may be a standstill in another. The art of being a successful parent with a happy toddler means allowing Nature to set the pace. You cannot hasten the maturation of your child's muscle or mind, but if you let yourself become anxious you may spoil the fun – for both of you.

Fifteen months

Walking

Your one-year-old could barely stand without holding on – now he or she is firm on two feet, independently. She won't be able to balance on one foot until she is about three. This is the time for endless walking practice. Jack was on the move non-stop and getting into everywhere. Sarah reminded herself that fifteen months is the peak age for accidents.

Jessica, like most children who go in for the bottom-shuffle type of crawling, was slower to get into the swing of walking. You could see the effort in her expression, her head held forwards, her feet wide apart, and lifted high for each step, arms waving. A baby-walker gave her confidence, but most of all she liked to push a wagon full of blocks, her bear, a squeaky doll, a rag book and all the bric-à-brac of babyhood. When she sat down, which happened suddenly and often in her tottery walk, she enjoyed unpacking all her goods and then piling them in again.

When she was holding Bill's hand in her proprietorial fashion, she stepped out more boldly, with short, erratic paces. When Jack was 'out for a walk' he preferred to hold on to the pushchair, rather than a parent's hand: a preview of an independent attitude. However, like Jessica, he was holding up his arms to be carried after a very short walk.

Jack was fascinated with throwing – toys, food, everything – but balls he found especially interesting. After seeing some boys playing football when he was out with Dom, he wanted to kick a ball himself. But after he had walked right up to his ball, his foot did not seem to know what to do.

Jessica didn't throw as well as Jack: she rolled her ball rather than sending it flying through the air. On the other hand she was expert at getting hold of her mug by the handle, but in her excitement she usually tipped it too quickly, so that she lost most of the juice. It was rather the same with her spoon. She plunged it deep into the dish, with her elbow held high, but somehow her spoon did not pick much up. Anyway, it kept turning upside down by itself before she could get it to her mouth.

Toddlers

Jack regarded his plate, spoon and mug and all the contents as play material. He particularly enjoyed putting his whole hand into the dish and then squeezing the food between his fingers. He would struggle with Sarah to keep hold of the dish when she wanted to pick it up and finish the meal with the minimum of mess.

Jack was confident now in balancing one brick on top of another: a feat of hand–eye co-ordination. If he had three bricks he would carefully arrange them in a row, and if there were more he made a pile. At this stage the method of testing every toy or new object in the mouth was in decline. People like Jack could do more constructive things with them now.

Both babies had started drawing. Jack used his crayon to make dots on the paper by a hitting action: at first these were very faint, but then he pressed harder, grunting audibly. Jessica, holding her crayon tightly in her fist, made a scribble of vertical lines, and was clearly pleased with the result. Both children, now that they were 'writing' as well as reaching and throwing, showed a preference for their right hands. Around ten per cent of boys and slightly fewer girls are perfectly normally left-handed. This may occasionally lead to some awkwardness, for instance with scissors, but it can sometimes be an advantage, for instance in tennis and other sports.

By the time they were one, Jessica and Jack had each acquired a small vocabulary: Jack scored three and Jessica seven. She streaked ahead between one and one and a quarter, and learned more than a dozen new words, then the rate slowed down. Ellie was worried, but needlessly. It is the usual thing for babies to go ahead with a rush after the first word, and then almost mark time from fifteen to eighteen months. Jack's progress was slower, but slightly more even.

Talking, at fifteen months, is like playing with sounds

Childhood Development

instead of toys most of the time, but occasionally using words as an aid to communication. Your baby uses his hands and arms to help you to understand that 'Mama' means he wants you to carry him, or he wants you to give him some article which he is pointing to, or that he is definitely not going to eat his dinner.

You may have heard about some babies who were clean and dry by some enviably early age. In fact, from around age one, babies' motions often tend to come at a regular time and you may have the good luck to 'catch' them, but the nerves to the bowel and bladder are only just beginning to convey messages. There is a rumour around that when a baby has learned to leave go of a toy and drop it at will, it means that he is ready for toilet-training. Unfortunately this is wishful thinking, and your baby won't have any control over water or motions until he is about two.

The first sign, which does arise now, however, is an interested awareness of a puddle on the floor or a motion in the nappy.

'Ooh,' said Jessica, pointing out a warm, damp patch on the carpet. At this stage a baby cannot distinguish, from her sensations, whether she has passed a motion or urine. She may not be able to do so for another six months.

Eighteen months

Halfway through the second year is a good time to take stock, and it is sometimes marked by a check-up at the clinic. In the last six months your baby will probably have put on 2–3lbs (1.5kg), grown taller than 2½ft (61.5cm) and have several more teeth. With any luck he'll still sleep thirteen hours at night, but he or she won't go to bed so willingly nor settle for his afternoon rest. In the latter case you may have to compromise with a shorter time and toys to play with,

Toddlers

while you re-charge your batteries, urgently.

Jack couldn't run yet, but he had a busy, important way of hurrying: it reminded me of a head teacher I once had. His movements were rather stiff and flat, but it was faster and different from his usual toddling walk. He could also walk upstairs if Sarah held his hand and come down on his own by crawling backwards. Jessica could come downstairs by herself, too, but her method was sitting down and bumping from stair to stair. Both toddlers could do a big jump off the bottom step, with one foot forward, and in Jessica's case, holding Ellie's hand.

Whether it was a form of emotional support or for plain pleasure, Jessica always took her doll with her when she walked round the room: tucked under her arm, like a lady's handbag. Other children carry such companions by an arm or a leg. At her granny's flat there was a little chair that Jessica loved to sit in: she could manage this quite neatly. Jack was keener to climb into the grown-ups' chairs, and he sometimes pushed one of them round the floor. As well as standing, sitting and lying down, he – and Jessica – could squat down or kneel, which was useful when they were playing.

Jessica had a lot of pleasure from a small doll's pram, but as well as pushing, the toddlers had learned how to pull a toy along behind them without snagging it at every step. Jack had a lorry and Jessica had a dog on wheels which waggled its tail as it moved. They could both walk further now, often running ahead of their mothers in the park. But progress was agonisingly slow for the mothers. Firstly, there was the insistence on bringing a toy to drag along, then numerous halts en route to look at some animal, vegetable or mineral that had caught the child's attention. We, as adults would miss out if we didn't have a very young scout to point out, say, a leaf scudding in the wind or a drain making a gurgly noise.

Childhood Development

Your toddler can drink fairly well by herself now – and will expect you to be on hand to take the mug directly she has finished. If you aren't ready, she's just as likely to drop it on the floor. Jessica had mastered the trick of filling her spoon with dinner or pudding; the big snag was that she still couldn't get it all the way to her mouth without its turning over. Jack was, if possible, an even messier eater than Jessica, and to make matters worse, his appetite was chancy. This is quite common at around eighteen months, but Sarah was worried when he hardly ate anything.

This is the age when fathers may be enrolled to cajole or compel their offspring to eat. The winner of such battles is always the child. Since the phase of poor eating is usually temporary, the wisest parent will try to curb her anxiety and be patient. The worst outcome is to make the child dislike mealtimes. Jack responded better when Sarah filled the spoon for him and left him to put it in his mouth as best he could. He wouldn't yet eat anything with lumps in it.

Jessica, the good eater, always handed her empty dish, like her mug, to Ellie, knowing that she was a Good Girl. This was one of the first two-word phrases she was to learn.

Jack could now balance three bricks in a tower most times, and on one occasion, four. Jessica could only do two for certain, but often three. Boys are commonly better with bricks and balls at this age, but girls lead in arts and language. Jessica was an enthusiastic artist. She scribbled round and round, all over the paper and off the edge, but with her extra confidence she didn't press so hard now. Jack did straight lines up and down and across. They both enjoyed painting when their mothers could face the clearing up afterwards. You get a dramatic result so quickly and easily. Neither of them felt a need to use more than one colour at this stage. Ellie chose red and Jack, unexpectedly went for black, completely obliterating one of his drawings.

Imitation is the child's royal route to learning. It can sometimes make you laugh to see these little ones aping their elders with absolute seriousness. Ellie often 'phoned her friends: Jessica had endless jargon 'conversations' into her toy telephone. Dom read the *Financial Times* at breakfast: Jack would just as solemnly peruse a single sheet of paper, trying to make it lean against his mug. Mother-care of a doll or stuffed animal occupied both children equally – feeding, hair-brushing, putting to bed, with a running commentary throughout.

Peg-boards and posting boxes were favourite puzzles, and beads as big as cotton reels to thread.

Language was consolidating, rather than growing fast at eighteen months. 'M's and 'd's were both mastered but some of the more difficult consonants were simply left out. For Jack 'i-ee' meant 'pretty' and 'ungy' meant 'hungry', Jessica had some real sentences: 'Who dat?' 'I do it' 'All gone' as well as 'Googirl'. Babies know a lot more than they say. It was easy for Jack to point out a dog, a car, or a man in his picture book, if he was asked, and he officiously turned the pages, two or three at a time, for Sarah or Dom. Boys are especially good at learning the parts of the body – eyes, hair, nose and mouth in that order are usually the first. Girls of one and a half are usually slightly better at talking.

Language, like teeth, is acquired according to an individual, in-built programme in the early stages, and it is not linked with the rest of development. What we have mentioned are merely averages, and it is perfectly normal for one child to have a wordstore of two at eighteen months, while another may already know 200. Because this comes under genetic control, late or super-early talking tends to run in families, but remember Albert Einstein saying nothing until he was four.

Toddlers love rhymes and stories with repetitive phrases like 'Fee, fi, fo, fum' or 'Eeny, meeny, miney, mo.' Jessica had one of her own. It was 'Diggle, doggle, daggle' and she would say it over and over while she played by herself.

Socially, toddlers are often shy with adult strangers, but they do their utmost to amuse those whom they know. They will repeat anything that has been praised as good or clever, and especially if it has made a grown-up laugh. Jessica would laugh herself first, as though that would be infectious. It often was. One of her favourite jokes was to 'hide' behind a chair, then toddle out and say 'Bo!' to Ellie. 'Bye-bye' was already a well-established social phrase for both babies, but Sarah was anxious to teach Jack to say 'please' and 'thank you'. In the end, he sometimes did, but usually not to important visitors.

The top social skill, of course, is bladder and bowel control. Jack and Jessica now seemed aware of an 'accident' in their nappy just before it happened, but not in time to convey the need for a potty. Sometimes Jessica would wake up from her nap dry, and she enjoyed being told how good she was. Both she and Jack sometimes cried in the night if they were wet. You might think that this signalled that they were ready for potty-training, but it was probably still too soon.

There seems to be a connection with walking, and it is certainly useless to hope for toilet control before walking is well-established. The best age to learn seems to be about two, when the mental and nervous pathways are completed.

Two years

The two-year-old is an unsurpassed charmer, more full

Toddlers

of fun than ever before, and more passionate in frustration. He or she is all opposites: half-hiding from you by putting her fingers over her eyes and peeping between them, giving you a toy or a half-eaten biscuit and then taking it back, swaggering along with a swashbuckling air one moment, then running to cling to you the next. It's also the time when a baby cot is exchanged for a proper bed, and a toileting breakthrough is on the cards. In the last six months he may have grown 2ins (5cm), put on 3lbs (1.5kg), and acquired a total of sixteen teeth.

On the athletics front, Jack could walk all the way upstairs without adult help, though he had to put both feet on the same tread before stepping up to the next one. The same *dot-and-carry* method applied for coming down, and now he could jump with both feet together off the bottom step. He could jump off the ground, too. That was all right, but Sarah's heart was in her mouth when he scaled the heights of the climbing frame in the park, or up the step-ladder to the slide. Jessica loved to slide down, but she wouldn't climb up to it by herself.

Jessica could run, but it was rather a waddle, with feet well apart: cornering was tricky. Jack could balance on one leg for a matter of seconds, and Jessica could stand on tiptoe. She often did, to reach things. In one area of climbing Jessica was a step ahead of Jack. She had discovered how useful a chair could be for reaching the interesting objects Ellie put on the higher shelves and surfaces, imagining them to be out of harm's way. Jessica could push a chair across the smooth kitchen floor, clamber onto it and hey presto! a newly baked tartlet was in her hand. It could just as well have been something dangerous. Ellie felt that nothing was safe.

Coached by Dom, Jack could manage to kick a ball – more of a nudge with his toe – after walking up to it. He was also nearly able to pedal his trike, instead of

Childhood Development

pushing the ground with his feet: he pedalled with his right foot and pushed with his left, at first. Jessica meanwhile was learning to catch as well as throw her big ball. She held out both arms and Ellie or Bill had to lob the ball gently into them: it often slipped straight through.

Two-year-olds relish every sort of bodily activity, and they have a characteristically physical way of expressing delight – dancing, jumping, clapping, laughing aloud and even screeching for joy. They have one big fault when you are on a walk, though: an inveterate tendency to dawdle. It's a phase that passes – after about a year . . .

Almost every day both children were acquiring new skills of the precision type. They could pick up the smallest crumb, or pin or button, and wield a pencil with confidence, making round and round drawings. In Jessica's case there were dots and criss-cross lines as well. Painting was energetic too, more like scrubbing the paper with one colour on top of another, resulting in a muddy-looking splodge. The artist clearly derived great satisfaction from this result.

Fitting pegs into round, square and triangular slots was old hat, superseded by small jigsaws with big pieces, and Jack in particular enjoyed building with interlocking bricks. He could build a tower six blocks high, but preferred arranging them in a row or other tidy pattern. Jessica wasn't so interested in bricks, although she could balance four or five without difficulty. She had learned to snip paper with round-ended scissors, and also managed to hack some of her hair off. Nowadays, if she dropped a toy or put it down when she was busy with something else, she didn't forget about it as she would have done six months ago. She would look round for it, even under cushions and other odd places.

Imaginative play is in the bud at two. Both Jack and

Toddlers

Jessica practised mothering techniques with dolls, toy animals and dolly-sized equipment, and traffic control with little cars and lorries. They talked all the time in appropriate tones, even if the words did not always make sense. This type of play shows the child inventing his own world. The next stage is 'Let's pretend' with another person, child or adult. This is unlikely before two and a half.

Eating is more or less under control at two. Jessica could pick up her mug with one hand, almost nonchalantly, drink from it and put it down, without spilling. With her dinners, she could at last get most of the spoonful into her mouth without losing too much. Nowadays, too, she could chew and swallow automatically, even if there were little lumps in the food.

Meals with Jack were not such a pleasure. He probably had as much hand control as Jessica, but he had a maddening habit of stirring his food round and round instead of eating it, or holding up a spoonful and watching the food slide off. Added to this he had learned the phrase 'Not nice' which he applied frequently, before as well as after the first taste. Dawdling, with Jack, extended to mealtimes.

Trying to persuade him to eat up, or telling him he was naughty when he went on messing about, was a waste of breath. Although he knew plenty of words, Jack was not yet capable of following a rational argument. That is why it is fruitless to reason with a two-year-old who is having a tantrum.

Easy-going Jessica sailed through the tantrum months – eighteen to thirty, give or take – with no more than an occasional display of temper, when she would stamp her foot and scream. Jack, the highly strung type, had a run of tantrums when he couldn't make himself understood, or if he did, when what he wanted wasn't forthcoming. The latter situation often cropped up somewhere public like the supermarket, and Sarah felt

Childhood Development

the eyes of the whole world were focused on her and her son. Jack would be beside himself with rage and frustration, jumping up and down, screaming and even rolling on the floor.

Once or twice he held his breath until he fell down with his face a dreadful blue colour. This was frightening for Sarah, and the first time she took him to the doctor for a check, to make sure that there were no medical reasons for the attack. The doctor reassured her that there was no danger that Jack would stop breathing altogether. As soon as he became faint, likely after about fifteen seconds, he would begin breathing automatically, and recover quickly and completely. Usually he had started breathing before that.

Various manoeuvres such as slapping or trying to force the child's mouth open do no good, and a reaction by the mother of upset and panic – natural enough – is wrong, too. The whole performance is a kind of blackmail – to get your attention and whatever he wants. What you need to do is check that your child is in a safe, comfortable position for recovery, then ignore the whole affair. When Sarah tried this, Jack had a run of even more dramatic attacks. Nevertheless, staying firm did pay off in the end, and the breath-holding ploy fizzled out.

In a way, tantrums are a sign of development. They are a side-effect of the little one's drive towards expressing him- or herself: he almost bursts with the effort but can't make himself understood, or can't convince the grown-up of how much it means to him to have or do whatever it is he wants. Unfortunately there is no wonder cure for tantrums. It is sensible to avoid the triggering situations without capitulating to the young tyrant's demands once he's started his tantrum. The only thing to do is to gather him or her up, hold him tight and tell him you love him, as you escape to

Toddlers

somewhere quiet or back home. This applies just the same after a breath-holding episode.

Talking

After walking comes talking, though of course they overlap. Since frustration, even to the point of tantrums, stems from difficulties in communication, language has a high priority at this age. There is an enormous leap in the number of words learned between twenty-one months and twenty-four. The average increase is over 150, so that the two-year-old has 200 or 300 words at his disposal – and in a few cases as many as 1000. Girls are usually a little ahead of boys, to make up for a lesser bent for construction toys.

The new words cover a wide range: inanimate objects, animals, people, actions and descriptions such as 'hot', 'pretty' or 'bad'. The terms 'mine', 'me', 'you' and 'I' appear in that order, as a rule, but two-year-olds often refer to themselves by name. 'Jack do it' was a favourite expression, and 'Eska a good girl' from Jessica.

It wasn't just naming things. Now the toddlers were using three- and four-syllable sentences:
'What's dat?'
'Where Daddy gone?'
'I don't want go to bed.'
'Granny go bye-bye.'
'Jack not like lady.'
Children of this age soak up, like blotting paper, anything you say, so it behoves you to avoid the phrases you don't want to hear repeated. It isn't only the swear words, but throw-away remarks about, say, your in-laws, made in a moment of irritation. Naming the details of pictures in a book, and carrying out simple

instructions, such as 'Fetch your wellies', are well within your two-year-old's compass, and make her feel important.

Although younger children can enjoy hearing stories it is only now that they are beginning to have real meaning. Some of the most riveting are about the listener him- or herself, but those from illustrated books have another delight. With her new, neater finger control Jessica could turn the pages over one at a time, dead on cue, when Ellie was reading to her. Jack, the mimic, liked to sit in his small chair 'reading' his book.

Although language is immensely useful, it does not mean that your child is backward if he says very little while other people's toddlers are chattering away. Up until this age every child runs to an individual developmental programme for language, but they all end up as talkers. Some of them appear to wait until they are sure of both pronunciation and grammar before they commit themselves: these are usually bright children. Sometimes an illness or tension in the home slows down a child's talking. From two years onwards, the input from parents and others has a major effect on progress in language.

Everyday skills now include washing and dressing. Jack liked to wash his hands 'by the self', as he said. He could dry them, too, though not very well. Jessica was interested in her clothes. She could not only take her shoes and socks off, if the laces were undone, but she could stuff her feet into her shoes. There was a fifty:fifty chance of their ending up on the right feet. She could also find the armholes in her frocks and coats. Jack could pull his pants down but not up, and he was interested in buttons, but he had not yet fathomed out how they work.

Toddlers

Toilet-training

By now Jessica and Jack had learned to distinguish, from their sensations, between passing a motion and passing water. They also – with their mothers' help – invented words for each function. Usually every family has its own toilet vocabulary and easy words like 'pee' and 'pooh' and 'loo' are quickly learned. Bowel control is the first to be mastered, particularly if a regular time of day for sitting on the potty is established.

One snag, which can be puzzling unless you know about it, is that a child who has usually passed a motion in the right place without any problem, may suddenly start to hold on to his motion at the crucial moment. In fact, the first stage of learning to control the sphincter – the ring of muscle at the exit – is how to tighten it. Learning to relax it, at will, comes later. This is similar to the way your baby learned to grasp things in his hand long before he could control the letting go.

Several aspects of childhood learning seem to go backwards. Undressing, for example, comes before dressing, and tipping things out before packing them away. It makes matters worse, that is, the sphincter tightens all the more, if there is a feeling of tension around potty-training. Of course you are pleased when a potty is used for the right purpose, but it is a mistake to overdo the pleasure. It can be muddling for a toddler who has – apparently – produced something wonderfully good in the potty, only to see his mother throw it away down the pan.

A lot of children manage to achieve fairly reliable bowel control at about two, but there are bound to be a few accidents. At the same time, rather tiresomely, toddlers want to pass water more often. They are practising responding to the particular sensation. A reasonable programme is to 'pot' the youngster three times a day after meals, and before bed as a routine and at other times if he asks. Jack became resistant to the whole concept when he felt he was being bothered too often, but Jessica would sit happily on her potty, thinking, it seemed, of other things.

Learning bowel and bladder control is like learning to ride a bicycle. Sooner or later, and in this case usually somewhere between two and three, the child discovers that he is actually in charge of what happens. This is a proud moment. At two, a dry night is an occasional treat for the mothers, but not something to bank on.

Three years

With the third birthday your child has graduated from toddler status into an official-sounding pre-school child. He or she is a sensible, serious individual who is just beginning to experience the immensity and strangeness of the wide world outside his home.

Jack still got enormous pleasure from running, jumping, kicking, throwing, climbing and tricycling – all the big muscle activities – but now he was spending more time on sedentary play. Concentration was conveyed in his expression and his every movement while he painted, drew, did a jigsaw, built a house or worked with a puzzle box.

Jessica's big advance was in talking. She was fast becoming a chatterbox, naming things with a know-it-all air, and making comments. While two-year-olds have a wordstore of 200, on average, by their next birthday this has escalated to about 1000. To Ellie it seemed that Jessica used all that number and more, all the time.

Some three-year-olds enjoy the melody value of words, and chant them in a sing-song way; some use the words for their meaning in exchanges with other people. Jessica was learning the real value of words by

Toddlers

talking to herself, her dolls and Rabbit as she played. She was both an actress and a commentator in these games.

The big bonus for the parents of a three-year-old is that, at last, you can bargain with your child. As well as being able to follow your explanations, she can imagine 'after tea' or 'tomorrow' and will accept your promise of a treat to come. In this situation of learning trust, your promises must be sacred.

Some young children can only be understood by their family because they haven't mastered the trickier bits of articulation. 'R's can come out as 'w's so that 'run' sounds like 'wun' or 'ride' like 'wide'. 'Th' is usually quite difficult for three-year-olds, but that doesn't hold them back from talking freely of 'dis' and 'dat' and 'dere'.

Questions are beginning to dominate your conversations with your child:

'What is dis?'
'Who is dat?'
'Where does dis go?'

Questions are so enjoyable that there may be a lot of silly or meaningless ones, not planned to irritate you, but part of speech development.

Three-year-olds are charming companions. They are naturally affectionate, although sometimes jealous, and want to please you. They feed themselves without help and are interested and involved in dressing and undressing. They can undo easy-to-reach buttons and unlace shoes.

Many children are dry at night when they are three, but others, due to a slower time-schedule in bladder development, may be four or even five before they achieve this. This is perfectly normal. It may help to 'lift' your little one when you go to bed. The touch of the potty will make him pass water automatically, without even waking up, in some cases. But it doesn't

Childhood Development

matter having a night-time nappy until his bladder can cope.

When they were three, Jack and Jessica could both go to the toilet by themselves, but would always mention the fact. They were not very efficient at wiping themselves. Sometimes when Jack was busy playing he would put off the trip to the loo. Then he would dance up and down trying to keep control until he got there, but not always avoiding wet pants.

Jack knew he was a boy and Jessica knew she was a girl, and they categorised others accordingly. When she went to the playgroup Jessica realised that boys stood up to pass water, but that she couldn't. Clothes don't give clues to gender any more, when unisex dungarees give way to unisex jeans and even haircuts are the same. Nevertheless there are fundamental differences in interests and skills between boys and girls. These are built in with the genes, and are not just a matter of parental expectations and the way they treat their offspring. Of course individual variations can buck the trend and a boy may shine in language and expressing feelings, while a girl may like machinery and construction toys better than dolls.

Helping your child's development

Helping your toddler to derive the maximum satisfaction from the magical years, one to three, and achieve his potential, doesn't mean your taking charge. You cannot control your child's development any more than you can make a plant grow and blossom. But in either case you can provide the best possible environment. The basics are freedom, with safety, to play and experiment, sufficient space and a variety of materials. You must also supply the stimulus of new scenes, new people and an introduction to the world of the arts.

Toddlers

This means hands-on involvement: music to hear, to sing and to play on a xylophone, toy piano, or tambourine; rhythmic movement in dancing or swaying or jumping in tune; and literature from books and stories from out of your head. Science comes in, too, with sand and water play. And of course, the whole package is wrapped in love and an interest in what, to your toddler, are his remarkable achievements.

The toy list (see p 246) grows and includes clay, sand, mud, stones and water, including soap bubbles and the equally messy finger paints. Equipment for playing 'house' comprises dolls, carry-cot, bed and bedding, cooking utensils, broom, dustpan and brush, and a toy telephone. You can set up a makeshift house with a table, chairs and sheets. Sizeable toys like a Wendy house; sandpit, bucket and spade; climbing frame and slide; swing and tunnel aren't practicable in a flat and may not be affordable even if you have plenty of space.

The local park may have some equipment suitable for small-timers, but one of the best ideas from two to two and a half is to consider pooling resources in a playgroup, or entering your toddler at a nursery school. Most children at nursery school are three- and four-year-olds, but it is worthwhile going along with your toddler and staying with him for a few sessions when he or she is two or more. She might benefit from going two or three mornings a week before taking it on every day. Playgroups run by mothers are more relaxed, and a gentle introduction to activities out of the home, in the company of other children.

There are two Don'ts in helping your toddler's development: one to do with athletics, the other with language. You may be happy for your young limb to use the home as a giant climbing frame and the sofa as a trampoline. Nobody minds the under-ones clambering about – so long as they are safe – but from toddler age, other people, even doting grannies, are unlikely to be as tolerant as you when their property looks like being wrecked. To save problems for your child – and you – it is better from now on to find opportunities for climbing and jumping out-of-doors, and make the sitting room furniture off limits.

The other Don't concerns talking. It can work in two opposite ways. Some parents are so keen that their child shall speak properly, that they are forever correcting him when he gets it wrong. But at this stage, talking at all is an achievement, which you don't want to inhibit. If you often talk with your child your example will be his best teacher, since at this stage he can only learn by imitation. He is trying his best, anyway.

The reverse mistake comes from being enchanted by the quaint way your toddler expresses himself. He or she is so serious when she tries out a grown-up phrase. Jack when he was three often heard his dad talking politics, and discussing the prime minister. Jack felt very clever when he talked about the Pie-man, who was always making 'stakes'. Sarah and Dom found this so amusing that they, too, referred to the Pie-man's stakes. It may have been funny, but it didn't help Jack, who was so anxious to communicate with dignity and correctness.

Father's role

Jack, the natural acrobat, liked nothing better than rough-and-tumble play with Dom, while Jessica particularly enjoyed gardening with Bill. She used her small fork energetically, copying him, and liked patting the earth with her plump hands. DIY is a magnet for people of one and a half plus and they want to be within inches of the action, helping.

Fathers are liable to do novel and exciting things,

Toddlers

not the dull household routine that mother and toddler know by heart. And fathers don't keep saying 'Mind' and 'Be careful.' The main fault in fathers is that they work, often early and late and bring extra home at weekends. Mothers who work outside the home usually make a superhuman effort to make sure their children don't lose by it.

A small son or daughter needs a dad as a source of confidence and a stimulus to adventure. It is a tragedy if he is so busy that he cannot fit his own child into his schedule. The loss for the child is enormous, but there's a loss for the man, too. What is needed, through ingenuity and determination if necessary, is quality time shared by father and offspring, not a ritual walk at weekends and a goodnight kiss in the week, if the toddler isn't quite asleep. In a recent study by Care for the Family it was found that around fifteen per cent of men don't see their small-timers at all during the week.

New men are thin on the ground and they may not make the most dynamic dads anyway. It is commonplace for a father to be sidelined or to sideline himself, during the babyhood period of nought to one. It is not too late to take on the fathering role at toddler-time. It is exactly the age when the more active approach of the male parent chimes in with the child's growing obsession with movement, muscle work, climbing, kicking and throwing.

Daddy's reading aloud is always special. There is the comfortable, safe, cuddly aspect without any babyish sentimentality. It adds dignity to the procedure to have a man's serious voice telling the story, and reality to parts about the Wolf or the Giant.

Grandparents' corner

Both grandparents can enjoy the toddler stage, and

grandfathers no longer feel irrelevant. They are not usually expert in nappy-craft or mopping up operations, but are first-class at entertaining a toddler who is mobile, likely to be relatively dry, and able to exchange a few words. Grandfathers are especially valuable where there is an absent father.

Grandmothers, as ever, are the key players, however. In the early toddler years your grandchild may still be going through a mother-clinging phase. It isn't personal and it doesn't last. It is up to you to be understanding and reassuring, and then it will pass all the sooner.

At toddler age baby days are over. Your grandchild is an individual with his own ideas and a will of his own. This is a time when you may find yourself at odds with the way your daughter or daughter-in-law, abetted by her partner, is bringing up the young innocent. For instance she may believe in complete freedom, letting the little one call all the shots. Or she and her partner may like to let him or her stay up as long as he can keep his eyelids open, or bring him down to join the adults, if he wakes in the evening. If you don't care for these methods, you must bite your lip. It is essential.

Equally, you may think that one and three quarters is too young for nursery school: but this is for the parents to decide. You may strongly disapprove that the couple still smoke. Again, it is not for you to pass judgement. And you may annoy the parents by using baby talk when their highly intelligent toddler knows that a horse is not a 'gee-gee' and a cat is just a cat, not a pussy-cat.

The greatest benefit you can confer on your grandchild is to create harmony between the generations: all three. Your reward will be never to be excluded from each funny, delightful stage in your grandchild's development. You are also likely to be exploited as an inexpensive resource for baby-sitting at weekends and evenings, but you can set the ground-rules for that.

It is even more gratifying now to give this fascinating little person presents and watch his delight. There is a danger in generosity. It is vital not to outdo a child's parents. If you really want to make a special, or expensive gift, it works best if you do it through your daughter or daughter-in-law. All you lose is some of the immediate kudos, but you will gain in the whole family relationship.

Something that you can give which will upset no one and give the toddler long-lasting pleasure is teaching her some of the old nursery rhymes and songs. Remember 'Ring o' ring o' roses', 'One, two, buckle my shoe', 'Ride a cock horse', 'Sing a song of sixpence' and a hundred others? If your grandchild picks up some of the words, she gets a fine sense of achievement straight off, and a long-term link with generations of children long past and those to come.

6

Three–Four–Five Child Alive:
the pre-school years

There's no doubt about it. There's a child in the house. The signs are everywhere, in sight and sound and feeling, and there's no pretending that you are not a family.

From three through five it's as though a fairy godmother were showering your little one with the most priceless gifts. She already has the basics of speech, but now it bursts into flower, and between three and four she – or he – makes a stupendous discovery. Taking her first peek at the world outside home, she finds other people. They are quite separate from her, unlike Mummy and Daddy who have always been there and are an integral part of her existence. A sense of personal identity clicks in, together with the vocabulary to go with it: 'me', 'mine', 'I' and, of course, her or his given name.

Jack and Jessica noticed that some other people were men, others women, or their junior counterparts: boys and girls. Then the final penny dropped. Jack knew for certain that he was a boy, and Jessica that she was a girl. Ellie said that Jessica had been well aware of her particular feminine charm since she was two, from the shameless way she flirted with her dad.

Four to five is the age of imagination, the magic wand of childhood that transforms an old tree trunk into a train, a boat or a bucking bronco – in the

Three–Four–Five Child Alive

twinkling of an idea. Anything is possible. Five years old, by contrast, is the doorway to thinking. Imagination is reined in by rational thought, with the word skills to express it. Now that Jack could communicate effectively, tantrums became a phase of the past.

A revolutionary change, which will influence the rest of your child's life crops up now. From three to five your young hopeful leaves home, at first for nursery school then for serious education, with sums and reading.

Rising four and four years

Physical progress. As well as exciting new adventures in the mind, your child is making steady physical progress. From birthday to birthday from years three to seven, your child is likely to grow 2½–3 inches (6–7.5cm) taller and to put on 5–6lbs (2.25–2.7kg); and there is a metamorphosis from toddler to schoolchild shape. The cuddly chubbiness of babyhood fines down: more noticeably in Jack than Jessica. The sticking-out tummy gets flatter, legs are proportionately longer and muscles sturdier. Your child's face alters, too, as the jaw bones develop to make room for the permanent teeth. They will start coming through at about six.

One part that doesn't grow as fast as the rest is your child's head. Both his head and the brain inside it were already more than sixty per cent adult size when your toddler was two. When he is five it will have reached ninety per cent. But the greatest miracle of all, development within the brain, is hidden from view. A major process, called myelination, is going on: the naked nerves are coated with a protective sheath without which they are unable to transmit messages. This conversion is now almost complete for the thinking part of the brain, and makes possible the fantastic advance in your child's mental powers at this age.

Childhood Development

Thinking, reasoning, imagination and creativity are all burgeoning from three to five, and are served by the word-power to formulate them.

Jack, at this age, was into high-speed living, with occasional stops for rest and refuelling. His mind was exploring everything, and his muscular equipment was geared for a lifestyle of running, doing a running jump, climbing, swinging by his arms and even skipping – after a fashion. He could kick, using his knee now as well as his hip joint. This was far more effective than his wooden-legged effort of a few months before.

He could throw overarm or with a wide horizontal swing, and catch fairly efficiently. Jessica, at four, could do all these things, but she wasn't much interested in kicking and her method of throwing didn't make the ball go as far as Jack. For some odd genetic reason girls tend to use a downward throw from the shoulder.

Stairs, of course, are a doddle by now, and walking along the top of lowish walls a particular pleasure. Confidence leads to a mild show-off tendency. Ellie and Sarah didn't know whether to discourage feats of daring, or to cross their fingers while their young ones gained experience through practice.

The finer muscle skills also develop apace at this age. Jessica was first to hold her crayon the grown-up way, and her drawings were beginning to have some resemblance to what she said they represented. At three and a half her portrait of Ellie consisted of a big oval with a squiggle in the middle for features and two draggly lines for legs coming out at the bottom. From four onwards she began adding further details: an arm sticking straight out of the big head, with a hand with lots of fingers. A second arm came later, then eyes and a mouth, then a body, then hair.

Jack's people had mouths like gratings, eyebrows straight across and a vertical line for the nose. Jessica put dots for nose and eyes, while the mouth was an up-curved, smiling line. Jack's men had long, straight feet sticking out horizontally, but Jessica's feet were round blobs, which later had shoe-laces.

We don't know how babies and toddlers see colour, but they seem to be vaguely aware of it at three months, and at toddler age they go for toys with bright colours. At four most children can name one colour, usually red, and by the time they are five, they can often identify yellow, blue and green as well. Painting can now involve blocks of different colours arranged with some design in mind.

Sometimes in a drawing or painting an outsize letter or number may appear, apparently just as an interesting shape. Jessica gave all her pictures titles, although they were impossible for an ordinary adult to interpret. She certainly felt that they were of value, and liked to bring them home from the playgroup to display on the kitchen wall.

Jack's creative expertise was most obvious in construction work, and he could now build a house or a bridge or a truck from memory. Both children liked handling play-dough. Big chunks were squeezed and pounded and small lumps pulled off to give to whichever adult was at hand. Jessica dressed and undressed her dolls and sometimes built a bed for them in the form of blocks arranged in a rectangle. This could also serve as a table if they were to have a meal.

Language. It was a thrill when your baby spoke his first word. Now he or she has more than 1000 at his command. It seemed to Ellie that Jessica never stopped talking except when she was asleep: to herself, to her Rabbit, to grown-ups or other children. The three- or four-word sentences were now linked with 'ands', and Jessica could cope with future and past tenses. Often she rambled on for the pure pleasure of it, and she was so confident in expressing her thoughts that she was quite dogmatic. 'People don't have tails,' or 'Tom is a silly-billy,' she would declare with scorn.

People of four are inclined to bolster their own self-esteem by pointing out the faults of others. Another favourite saying of hers was: 'I've done that before.' Like Jack, she always wanted to do something new. For instance naming objects in a picture book was old hat, but she knew there was more to books than the illustrations.

While Jack, at three, asked more than 100 questions every day, they were mainly of the what, who and where variety, but their number and complexity escalated to a plateau at four through six. 'Why' is a regular opening among four-year-olds. Jack wanted to know: 'What makes a car go?' 'Why has that lady got such a big tummy?' Jessica was interested in why babies cry, what makes a flower flower, and why Ellie looked 'worroed'. The hypotheticals – what if – would come later. Jokes come into the conversation from about four, and cover anything with an element of incongruity. Jack laughed like anything at the thought of a cat going 'Woof-woof' and a dog saying 'Miaow'. Like an old man, he repeated it to everyone, explaining if they were slow to catch on.

Your four-year-old may still have difficulty with some of the consonants, especially the double kind: sh, ch and th. R may still be tricky as Jack found, or rather, his parents noticed. He was prattling away happily enough, about 'winning a wace' or hating 'wice pudding'; but Sarah and Dom were tempted to correct him and check what they saw as a mistake in articulation becoming established. Difficulty with articulation runs in families. It has a genetic origin concerned with the time-table for nervous maturation, and is sometimes linked with delay in achieving bladder control at night. It has nothing to do with intelligence.

Sarah and Dom consulted the granny generation, and, sure enough, Dom himself had been through a phase of mispronunciation. He has certainly grown out of it. The danger of interrupting and apparently criticising a child's efforts at speech is that it may disturb the complex, delicate, and as yet imperfectly integrated arrangements. Insecurity and self-consciousness act like stage fright and hold up the child's progress.

Stuttering to a mild degree is common and this, too, is best ignored. It is usually because a bright child's thoughts tumble out too quickly for the words to keep pace.

Numbers. The parents of three- and four-year-olds, and a few twos, are often proud of how high their youngsters can count. They can usually recite the numbers up to ten by the time they are four and mention huge, impressive numbers like ninety-a-hundred. Jessica, like most of her sex at this age, was ahead of the boys and could manage fifteen. This was no indication of what she understood. If you asked her what two and one comes to, or suggested she could count out six beads for a dolly's necklace, she would look flummoxed.

Jessica did best when the objects to count were sweets, and when she was just four, she could count out three sweets, and knew, if she could handle them, that two sweets and another one made three, or if one sweet was taken away (by the hand of a giant) instead, there was only one left. She could not yet cope with more than three objects to count and manipulate, and talking about numbers in the abstract was too difficult. Jessica was a bright little thing, and well up to the average.

Fortunately help is literally at hand for the tyro mathematician who can't hold numbers in her head. She has fingers, which she can see and touch. Jack liked to count aloud, like a poem, and he also learned to write a large four, which he knew was especially about

Childhood Development

him. 'You are a big boy: you are four,' people told him.

If one major branch of knowledge – arithmetic – was beginning to bud, so were the others: reading and writing. Children of four have already worked out that drawing and writing are different, and that writing in books can tell a story, or on a piece of paper will tell the milkman to leave an extra pint. At this stage your child may form a few letters as well as numbers, scattered anywhere on the page. At first they are only patterns he's seen before, like circles and squares, but gradually they are seen to have a meaning.

Both Jack and Jessica could draw a big 'J'. All their letters were different sizes, but large.

Another fundamental feature of writing – in English – is that the lines run horizontally and from left to right. Jessica wrote her mother a letter of wavy lines across the page: pretend writing. Reading and writing go hand in hand, and if your child sees you reading, apparently for pleasure, he or she will naturally want to do it too – and find out how. The eager hunger to learn is never stronger than at this stage, and such a precious commodity deserves encouragement. The period of rapid physical growth is tailing off, while mental development is on the fast track.

Underlying the development of these two great human skills, numbers and letters, is a phenomenal advance in your child's ability to think and understand. Children learn best by doing. That's why, a little later they cope so easily with computers. They press the keys and move the mouse in the same way that they learn to ride a bicycle. The hows and whys come afterwards.

At four to five your child is happiest of all learning from you and your partner. Enjoy this while it lasts. Your opinions and know-how will never be more willingly received than now. Another plus is that the butterfly attitude of the toddler is being replaced with a longer attention span: although short by adult standards. Ten minutes is a very long time. Memory is improving at the same time, for things that have happened, people and places. Jack was becoming a useful landmark spotter on car journeys. He could remember a bridge or building they'd passed some weeks before.

Sarah sometimes thought that Jack must be hyperactive, a condition that affects boys more than girls. In fact, he was a normal lively four- to five-year-old with an enormous need to let off steam by rushing around, and a propensity to get over-excited. Jessica wasn't exactly serene, but she was busy at a less phrenetic pace than Jack.

Imagination. Imagination is the hallmark of three–four–five, and another aspect of growing intellectual powers. Make-believe play can still be solitary, but the co-operation of one or two other children enhances the enjoyment. Can't you remember making a den or house with a friend, a place where you could be whoever you wanted to be?

A touching aspect of the innocence of little children and their faith in our adult wisdom is their readiness to believe in Father Christmas, the Easter Bunny or the Tooth Fairy. The whole world of fairy stories, including those about space and ET, depends on our children's gift of imagination. The down side is fear.

Tinies of under two are afraid of strangers and of being abandoned. After that, with their greater comprehension of words but almost no knowledge of the shadowy places of outside home, fears of wolves and witches, monsters and ghosts, seem realistic. These horrid creatures may be especially troublesome from about three. Jessica was afraid of a wizard with a pointed hat who lived behind the curtains in her nursery at night.

Jack had caught his fear of spiders from Sarah. Some children are infected by an adult's dread of snakes or thunder. Others have a more rational fear of dogs or other animals either because of dire warnings or because they've been nipped. Jessica's short-lived anxiety lest she should be sucked down the plughole of the bath was based on her feeling the pull of the water as the bath ran out.

The dark, especially the lonely, silent darkness of the bedroom when the grown-ups have gone downstairs into the light and the warmth, can develop as early as two and go on past five. Children all the world over, in every culture, are afraid of the dark.

Fear of failure is something we associate with adults, but it can also haunt a person of three years old plus. It is evidence of growing insight when a child stops feeling omnipotent and finds there are things he can't do. The frustration that led Jack into tantrums was part fear, part anger. Some children in the three-to-five age group can be quite aggressive, especially, but not only, the boys. As well as making fierce remarks they may even strike out. This is most likely between three and four. Four- to five-year-olds are better able to express their feelings in words. As with fear, family example is paramount.

Social skills. At four, many children are learning to dress and undress, without much help except for hard-to-reach buttons. Before this, although Jessica made a brave attempt at doing it alone, she was just as likely to put clothes on back-to-front as the right way, and with socks there was often a bulge on top where her heel was meant to go. Sometimes Jessica would dress and undress for the fun of it, and both she and Jack liked dressing-up games.

Because they can manage their clothes fairly well, four-year-olds become independent about visiting the loo. Even if they are not very expert at wiping themselves, they need the practice for when you aren't there, for instance when they go to school. It is natural, at this age, for them to take a close interest in the process.

Another sign of your child's growing independence is that now he prefers to serve himself from the dish at mealtimes, and as well as telling you what he or she doesn't like, he may be full of suggestions on menu-planning. Fish fingers figured prominently with Jack. He had also found that he could talk with his mouth full.

Sleep. At four the formal nap is definitely out, and going to bed in the evening is unpopular. Jack put it off as long as possible, becoming whinier by the minute, while Jessica staggered to bed – still – with an armful of dolls and animals. Most parents get their four-year-olds in bed by seven – and wish it were six.

Eating. This is no special problem, with spoon and fork both coming into play, with more or less help from fingers. The one worry you may have is that although your child is expending limitless energy, his appetite has fallen off. This is not invariable, but it is a normal response to the slowdown in physical growth and picks up later. No one is too concerned about table manners if the nourishment is going in.

Friends. Until this time your little one has had likes and dislikes among the people he knows – mainly grown-ups – but has only looked at other children with interest. Birthday parties are an indicator of a child's social progress. On Jessica's first birthday Ellie invited another mother and her eighteen-month-old daughter and a gaggle of aunts and grandparents. When she was two, there were two others of the same age and they played together such games as Ring o' roses with the mothers taking a leading part.

On her third birthday Jessica had three friends to tea and they played with Jessica's toys and those the visitors had brought. When good humour degenerated into disputes about who could play with what, Ellie and another mother started some singing games like

Childhood Development

Nuts in May and soon everyone went home.

Making friends with other children develops from about three and going to a nursery school or other group is a tremendous help. Your child doesn't know naturally about sharing and co-operating, but he is at the right stage to learn. When she was three Jessica said she liked Katie best because she had a swing in her garden, but by the time she was four Jessica explained: 'I like Katie best because she likes playing shops, too.' They didn't quarrel as much as when they were three, but Jessica was distinctly bossy at times.

Jack had an imaginary friend called Buffy. He was exactly the same age as Jack and liked all the same things. He was always there. Buffy said the healthy spinach that Sarah wanted Jack to eat was yucky; and when Jack paddled in the edge of the pond and his shoes and socks were soaking, it was Buffy who had told him to do it. Sarah was worried that Buffy was a sign that Jack was lonely or diffident. In fact, Jack was practising with Buffy: assertiveness, discussion, kindness and suchlike useful skills. It made him all the more competent at coping with real little boys at nursery school.

Playgroups and Nursery Schools

Whether your child is a bubbly extrovert like Jessica or more thoughtful, like Jack, the experience of a playgroup or nursery school will be of benefit. For starters, there is the freedom to make the maximum mess with water, paints, paste or clay, such as would wreck a normal home. There is room to let off steam in activity, and the opportunity to make – with others – more noise than a mother could tolerate. There is a wide range of toys, materials and equipment – and the priceless boon of other children to play with, talk

Three–Four–Five Child Alive

with and copy. The easiest way to learn is by copying.

There will also be a knowledgeable adult who has nothing else on her mind but to help and guide the children into developing their latent skills.

To learn to co-operate and mix easily with other small-timers, to conform to a few rules and even to sit quietly for short periods – all will ease the transition to real school later. Equally important is the chance to practise going to the loo unaided – and asking beforehand – and managing to eat and drink tidily.

While playgroups usually run for mornings only, the nursery school schedule may extend after lunch, and there will be a qualified teacher. Depending on her age and maturity, and what is available, your child may go for mornings or afternoons only, or for the full day. Nursery schools differ in the pre-school programmes they offer. One type concentrates on direct preparation for formal education, with the rudiments of reading, writing and arithmetic. At the other extreme is an extended play period with the teacher taking a supporting role, as the children choose their own activities. The third approach is for the teacher to suggest projects and provide the necessary materials, with advice only if asked.

The physical setting may be spacious and school-like, or even part of a primary school with bigger children charging around the playground, or more like a home. Essentials, either way, are some facilities for outdoor activity and caring, unflappable staff.

You will choose a nursery school, from what's on offer, according to your child's personality and needs. Jack certainly needed a chance to race about and encouragement to release his tensions with music and movement sessions, but he was not ready to cope with a large number of other children. He took a week or two to settle in.

Jessica had no problem with making friends. She

Childhood Development

took to the whole scene like a duck to water, but it was useful for her bright little brain to be focused on serious matters some of the time. For example, she particularly enjoyed sitting on the floor next to her friend, Katie, listening to a story about history, and when they all sang and played clappers and triangles and tambourines.

Your child's experience at nursery school matters. It can colour her attitude to the whole educational world, in which she will be involved for years to come.

Five years

Five years old is a golden age. The harum-scarum four-year-old who would run off into danger without a second thought, has matured into a reliable, responsible young person. Outbursts of temper when he can't have what he wants are being replaced by diplomatic negotiation. That is, if he has been provided with an example of civilised behaviour at home. This has never been more important than now, for at five your child is building a personal set of moral values and developing a conscience.

Five is a nodal point in your child's life. The winding, changing path through infancy and toddlerdom has brought him to the brink of a totally new way of living. At present you, his mother, are the centre of his universe, although his father has an important slot. Secondarily, the nursery school teacher is, hopefully, 'a nice lady'. All this is about to change, and change for ever.

School, a whole new world of other people, will absorb much of your child's day. It cannot help but influence his thoughts, ideas and beliefs. You and his father will no longer be the fount of all wisdom. Jessica felt it necessary to inform Ellie that the sun doesn't go to sleep at night, as she had thought, but hides round the other side of the world – and pops up again when we have to get up. Jack gave Sarah the hot news that a boy called Edward never went to bed before eight o'clock, and sometimes stayed up all night. With all this information to impart, your five-year-old is eager to talk all the time he is with you, through bath-time, mealtimes, any time.

Physical progress. Physically, the interesting bit is not so much size as the development of a particular bodily type. Jessica measured 3ft 9ins, and although she was taller and stronger and sturdier, she still seemed comfortably huggable. Jack was exactly 4ft tall, and a thin, wiry type as befitted a live wire.

The range for height is 3ft 6ins to 4ft 2ins (102–120cms) and a little less for those with Asian blood, but each child is following an individual programme. Breathing and heart-rate are noticeably slower now: this allows of a greater reserve for situations requiring extra effort.

Balance and control are the watchwords of five years old. Jessica could hop, skip and jump – and gallop – and it was a delight to see her using all these methods of progression in pure happy spirits. She also liked dancing and had joined a dancing class. Most children of four to five enjoy marching round and round while their teacher bangs out a tune on the piano. Jack was more of a gymnast and liked to do a head-over-heels, although he often rolled sideways in the middle. He had ambitions to do handstands, as well. He could hang upside-down on the climbing frame bars.

Jessica, meanwhile, had discovered that trees were to climb, and there was a little scrub-oak on the common which was a positive invitation. In the summer swimming was a new adventure. Some children start much earlier, but Sarah wanted Jack to feel confident enough to enjoy it from the first. Jessica didn't get blue and cold, and looked upon the children's pool as a place to jump and splash in.

Both children were now super-experts on their trikes, wheeling and turning in the most complex manoeuvres. Jack was desperate for a two-wheeler with stabilisers. If Jack was ahead of Jessica in ball sense – he already had a grown-up-looking stance for throwing, with his left foot forward – Jessica was better in matters of fine muscle control. She was proud to have her own knife, fork and spoon set and she could use them to the manner born by her fifth birthday.

Drawing and copying and then writing, the basis of literacy, depend partly on opportunity and encouragement, but also on the stage of development of the nervous system. Jessica could copy a circle, a cross and a square, but a triangle, with its sloping sides, was tricky and a diamond shape right out of range. Jessica's portrait of Ellie now gave her a head, body and four limbs, with such refinements as fingers, hair, eyes and mouth and clothes. Men could be distinguished by having hair only on top and no skirt.

Jack's masterpiece showed a square house with a door and two windows and a roof going up to a point. There was a huge yellow sun just above it, with rays all round, and the sky went straight across at the top of the picture. Sometimes he drew a tree with branches and leaves or fruit and two plants on each side with round flowers. You could tell what the subject was without any need for interpretation by the artist. As well as original creative work, your five-year-old will enjoy colouring books and as his hand–eye co-ordination improves, more of the colour will stay inside the lines.

With a little help your youngster will be a keen exponent of DIY, using such tools as a hammer, a screwdriver or a spanner; of gardening, with spade and fork; and cooking with mixing bowl, spoons and a measuring jug. The whole world of human activities is unfolding before your five-year-old and his or her games are taken straight from real life. Playing house, or hospital, firemen or explorers can also give way to more complicated re-enactments of television programmes or stories from books.

Playing shops is a step towards understanding money. Three- and four-year-olds assume that their fathers have a limitless supply of the stuff and that the goods in the shops are just there because that's where they belong. It is useful to play with toy money, and to pay with real coins for small items in the real shops. The idea of work being necessary to obtain money only comes in when pocket money to spend is related to something practical and useful – not just 'being good' or going to bed without grumbling. Any money earned should be converted into goods bought; the concept of saving comes later.

Helping your child's development

The most important task is to prepare your three- to five-year-old for the big bang – school.

These are the things to inculcate:
- top priority is convincing your pre-schooler that going to big school is very grown-up and important; that school is interesting and the teacher is there specially to help him or her; that teachers are kind and clever. Jessica was taken with the idea of lots of other children to play with. Jack had heard that you did science, with proper experiments.
- asking 'May I go to the toilet?' or 'Please may I be excused?' in good time.
- managing the toilet alone, including wiping, getting your clothes straight, and washing your hands.
- taking outdoor clothes on and off, and probably some other changing for exercise periods.

Childhood Development

- taking shoes on and off. At just five, shoe-laces seldom co-operate with small fingers, but the elastic sort don't have to be tied and untied during the learning period.
- listening and following simple instructions – from the teacher.
- sharing and taking turns.
- managing your own lunch, whether packed or at table.
- learning to say your name and address. Jack had it off pat: 'I'm Jack Larcombe and I live at 21 Waverley Lane, Tilford, Surrey and my mother will be worried about me.' He didn't have to say the last bit unless he was lost. Telephone numbers are useful, too, but they are more difficult to remember and usually they are obtainable from the name and address.

Of course you want to give your child a headstart with the basic school subjects, or at least ensure that he is not floundering while the others know what it's all about. It amounts to his becoming familiar with the concepts of reading and numbers. Reading may be taught by the look-and-say method, coping with whole words at a time, phonetically: C-A-T, and 'reading for meaning' a kind of guessing game in which the child tries to work out from the context what a phrase is likely to say.

Most children learn by a mix of all three methods, but it is best for parents not to jump the gun, so that whichever way the teacher starts off, the child isn't muddled. Reading stories and the odd notice or advertisement can do nothing but good. Similarly with numbers. You don't want to get involved with modern mathematical strategy, but you can give your child a feel for numbers. Opportunities to count crop up everywhere, for instance how many red cars there are in the car park, the one-to-one principle of putting out the knives and forks for a meal, and she can tell you the names of her three best friends.

Three–Four–Five Child Alive

Jessica boasted that she had five candles on her birthday cake, but it was quite difficult counting them. She had acquired an idea of size from her Russian dolls, and she was spot-on in assessing the biggest and smallest slices of cake. Jack had a fleet of little cars: he learned to sort them into different makes and models as he played.

On the social side your five-year-old can eat with a knife and fork, only a little awkwardly, brush her teeth and comb her hair. Jessica had a way of going round the tangles, so Ellie had to check. Your five-year-old is a fluent conversationalist, ready to tackle any subject. His or her outlook is down-to-earth and pragmatic, and this may be mistaken for callousness. Matters such as illness, death or accident are discussed with interest but unemotionally.

Ellie was horrified when her mother was ill with bronchitis and Jessica asked 'Are you going to die?' Jack showed a keen concern for what had happened to the vehicles in a motorway pile-up – did the airbags all blow up? – never mind the human victims. The plus side of this age-related practicality is the courage of five-year-olds when faced with painful procedures in hospital. The four- and five-year-olds who were terribly injured in the horror at Dunblane in 1996 amazed the medical staff by their stoicism.

Guiding your child's moral development begins to be an issue on the brink of school. Younger children are naturally egocentric – the sun shines especially on them, or ice forms for them to slide on. Sometimes a toddler can do something that seems touchingly thoughtful, like picking three daisies for Granny or patting the crying baby and saying: 'Poor baba.' This may be pure, golden kindness, or it may be to please you.

It isn't until four and a half or five that a child begins to understand that other people feel and suffer. Girls are said to show more concern for others than boys, but it could be that they express it better. Jack was tenderness itself when he found a bird with a broken wing: he made a nest for it in a box and tried to feed it with biscuit. He and Sarah took it to the vet, an understanding man, who said the little creature needed immediate hospitalisation, and kept it at his surgery.

Ideas of right and wrong are rudimentary at this age. Wrong is when the grown-ups are cross, right is all the other times, and being kind is good. The idea of sharing and taking turns is bound up with being fair, and develops particularly at nursery school and later. You are likely to hear the wail regularly from now: 'It isn't fair!'

One of the sad aspects of learning right from wrong is that children can misinterpret an event that makes them unhappy as a punishment. When Jessica had a bad tummy-ache and the doctor came, she asked her: 'Have I been naughty?' And it is well-known that children whose parents divorce often believe that they themselves were to blame. Now that your child is a sensible five you can explain why some things are wrong, and punishment becomes a secondary issue.

Lying and stealing

Five is the age for fantasy. Jack, whose grandfather had given him £25 to start a savings account, told his pals and his granny that he had got millions of pounds and could buy an aeroplane if he liked. This wasn't lying. Since the other children at school wouldn't believe him, such fantasising would die a natural death.

The other sort of untruth is to get out of trouble. Jack used to use Buffy, his imaginary companion, as a scapegoat, but no one else believed in him. That meant that when the fridge door was found open, or a broken cup turned up mysteriously behind the sofa, either a bad man had got in, or the door, for example, had opened by itself. Anyway, Jack hadn't done it . . . Sarah's ploy, a good one, was to say to Jack: 'You mean that's what you wish had happened, don't you?'

The only way to ensure that your child usually tells you the truth, especially before he is ten or eleven, is to guarantee – convincingly – that you won't get cross or punish him or her, whatever he says.

If a child of five or under takes another child's toy or helps himself, without concealment, in a shop, it is analogous to his telling you what he wishes as though it were the truth. It can be an acting out of the hopeful, juvenile idea that 'wishing will make it so'. He wishes the article was his. There is no cause to be scandalised, but clearly the idea of ownership – other people's – needs explaining firmly whenever there's a breach, and whatever has been taken must be returned at once.

Jessica liked to take a miniature Teddy bear with her when she went to nursery school – a little piece of home. Equally, she sometimes brought something back, such as a crayon, a little reminder of school. Taking home a picture she had painted fulfilled this desire even better, and that was all right because the teacher had said they could.

'Stealing' money from his mother's purse may merely be a way of having something small of hers, a kind of reassurance. This childish form of taking what doesn't belong to him is usually a temporary phase. It calls for understanding and explanation.

Father's role

Three–four–five are the years of endless questions and fathers are the chief target. Rightly or wrongly, regardless of whether the mother goes out to her own

Childhood Development

prestigious job toddlers tend to think their father knows everything. Conversations with Dad introduce a wider, non-domestic vocabulary and at this age your child soaks up words by the thousand. He or she understands many times more than those he actually utters.

Communicating with young children is a mix of making some things simple but not talking down to their level all the time: or else how will they learn? Matters of right and wrong, why we should be kind, especially to smaller weaker people, and matters of ownership are all good subjects for occasional discussion. Opinions have more impact coming from Dad than from mother, teacher or grandparent.

At this age a child can be an effective helper. He or she can follow simple directions and enjoy the responsibility of doing so. Computer and fax machines fascinate them as much as carpentry tools, and it can do nothing but good to introduce them early on. One advantage is that a child cannot hurt himself with this apparatus, although he may do harm to it if not well supervised.

Going for a walk with Dad can open a child's eyes to different facets of the familiar local world. Bill loved cars and he soon taught Jessica to recognise the different makes. There was another game he and she enjoyed, too: the listening test. With eyes shut, in turn, they would try to guess from the engine sound whether it was a van, a container lorry or a sports car going by. Ellie would have made the walk an exercise in nature study.

Special expeditions, perhaps to see one or two special exhibits in a museum, or to watch people playing tennis or football in the park, can be 'father' activities. So, of course are ball games. These come into their own now that muscles are stronger and hand and eye work together better.

Exercise in general tends to be a dad responsibility

Three–Four–Five Child Alive

– isn't he, after all, the strong man of the family? Children of the twentieth and twenty-first centuries have two interlinked health problems. They don't take nearly enough exercise and there is a tendency to fatness, in the long run increasing the risk of killer diseases, heart attack and stroke. Children naturally enjoy games and physical activity of all kinds, and it is up to fathers to foster this healthy outlook. A dad who slugs around is no model for the coming generation, and no father should miss the pleasure of introducing his son or daughter to various sports and helping them develop a skill.

Grandparents' corner

Your main job as a grandparent is to counteract the stress of being a pre-schooler. Starting big school is a momentous step and the thought of it can be daunting. It is up to you to help your grandchild to savour to the full the freedom and spontaneous fun of the few years before school makes him grow up. Going for a walk with Granny should act as a tension-releaser. In the summer, rolling down a grassy slope is a lovely, funny feeling, and in winter splashing through puddles in wellies is satisfying. A granny can concentrate on pleasure, and you don't have to be more grown-up than you want to be with her.

A good granny can be relied upon to admire your achievements – like balancing on one leg while you count to ten. She will find that greyish lump of well-pounded pastry delicious after it has been baked (and, hopefully, sterilised by the heat). A good granny is frequently amazed at your cleverness, kindness or courage. Confidence-building is especially valuable when a person is about to set out into the competitive world of big business – or school.

Childhood Development

At this time the parents will be considering your grandchild's first school. You can safely be a sounding board, but if you have strong views keep them well hidden, unless you are specifically asked. Your stock will go down sharply with your child and child-in-law if you air opinions that differ from theirs.

Another risk area that crops up especially with the three- to five-year-old age group is spoiling. Of course you love your grandchild and you want to be loved back. Also it is a delight to give him or her pleasure. But beware of:
- outdoing the young parents with gifts
- siding with your grandchild if there's a dispute about going to bed, finishing dinner, or saying 'thank you'
- being over-protective and fussing about cold, rain, dangerous climbing etc
- laughing when he or she is cute but naughty
- encouraging him to repeat babyish mistakes in what he says, however quaint

7

Love, Life and Laughter:
taking stock

It is time to take stock. Your child stands on the threshold of life in a wider world, where you cannot go with her or him: school and the unknown that follows. You have brought her safely through the first five years. There are fifteen more to go before she reaches adulthood, but none of these will be of such far-reaching importance.

Already your little one's bodily type is firm-set, and you can forecast some of her physical attributes as an adult. Is she a sturdy mesomorph, with a built-in advantage in sport and leadership? Or a lissome, willowy ectomorph with a gift of imagination? Or a rounded, warm-hearted, appealing endomorph? Most likely he or she is a unique mix of all three.

If he was tall at three, he is likely to be tall at seven and twenty-one. Most children have achieved seventy per cent of their adult height at six, but from then on their growth advances in fits and starts, depending on the timing of the great pre-pubertal growth spurt. This is wildly variable from child to child.

If the plan for physical progression is already delineated, the foundations for the far more complex emotional and psychological development have also been laid. A hundred years ago Sigmund Freud believed that: 'The little creature is often completed by the fourth and fifth years of life and after that merely brings to light what is already within him.'

Childhood Development

It is certainly true that most of what is in your five-year-old has come from you: from the genes you and your partner have handed on to him or her, the way you have cared for him and the example you have set. It was your practical care, including nourishment, sweet fresh air and exercise, and protection from danger, that enabled his marvellous physical progress.

Just as essential was your input of tenderness, which has given him the security of knowing he is loved and lovable – always. It is this that gives him in turn the capacity to love the people close to him and by extension, his world and the creatures in it. It is from you that he has acquired his survival kit: the emotional strength and core values which will guide him come what may, when he ventures outside your arms, his home. First it will be to plunge into the unfamiliar community of schoolchildren and teachers, a practice-run for what comes after – our tough, materialistic, each-for-himself, adult scene.

The most important lesson for a human baby is about love. You started right in on Day One. In fact you were probably there ahead of him, with a store of tender feelings in readiness, even before you knew you were pregnant. During the pregnancy, he was literally surrounded by your loving warmth, but from the moment he was born, when you came face to face with your baby, you began teaching him.

When he was helplessly dependent, and could offer you nothing but his weakness and his cries of bewilderment, you loved him and fed him, tended and comforted him – however exhausted you were. None of this was wasted. Jessica can't recall the manhours and womanhours Bill and Ellie devoted to her, dumping their hopes of a mountaineering holiday, a night on the town, or simply a long lie-in on Sunday. Jack will have no conception of Sarah's and Dom's sleepless nights when he had the colic.

Love, Life and Laughter

Yet the experience of being loved so much that their needs had priority over everything else will have soaked into the being of both these babies – and yours. They will carry within them, always, the knowledge of being held dear and personally protected from harm. This perception will have been confirmed again and again during your child's infancy, toddlerdom and pre-school years.

Love is a commitment to care, plus pleasure in the loved one's existence. In the early weeks and months your baby learned about it from the receiving end. She could enjoy your loving her and see it in action. From about six weeks your baby smiled to herself, conveying that she felt satisfied (feedwise), comfortable and safe. At eight weeks her wavering smile was definitely directed at you, the source of all goodness: the very first step towards loving you back.

At three months her joy in your company bubbled over into chuckles, and laughing out loud at four months. Laughter is linked with the happy side of love. For tinies and adults alike it dispels fear and tension like nothing else, relaxing the muscles to the point of weakness, and quelling anxiety. You must have noticed how much children laugh among themselves, often at the silliest, most meaningless things. For some reason it acts as a stimulus to the developing brain.

Three-year-olds laugh much more than when they were at the serious age of two and a half, with weighty problems of potty-training, finding effective ways of communicating, and separations from mother, perhaps at nursery school. Play with words flourishes at three and four. It is a giggly game to say 'izzy, wizzy, bizzy' or some other nonsense syllables back and forth with another child. Soon the more adult humour of the incongruous and the ridiculous, and semi-adult punning come in. Parents themselves need a sense of humour to safeguard their sanity.

Childhood Development

At around eight months your baby was selective with his smiles, beaming and chortling for you, but solemn with appreciation with an 'aunty' he did not know. Jessica, at ten months, showed her first signs of feminine wiles, holding her head on one side in a provocative way when she smiled. Boys are less inclined to do this: Jack didn't. (However, he did propose to Sarah a couple of years later.)

At one and a half your baby began to imitate the love and care you showed her. Jack hugged his bear and his wooden car, and Jessica 'fed' her dolly with a spoon and carried it around with her, either under her arm or swinging by a leg. Your two-year-old was demonstratively affectionate to you, especially at bedtime, and without the slightest self-consciousness. The goodnight hug and kiss became part of the bedtime ritual.

At two and a half, if not before, your child's innocent, untrammelled love may have been marred by jealousy. This, of course, is especially the case if a new baby has sneaked into the family. Jack became very possessive towards Sarah, mentioning the word 'love'. He did not have a baby brother or sister, but he had begun to resent his father monopolising his mother's attention at times. Jessica, in a similar position, reacted by being a show-off, doing anything to divert her parents' interest from each other onto her. Jack's ploy was boasting, and telling the long boring riddles he'd learned.

Luckily, by five, if there have been no unexpected setbacks, for instance through illness, your child will be more reasonably affectionate, confident in his own powers and satisfied with his status within the family.

Feeding, physical care, hugging and kissing – these are the bare bones of what you've taught your child about love: vital but not very different from what a mother chimp might do. There is much more to human love than that.

Love is about sharing, sharing with the other person

everything good or beautiful, interesting or wonderful, everything that has given you pleasure. It is one of the joys of being a parent that you have a cast-iron excuse for re-living the delights of your own childhood – making a sand castle with a moat, re-reading *Peter Rabbit* or *The Wind in the Willows*. With your child, to whom it will matter so much, you can look afresh at the marvels of modern technology and today's new knowledge – and share the best bits.

Your interest and enthusiasm for a subject, and the fact that you spend time on it, will kindle a flame in your youngster's enquiring mind. In turn her – or his – round-eyed wonder will boost your own curiosity.

Language and literature

Words are the master key to unlock all the knowledge of mankind, and on a personal level allow us to express and exchange our feelings, hopes and fears. Like any loving mother, you used to talk to your tiny baby, long before she could have any notion of the meaning of words. This may have been sentimental, but it wasn't silly. You had begun to teach her about the rhythm, the music and emotion of words. Whatever you said, your words would comfort your crying infant, a form of contact apart from touch.

You need never be afraid of using language way ahead of what your child can understand. Babies and toddlers simply love the sound of their mother's voice. They like hearing such old rhymes as 'Three Blind Mice' or 'Pop Goes the Weasel' not for the content, but because they become familiar. At three and a half, Jack was very pleased with himself when he could recite 'Jack and Jill' (his favourite) all through.

It is a good idea to widen the range with genuine poetry, combining charm with the rhyming. Jessica liked the lilt of Tennyson's 'Lady of Shalott', the absurdity of Edward Lear's 'Jumblies', and the exciting, if incomprehensible poem that begins 'The Assyrian came down like the wolf on the fold . . .' (Byron's 'Destruction of Sennacherib'). It doesn't matter that they are about sad or disastrous events. So is 'Rockabye Baby', and 'Humpty Dumpty' didn't end up too well.

Jack and Jessica enjoyed words, as all children do, and had no dislike of the long ones. The Beatrix Potter tales prove this. Later on children need a mixed mental diet of the old and hallowed and the new and sparky stories. The readers are parents, grandparents and teacher, at first. This provides the children with a rich store of vocabulary, invaluable for school-work, and an aid in all communication. (See book list, pp 254–62).

Nature's seasons

One of the attractions of language is its rhythm. Rhythm is at the heart of nature, from the regular alternation of night and day to the great, sweeping changing of the seasons. To be in harmony with these is to live the year through always with something to look forward to. You can help your little one to achieve this in the years before school, when you are by far the biggest influence in her life.

Spring. Spring, especially is in tune with childhood, when the dead, black earth comes to life and everything grows. You can show it happening for your child by pre-planting grape hyacinths, dwarf daffodils and crocuses indoors in a bowl or outside in a sheltered corner. A walk in the most unremarkable countryside or on a common provides hidden treasure in the shape of twigs to bring home. Warmth and water will induce sticky horse chestnut buds to stretch out their green hands, and the little tight sausages on the hazel to turn into fluffy lambs' tails, and the most ordinary leaf bud to unfold.

The earliest spring flowers are precious for their rarity and their message of the glories to come. It is not too hard to find the cheerful yellow face of a dandelion, an imitation sun in miniature, by the wayside, or to spot the varnished gold of a celandine. If you are very lucky and remember where to look, your little naturalist may discover the shy flower of the sweet violet.

Collecting treasure gives purpose to a walk. A small basket is perfect for transporting the interesting objects your child finds: stones, a piece of bark, an old acorn, leaves and twigs. A satisfying conclusion, when you reach home, is arranging them on a bed of damp moss or earth. Unlike an expensive, boring, shop-bought floral decoration, this arrangement is meant for instant pleasure. It doesn't have to last.

The miracle of spring is celebrated in religious festivals all over the world: by the Hindus and Buddhists in the East, the Jewish people's Purim, and Easter, when Jesus came to life after being dead. For little children there is the happy Easter Bunny who hides presents in the garden – or indoors if he must – and the annual sport of painting faces on hard-boiled eggs.

Nor should your child miss out on the fun of playing with the March winds. The toys that take part are windmills, kites, sailing boats and simple flags. Sarah, with Jack's help, tried her hand at making the first two with paper, glue and dowel rods. Ellie found them very cheap to buy.

The other spring special is the cuckoo. If you know a wood where he visits, be sure to take a trip there in April or May. His cheeky song is like no other and it's a guarantee of summer on the way.

Summer. This is the playtime season for parents as well as children. It brings the blessings of warmth and

Childhood Development

sunshine, but beware the ultraviolet rays on your child's petal-thin skin. Blondie Jessica was especially vulnerable, and her red-haired friend more so. The top summer play material is water: from the limitless Atlantic to a tinkling stream, a boat pond or a paddling pool – or a washing-up bowl that doubles for the sea with an island of stones and moss, twigs for trees and boats made of bark or walnut shells. You have to use play-dough for fixing masts and to make them balance. Swimming, of course, is the ultimate water activity – when your child is ready.

Autumn. Autumn brings the Hallowe'en pumpkin (witches can be too frightening), shiny conkers, leaves to sweep up and chase, and smoky bonfires. Planting bulbs in the still warm earth is enjoyable in itself, so long as no one hopes for a quick result. Fireworks for Guy Fawkes are the high spot of autumn. They are fascinating and exciting for children – and major responsibility for their parents. For the under-fives a sparkler in the hand is worth two rockets in the sky, however spectacular, set off by a professional. But even sparklers can cause a nasty burn, without thick gloves and great care.

Indoors, autumn means making leaf prints. Jack loved sloshing the (non-spill) paint on each leaf and then pressing them, wet side down, on a piece of paper. Jessica liked to make a decorative feature of polished apples, to look splendid in the middle of the table – and to eat.

Winter. This is the season to set up a birds' restaurant on the window-sill or a table outside. In Jessica's restaurant the speciality of the house was bird-cake, made of bacon and cheese scraps, nuts and seeds, mixed in lukewarm melted fat and left to harden. Jack preferred a trip to the pond to see the ducks, at this time of year, glide eagerly across when they saw him standing on the edge. Then he would break the bread into beak-sized pieces, and they would quack 'Thanks'. The birds really need the children's help in winter.

Snow, if it comes, causes chaos for adults, delight for the young, and frost on the trees can look beautiful, but with shorter, colder days you are certain to spend more time indoors. Jessica liked, most of all, to have her friend Emily round to play. The high spot was dressing up in Ellie's clothes and acting a play, two minutes long, for the mothers. Jack and his mate Edward usually got down to serious construction work with Lego, interspersed with rolling on the floor in harmless mortal combat – like two puppies.

It cheers up a dull patch, when familiar toys have lost their interest, to introduce something special to mark the season. Christingles are easy and satisfying to make with small-sizers. You cut a cross in the top of a round-shaped orange, press some foil in and then stick a candle in it. Cocktail sticks, speared with raisins are pushed into the peel here and there and the whole made festive with a ribbon round the middle. They look good and they have a pleasant orangey aroma when they are lit. A Christingle is meant to celebrate any of the happy things in life, from a circus clown to a brown egg with speckles.

There's a lot to be glad about at this time of year. Roasted chestnuts, baked apples with the summer's honey, potatoes in their jackets – all these are a part of King Winter's feast which won't be a strain on a small child's digestion. Mince pies, plum pudding and turkey with stuffing may be all right for adults to eat but for young children, more importantly, they provide the fun of making wishes – stirring the pudding or at the first small bite of a mince pie. Wishes are best double: half for oneself, half for someone else. It's a minor antidote to the all-for-me attitude that can creep in.

The run-up to Christmas means making cards and presents and decorations. Vegetable prints made from

Childhood Development

carrots and potatoes cut to a shape at one end and dipped in non-spill paint make colourful, fashionably 'organic' cards. A home-made crib on a tray reminds everyone what Christmas is about, and is an exercise for imagination and ingenuity. Apart from the Christmas tree, 'flower arrangements' of bare twigs hung with Chinese lanterns look effective.

The only presents an under-five can truly give are articles he has made himself – not those bought by his mother. The pocket money – if any – for a child of this age goes nowhere when you are buying for an adult. Little bowls made from self-drying clay then painted can be used for sweets, or with a night-light converted to a lamp. Painted stones, explained as paper weights, are useful, and the quickly manufactured bookmark is a handy standby.

Keeping in step with the seasons involves natural history, a subject that is always of interest to children. Birds were frustrating for Jack. They always took off when he was trying to get to know them. Beetles, on the other hand, the outdoor varieties, made a much more satisfactory study. Although Sarah said he couldn't keep them as pets – it wouldn't be kind – he set up a temporary rest place for them. It was a shoebox, lined with grass and leaves and stones to be comfortable while he observed the newest find. Sometimes he found a caterpillar or a centipede.

His best present ever, Jack said, was the stick insect Dom bought for him at the pet shop. This was one he could keep, with its long legs and fascinating swaying body. Jack and Dom and Sarah soon knew every privet bush in the area, since privet is a stick insect's sole diet.

Television comes into its own with natural history. There are some brilliant programmes, but for our children to benefit we, too, much watch and discuss them. A whole hour is too long for most small children and busy adults, but a snippet of fifteen minutes is well worthwhile. It is tempting to let children watch by themselves – while you 'get on' – but because there is no interaction, children who spend a lot of time with the box become backward in their speech. You can't have a conversation with the presenter.

Music

Music should be a lifelong pleasure, involving a different part of the brain from anything else. It can fit a person's mood, or change it: soothe or inspire. Children can hear before they are born, and this includes music. Babies listen to it deliberately long before they can talk. They respond with their minds and their bodies also, by swaying, clapping, stamping or even marching.

Most people, apart from self-conscious adults, enjoy singing. Babies do it to themselves. Ellie wondered why Jessica's singing, when she was about two, didn't have much more tunefulness than talking. At that age she would only have a range of five tones, but these would increase to twelve by the time she was five. Then she could sing more songs, more musically.

It is worthwhile to let your child hear music from whenever consciousness develops – but there is no definite moment for this. It comes on gradually. It must be something like waking from sleep, but taking weeks over the process, and imperceptibly becoming aware of various sounds including music. In ordinary sleep, our hearing is the first of the senses to surface.

It is at around three that most children take a definitely intelligent interest in music. At that age Jack could sing four songs, two pop and two trad, and could recognise a dozen more. He knew the difference between high notes and low, slow and fast rhythm, and between loud and soft. He had a shaker made of beans in a plastic bottle, and became adept at following the rhythm of a piece; but he wasn't able to pitch his voice to suit, yet.

All music is good music in the right circumstances, and to give Jessica the best chance of learning to appreciate it, Ellie bought a few tapes to play often. She chose some Scott Joplin, 'The Teddy Bears' Picnic', 'Peter and the Wolf' and Ravel's 'Bolero' for starters, then she introduced Beethoven's 'Moonlight Sonata' and Mozart's 'Eine Kleine Nachtmusik'. The nub was repetition. Sometimes Jessica listened thoughtfully, but more often she joined in by singing or tapping out the beat.

When he was four, Jack discovered his aunt's piano, and was fascinated to pick out different notes: his aunt was as tolerant as she could be about his sticky fingers. Jessica had a toy xylophone to experiment with.

Art

Most children enjoy using crayons, paints and clay as soon as they can handle them. Sarah wasn't prepared for the vigour and enthusiasm of Jack's artistic creativity – the amount of paint and water on the floor, the table and everything else within range, and clay and plasticine firmly attached to various surfaces and Jack's multicoloured clothing. 'Free experimentation with the various media' is the most valuable foundation for formal teaching in art, they say. Saying repressively: 'Look what a terrible mess you've made,' is no way to encourage self-expression.

Sarah learned. Jack needed protective clothing – an overall – and an area of operation that was washable: in this case the kitchen. At two Jack used his paintbrush to scrub the paper in the middle, sometimes making a hole right through. Then he altered his technique to slosh and sweep a dripping brush all over the paper and whatever it was resting on. His whole body was involved in his painting, energetically, joyously. When not a scrap of the paper was left uncovered, he pronounced the picture 'done'.

Blocks, or more accurately, pools of different colours began to appear in Jack's pictures, then lines going one way or another, at random. The stage of choosing a subject and planning the painting can begin as early as four, or be delayed until six or seven. This is partly a matter of maturity, but also depends on the opportunity and encouragement the child receives. Jessica, at four and three quarters, often had to alter what she had intended as a house or a person into a 'pattern', when it wouldn't come out right.

Children's art, so full of life, is full of information too. It gives a marvellous insight into what is going on in the artist's mind. For example, a predominance of black and brown indicates a low mood, while red, yellow and orange, the sunshine colours, show the reverse. Sometimes the bright colours are covered over with the darker shades, spelling a major disappointment. Lines crossing each other may reflect conflict at home, and lines curving upwards, like a smile, are happy.

Either way, self-expression in painting, with no rules to conform to, releases the tensions of growing up in a complex world, often with personal or financial difficulties at home. We adults have lost the gift of painting in this free fashion, but it is of great benefit to our children.

Moral values

Arnold Gesell, the great guru of child development, wrote: 'The intrinsic charm and goodness of childhood still constitutes the best guarantee of the future perfectibility of mankind.'

Childhood Development

In a word, your child and mine, in their innocence, have the potential to make the world a better place. It is our massive responsibility to cultivate the essential goodness in our children, despite the popular philosophy of 'I'm all right, Jack.' And the vital first five years, when the foundations for character and behaviour are laid, belong to us, the parents.

The trick is to play along with your child's natural development. That way you can help your baby, whose instincts are totally centred on self, into becoming a sensible, thoughtful, lovable five-year-old with a sense of self-worth and a set of principles. He is on course for developing into a responsible adult who will win respect and affection wherever he is known.

During the first two years the best you can do is to provide your baby with a happy, loving home where he is wanted. Babies soak up atmosphere. They are sensitive to anger and tension, and the slightest whisper that they were not wanted. The idea that babies don't understand is wishful thinking: they understand with their feelings months and years before they've mastered the intricacies of language.

From the time your baby can smile, you can see for yourself that he or she responds to your actions. She is already following your lead.

It is pointless to tell an eight-month-old baby that she is 'naughty' when her waving arms knock her mug over, but by two, young Jessica had a clear idea that she was a 'good girl' when she ate up all her dinner, or provided what her mother wanted in the potty. Jack, too, was learning that goodness and badness meant what Sarah wanted, or didn't. This was the beginning of realising that another person's wishes counted as well.

At two and a half most little ones try pitting their will against their mothers'. This is a normal, natural stage in development: testing out what they can get away with. By three, your child begins the other tack. She wants to please you – mostly. Jack often asked 'Dis way?' when he wanted to get it the way Sarah wanted. Both he and Jessica blossomed in the sunshine of praise and were abashed by disapproval. However much your toddler wants to be in your good books, you can't expect him, at three, to understand rules or the reasons for what is good or bad. For him it is purely a matter of how you react.

'I can discuss absolutely anything with Jack now,' Sarah declared proudly. It is true that a four-year-old, with his newly won grasp of language, comprehends much more of what you tell him. This means you can explain, for instance why some things are dangerous; he is open to persuasion if you promise something in return; and he is beginning to get the idea of rules.

Little by little, as the occasion arises, you can tell him about being kind and helping each other; not taking someone else's possessions; saying things like 'Please' and 'Thank you' to make other people feel comfortable, especially grown-ups; looking for the best things about people and places and talking about these – not the nasty bits, which you wouldn't like the other way. The difficult part is that you have to practise all these things yourself. Example speaks louder than words.

Telling the truth is not included yet. It comes later, when your child is mature enough to value truth even when telling it makes you – or some other important person – cross. Up till four, fiction and fact are blurred in your child's mind, and even a five-year-old will make a flat denial if he is confronted with his guilt. The canny parent never corners the child, since it only makes matters worse if he is afraid to admit what he's done. Sometimes, when he was coming up to five, Jack would whisper 'Had an axicant,' when, for example, he'd managed to turn the tap on but not off and flooded

Childhood Development

the bathroom. Usually he blamed someone else, real or imaginary or a mysterious spontaneous event.

At five years old Jessica and Jack had both worked out that being good involved doing what the grown-ups told them. Jessica even started asking permission before doing something: 'May I go in the garden?' 'Can I have an apple?' This is a useful attitude for someone just about to start school. Time enough to cast aside parental values – supposing they are reasonably good – in adolescence.

There are horror stories in the news about unmanageable, even vicious, five-year-olds entering school and plaguing both teachers and the other children. There must have been some catastrophic failure in their upbringing. In the ordinary way, five is a most satisfactory age for parents and child. The various threads of basic development have been drawn together, so that your child can do most things for himself. Yet he is still strongly attached to you and to his home and genuinely enjoys being helpful and winning approval.

By this age your child's character has formed sufficiently for you to picture what sort of adult he or she will be. Jessica, at five, was a sunny, generous little soul, full of practical sympathy for someone sick or sad, an injured animal, or even a flower whose stalk was broken. She expected that everyone would like her and usually they did. This must have had something to do with Ellie and Bill.

Jack was a different type: quieter and more thoughtful. Whatever he did, he was anxious to get it exactly right. He was probably just as kind as Jessica, but not so spontaneous. His eager interest in everything round him – animal, vegetable or mineral – landed him in a few scrapes. He was always surprised when a good idea misfired. Sarah didn't appreciate it when he put a half-eaten mouse in the fridge, to keep it in prime condition for when Jezebel, the new cat, had her supper. 'But there was a fly on it,' he explained.

Everyone thought that dear little Jessica was no trouble, but her ideas didn't always work either. At her fifth birthday party she insisted on giving a younger guest, a three-year-old called James, the wooden clown who climbed up a stick, which her godmother had brought for her. 'I'm much too big for that,' she explained. Her godmother was there.

Ground rules

There are certain ground rules which should act as a background that helps your child's moral views develop so that he or she will be liked and respected wherever he goes, and he can feel good about himself, too:
- encouragement: to build confidence
- praise wherever possible: to teach appreciation of everything good or beautiful
- sharing what you have: to teach generosity
- tolerance: to emulate and to teach patience with other people
- fairness and reliability: to lead to trusting relationships
- good humour and reliability: for the gift of making friends
- effort and imagination to be valued as much as the achievement: to boost creativity and resourcefulness

It is you who must show all these factors in action, and the whole must be liberally seasoned with love: Mother-love, which is given but cannot be won, Father-love, which depends in part on merit: the necessary spur to effort.

These last five years of care and love and laughter have prepared your child to face the world of school – and enjoy it.

8

School-time:
five to ten years

School is a new, untried stage in your child's life, but it should also be a continuation and a transformation of all that has gone before. From the moment he or she goes through the school gates, a new, powerful force will influence his future development. Choosing the right school is of paramount importance.

Within the constraints of what is available and financially possible, there are three main aspects to consider:

1. *Where you hope your child's education will lead him*:
– a professional or academic career
– something artistic, creative or perhaps green
– practical, down-to-earth know-how, fitting him or her for getting on in the real world
– scope for his special talent or interest in music, sport, science, art or drama

The first school after nursery days matters: it sets the tone for the whole of your child's education, including his attitude to study and to discipline.

2. *Your child's personal characteristics*:
– lively and extrovert or shy and quiet? Will she relish joining a large number of rumbustious other children or be overwhelmed?
– a leader or a follower, or put it another way: bossy or obliging? In the latter case, too relaxed a regime can lead to problems.
– industrious or lazy? The first type needs good facilities,

the second a framework of rules, and they both need encouragement.
- a self-starter or one who waits to be told what to do? The latter needs a stimulating environment and a patient, committed teacher.
- special abilities? These require adequate facilities and a teacher with expertise and enthusiasm for the chosen subject.

3. *Your child's level of maturity. Is he or she ready for school?*
- has he the practical skills of self-toileting, taking shoes and coats on and off, managing meals without help? These may need a crash course before The Day, and reassurance about asking the teacher if he is in a fix.
- how easily does he mix with new people? Find out in good time who else is starting at the same time, and make contact with the other mothers. It is handy if there is someone who lives near you and can share the twice-daily school run or school walk.

What to look for in choosing a school

It is essential to visit the school to suss it out, and meet the head and the form teacher.
 Focus on:
- atmosphere: busy, friendly, controlled, chaotic, noisy
- style of education:
    formal teaching, with some interaction, covering the subjects necessary to get into prep school or chosen secondary school
    child-centred, with the pupils deciding, individually, what they want to do
    combination of formal set projects and the children left to approach them either in groups or separately, with advice at hand

Childhood Development

- personality of the head and his or her goals for the school
- academic programme and expectations of progress in basic subjects: reading, writing and arithmetic
- time allocated to sport, including swimming, and free play
- facilities, eg computers, science, gym, library
- inclusion of music, art and drama, after school if necessary; clubs and societies?
- homework set regularly, marked promptly?
- discipline and bullying: any problems? Teachers' views?
- size of school; size of classes
- test or exam results
- your child's views (usually depends on whether he or she has friends going there)
- will the journey be difficult?

Don't be disheartened if you cannot get your child into the school you would have chosen. Anything the school does not provide, you probably can. There is no area of knowledge that you cannot explore with your child, and make really interesting, and there are extras you can buy fairly cheaply: sports coaching, dancing classes, music, and any of the standard school subjects that need a boost.

Locally there may be young naturalists' or swimming clubs and the like, and on your own account you can arrange outings which will make history, geography, art or architecture come alive. Even six- to seven-year-olds may enjoy some concerts, though perhaps not all the way through.

Jack enjoyed brass-rubbing trips – with proper permission – crawling on the floor with paper and fat wax crayons in various churches. Jessica's dad took her on fossil-hunting forays: parents learn a lot from planning outings for their children.

School-time

First reactions to school

The first day your child goes to school can have just as big an impact on you as on him. You have lost, if not your baby, at least a very special companion for whom you were the centre of the world. You shared his life, down to the most intimate details, for years. Home is so quiet on this day, and you can't help thinking about how he is getting on, if the other children are being nice, if he ate up his lunch . . .

Ellie met Jessica at the school gates. She came bouncing across the playground, her coat on the wrong buttons, with two other little girls. 'These are my friends,' she announced and Ellie knew it was all right. Jack was nearly last when he came out, his shoe-laces draggling. There was a chattering bunch of boys and girls just ahead of him but he was walking on his own, clutching a piece of paper in his hand. It was his picture of a volcano and the teacher had said it was very good. 'And she knows everything,' he added.

Some children don't settle into school easily, and may cry all the way there for the first week or two. Of course, as soon as their mothers have gone, the youngsters recover their spirits – but the mothers don't know that. Common reactions in the early days include:
- 'accidents' at school because they are diffident asking to go to the toilet or are afraid of its strangeness
- bed-wetting, in someone normally dry: if the minimum of fuss is made, this is likely to get better as the excitement of school subsides
- symptoms of being very tired after school: outbursts of bad temper, whining and pestering, unusually quiet, plain sleepy
- tummy-ache or feeling sick on school mornings
- thumb-sucking or other babyish behaviour: a matter of wishful thinking

Childhood Development

There is no need to worry if any of these reactions crops up for a few weeks when your child first goes to school. It is a help if he can talk about school, and how he feels, but sometimes they clam up. Sarah found the best time was when Jack was safe and warm and relaxed, in bed but with his bedtime story still to come. Stories are an antidote to the worries of the day.

School-starter

Five, as we have seen, is an easy age for parents. Jack and Jessica weren't alike, but they were both sensible, willing to help, competent to deal with the simpler tasks of everyday living – and hardly ever ill. Their parents were the cleverest people in the world. Your child feels the same about you.

By five and a half the rot has set in. There's a new hint of brashness and uncooperativeness creeping in, interspersed with times when he or she is as delightful and companionable as ever.

Six years

'He's a different child,' said Sarah of her six-year-old Jack. 'I don't know what's got into her,' wailed Ellie, about Jessica: 'she doesn't even look the same.'

Physically as well as psychologically, six is an age of transition. Between five and seven the jaw changes and lengthens to allow for the larger number, bigger permanent teeth. It meant that Jessica's little round button of a face was altering to oval. At around six the first teeth of the second set, the molars, come through, and the milk teeth, now looking absurdly small, start wobbling their way out. It's 10p a time if you believe in the Tooth Fairy, for very little trouble or discomfort.

Over the next five or six years all twenty-eight of the

School-time

permanent teeth erupt, replacing the twenty baby teeth. The wisdom teeth come later. Five to seven is the tombstone stage. The new teeth come through at different times, so your child's smile shows a mixture of gaps where some new teeth have barely broken the surface, while others are at different heights – for all the world like the irregular stones in a churchyard (see tooth chart p 271).

It isn't only new teeth which are erupting at six: new feelings, new impulses, new actions are all emerging. The person who is most confused by all this is the child.

Jessica swung from one extreme to the other. Ellie was the best mother in the world at one moment, and her daughter was stamping her foot the next, and saying just as passionately: 'You're horrible. I hate you.' Jack's problem was that he couldn't make up his mind, even between vanilla and strawberry, or choosing a present when his granny took him to the toyshop on his birthday. He had so much to think about – decisions, decisions – that he became an inveterate dawdler, although he never actually stopped still.

At five his ideas had been clear, his choices pragmatic and definite. What was happening now was in reality an intellectual step forward: in common with other six-year-olds he could see both sides of every argument, the pros and cons for any course of action. This kind of strain easily leads to tears. The good side is that six-year-olds' tears are quickly diverted into laughter.

The propensity to see two possibilities in everything was neatly illustrated by Jessica's attempts at writing the capital letters. Sometimes the straight side of a 'B' was on the left, but just as often to the right. Ellie thought at once of dyslexia, envisaging her daughter's schooling handicapped from the start. At this age back-to-front letters mean nothing more than the normal

Childhood Development

ambivalence of being six. Right and left are still problematical. Although your child knows which are his own right and left hands, he can't yet figure out how that works for other people and other things.

Just as physically your six-year-old is constantly on the move, so he or she is in a constant state of emotional ferment. This may show in a tendency to blinking, tics and stuttering, and also to using any bad words he's managed to pick up. They are one addition to his vocabulary your child acquires without trying. His mood is swayed – immediately – by outside events or what someone has said. It means that praise and approval go down extremely well, while criticism is totally unacceptable. Punishment doesn't work, either.

When Jack was fractious and obstinate, Sarah found the only way to get him to do what she wanted was to make a game of it. 'If I put the knives out, you put the forks and the one who finishes first can do the spoons . . .' Jessica had acquired a confrontational attitude which seemed right out of character. Hands on hips, she would state baldly 'I won't,' or if Ellie told her of something she thought interesting, Jessica's favourite response was 'So what?'

Jack was particularly resistant to Sarah's plea of 'Do hurry up.' He would immediately drop from half-speed to a quarter. Oddly enough – it seemed to go with being six – he could often be jollied along by counting: 'When I count to three – or five – or ten – you must clean your teeth' or whatever.

Because children are capable of thinking more at six than when they were five, they have a new bunch of frightening thoughts. Jack was afraid of big dogs, which was not unreasonable, but he was also scared of lions and tigers and crocodiles which came into his room at night. Oddly enough, these creatures never infested Sarah's and Dom's room, so he was safe there. Fortunately Dom could clear them out of Jack's room too, by brandishing a big stick and telling them off. This process had to be repeated quite often.

Stories featuring beasts and monsters or bad men are not suitable for bedtime reading at this age. Later they will be top favourites. Some scary dreams come from daytime fears. A common one is of the house being on fire. Jessica dreamed about menacing faces at the window or her mother being dead or lost. Not all six-year-olds' dreams are unpleasant; some are enjoyable, such as flying like Peter Pan. You can sometimes tell that your child is caught up in a compelling dream – this is an age when he is likely to talk in his sleep or even laugh.

Sex has begun to figure in the six-year-old's life. Even before he started real school, Jack would tend to play with other boys. Their games were full of imagination, adventure and aggression, while Jessica preferred to practise real life, playing schools, shops and – still – mothers and fathers. Doctor games have begun to lose their interest at this stage. They wouldn't do at school, anyway. Six is a fine age for painting, and again there is often a difference between the sexes. Little boys show a preference for picturing cars, planes and spacecraft, while girls tend to focus on people.

Six-year-olds are growing fast and also spending energy non-stop. This, added to the demands of school and their own unsettled feelings and thoughts, leaves them extra vulnerable to coughs, colds, sore throats and earache and any other infection that is not under the immunisation umbrella. Mothers often plan on going back to work when their child starts school: it is not as easy as they had thought.

Sarah found that Jack was off school almost as much as he was there, with a run of minor illnesses every few weeks. This six-to-seven age group is also particularly vulnerable to fractures – usually of the arm, after a fall. It is not only that they climb about more and seem to

Childhood Development

have no fear. As my grandmother would say: they've outgrown their strength. The limbs are longer but the bones are not yet consolidated nor the muscles fully developed.

One plus point in all this was Jack's increase in appetite. He had been a fussy eater before, but now his eyes were sometimes 'bigger than his tummy' and he would pile his plate with more than any child could have managed. Jessica went off puddings, which used to be her favourite. She developed a taste for raw vegetables and what she called 'bitey' foods, crisp but not chewy like meat. Sauces and gravy and juice were out of favour, too.

There's a propensity at six not only to stuff the mouth very full, but to talk through it. And of course, being six, any criticism produces a rude reply. A firm adult voice cuts no ice: it is the trigger to defiance. You can't win. Ellie liked to think that Jessica's dreadful manners and cockiness were due to the bad influence of the other children at school. It was true in a way. Not that they had been brought up to be ill-mannered any more than Jessica: they were just being assertive, which everyone agrees is a good thing. But being assertive in her own age group came over as appallingly rude when applied to adults at home.

Another unattractive feature is the way your six-year-old will flatly deny it or try to blame someone else if he has done something naughty or had an accident. The best approach is if you broach the matter in the form of a question, such as 'Where did you find the matches, darling?' The chances are he'll tell you and then you can discuss the subject sensibly.

Television

Six to eleven is the peak period for televiewing. Your

child is at the beginning stage. This is the time to work out a policy, while you still have a modicum of control. TV is a fact of twentieth – and twenty-first – century life, particularly for youngsters. I remember visiting a family with young children in desperate poverty. Food was scarce and they had almost no furniture – apart from a large television set on the floor. The average viewing time for children under sixteen is between two and four hours a day – some much more, others less.

There is no doubt of television's educational value: it is used in schools, colleges and the Open University. At home it is likely to be turned on for pure entertainment by parents and children alike, unless there is a special effort made to select worthwhile programmes. The screen has an almost hypnotic effect, but barely engages the intelligence at all, unless it is shared – as it is at school – with an adult who will discuss it later.

Children who watch a great deal of TV at home, fall behind at school in reading and writing skills, but more essentially in the ability to express themselves verbally. They see actions without words and hear words which they never need to answer.

Mothers are human, and busy humans at that, and it is convenient to have your child happily and harmlessly occupied while you get on with making supper or work out your tax returns. It is an easy option for the child too – he doesn't have to think of anything else to do. TV is like ice-cream: it goes down easily and pleasantly, but on its own it is poor nourishment for the mind and provides zilch in the way of healthy exercise.

Violence on the box is a long-term subject of controversy. It is estimated that by sixteen the average American youngster will have seen more than 13,000 killings and countless brutal assaults at home, on the screen. It is much the same in the UK and Australia. Whether or not it increases the likelihood of violent

Childhood Development

behaviour later in children like Jack and Jessica, from normal, loving homes, it does seem reasonable that it may blunt their feelings and make brutality more acceptable as part of life.

At this age you can choose which programmes your child doesn't watch, and by your interest guide him towards those of value. Natural history, exploring the frontiers of science, introducing the people of other lands and films of the classics can all be excellently done – and worth watching for any of us.

Computers

Somewhat similarly, computers have a fascination for some children which is almost as pernicious as television. They very readily learn how to operate them. Sarah and Dom were delighted at the blotting-paper-quick way young Jack took to their home computer, and at school, too. They were proud that their son was so truly a child for the twenty-first century. For Jack computer games were the magnet and they could become an addiction.

A power cut reminded the whole family that board games with other people were actually more fun, and paper and pencil an effective method for recording information and ideas. Most of all they were reminded that there are other things to make and do, and that little boys and little girls thrive best with plenty of outdoor exercise, playtimes with their peers, and novel and stimulating activities with their parents.

Seven years

Physical progress. During the years from seven to ten, boys and girls grow at much the same annual rate: 2–3ins (5–7.5cm) taller and 5–7lbs (2.5–3kg) heavier

School-time

(see the growth charts, pp 279–84). There is a slight increase in the proportion of fat on the body, especially for girls, but you would hardly notice it except in those with an inborn tendency to chubbiness. It acts as an insulation against cold and a reserve fuel store for the muscles.

Your seven-year-old uses his muscles in great bursts of energy, but now there are longer periods when he or she concentrates on drawing, building or reading. One of Sarah's happiest snapshots is of Jack racing round the garden with his friend Stevie, throwing paper aeroplanes as far as they could. They had seen grown men doing the very same thing on television.

Jack was introduced to team sport at school. He was not particularly good at ball games so he didn't enjoy them as much as free play with his pals. On the other hand he was one of the first to discover how to swim without one foot on the bottom. In fact he was like a wriggling fish in the water. Jessica liked rounders and she was keen to play tennis. Her neat footwork and muscle control made her a humdinger at skipping games and hop-scotch.

'Doing gym' was a favourite lesson with everybody at school. For one thing, it was a relief to do something active after sitting still. Another particular pleasure at this age was riding their bikes. Those seven-year-olds who hadn't already got two-wheelers were piling on the pressure at home. Jack and Jessica had each worn their parents down successfully before this.

Three or four new teeth are likely to come through this year. Meanwhile Jack had an irresistible urge to wiggle his loose tooth with his thumb, whatever else he was doing. Jessica's teeth seemed to Ellie to be growing all higgledy-piggledy. She was worried and asked the dentist if anything ought to be done to make them straight. The dentist said that she was quite right to have brought Jessica along when she did, and that he would keep an eye on those front teeth. Orthodontic treatment isn't usually necessary, if at all, before the age of eight or nine. At the same time as the appearance of her permanent teeth, Jessica's cheek-bones and forehead grew more prominent. It didn't make her look more grown-up, but touchingly vulnerable. The changes show up best if you compare photographs taken a year apart, around this age.

With active growth and fast living, your seven-year-old needs plenty of top-grade nourishment. As well as three proper meals – breakfast is a must – he or she is likely to want top-up snacks in between. An especially hungry time is when she has just come in from school. This is no time to say: 'It'll spoil your supper.' It won't.

Reading, writing and numbers. Reading, writing, numbers and painting are all part of your child's development at school. The style of teaching will obviously affect the way your child learns. Repetition is one key – actors use this method – finding out and doing are others. It helps your child in several ways if, at home, you encourage any tendency to collect things. It doesn't much matter what, at this stage, whether shells or stones or check-out lists from the supermarket. They provide practice in handling numbers and in classification.

Reading and its first cousin, writing, are the most important school subjects at seven plus: the essence of human communication. Books are the key to all other knowledge, and a portable pleasure which you can use in places where you can't plug in a TV or computer. They can take your child on exciting adventures – but he won't get hurt – or on trips to foreign lands which would cost a fortune in air fares. Time and space travel are within range, too.

Jessica was 'a good little reader'. Her teacher said so, but she also loved Ellie or Bill to read to her. They could share those stories which were too difficult for

School-time

Jessica on her own – like *Alice*. Alice was seven, like Jessica, when she was in Wonderland, and seven and a quarter 'exactually' in *Through the Looking Glass*. Jack, sitting bolt upright in bed with the excitement of the story, liked to read before going to sleep, like his dad. His favourite author, to start with, was Allan Ahlberg, and *Mr Biff the Boxer* his favourite book. Then he found that he could read the *Dilly the Dinosaur* books – he was keen on dinosaurs. But when Sarah read to him he liked to hear about King Arthur and his knights and some of the Greek myths.

The best boost to a seven-year-old's interest in reading for himself is to see by example that it is a grown-up thing to do. Trips to the library should count as important and enjoyable for parents as well as juniors, and a mixed collection of books at home is a valuable stimulus to find out more. (See book list, p 254).

Writing is a matter of practice. Ellie used to ask Jessica to write her shopping lists for her, and sometimes a note for the milkman. As precise hand control improves, so your child's writing gets smaller and more even. Punctuation, in the form of full-stops, is included.

Drawing and painting are progressing, too. At just seven, Jack did a strip of green or brown at the bottom of his pictures for the ground, and a strip of blue along the top for the sky.

Soon he began putting in a few black clouds hanging down from the blue bit, and by the end of this year there was a horizon, where earth and sky met. Some of his 'best' pictures, for instance the one of a racing car, he would repeat over and over, almost exactly. (The great Italian painters did this, too, with their famous works.)

Jessica's subjects were a house, a tree with fruit and a bird in it, but most often, people. They all had bodies and limbs as well as heads, now, and hands with fingers, clothes with buttons and shoes with shoe-laces. They had two hairstyles: a fuzz all over or dead straight and spiky. Their faces had smile-shaped mouths and dot noses: girls had skirts. Jack's men had black eyebrows in one horizontal line, straight vertical lines for their noses, and mouths like gratings, full of teeth. The difference between Jessica's people and Jack's is typical of the sexes of the artists.

All children are creative. At seven their thinking hasn't yet been guided and organised, so that originality and the free flow of imagination are flourishing. These are precious. Children's silliness can be irritating, but it helps to keep their minds open to any ideas, however absurd. Great discoveries and great art depend on this.

Seven-year-olds are calmer and easier to live with than six-year-olds. They don't have so many colds and they are not as severe, and school morning tummy-aches are less likely. They can dress themselves, except for odd bits that need tucking in, and comb their own hair, especially at the front. They can just about take themselves to bed unaided, but you must go to say goodnight, have a little chat and read a story (it won't discourage his own reading). He is also reassured that he is snug and safe, and there is no way you might forget about him or her.

Jessica still needed Rabbit in bed with her, and Jack had his now one-eared Ted. Bad dreams are less frequent than before, but imagination can still play nasty tricks. The window curtain rippling faintly because of a current of air looked awfully like a ghost to Jack.

Seven-year-olds are not very big and brave, after all, and they are easily demoralised if anyone laughs at them. They are ashamed if someone sees them crying or if they have made a mistake. The cheeky defiance of six years old has subsided – it was a sham, anyway – and at school he is dependent on his teacher and needs her say-so before he does anything new. At the same

School-time

time, your seven-year-old is becoming a little detached from you, his mother: this is a normal development. It doesn't mean that he or she loves you any less.

It's a side-effect of his wobbly self-confidence that your seven-year-old is a bad loser. He or she strongly believes in luck, and is convinced that other people have all the good luck and he has bad luck. A seven-year-old can concentrate much better than at five or six. Sarah often found Jack lying on his tummy reading or drawing, oblivious of everything else. In fact, at one time she seriously wondered if he was deaf, since he seemed not to hear when she was calling him. He wasn't deaf – just in another world.

One result of the seven-year-old's increased capacity for thought is 'seeing through' Father Christmas, and the Tooth Fairy. Jack, who was always a deep thinker, realised that it was better and kinder to go along with grown-ups like Granny, who liked to pretend they were real. Now that he could tell the time, Jack was desperate for a watch this year, so he hedged his bets. He wrote to Father Christmas and told everybody what he'd asked for. Jessica had found, to her relief, proof positive of the Tooth Fairy's existence. The tooth had gone from under her pillow and was nowhere to be found when she discovered the silver coin, left in its stead.

Now that there are critical doubts about Father Christmas some seven-year-olds wonder about God, too. This is an age for serious speculation about the fundamentals of life and death. Jack and his contemporaries of both sexes were refreshingly matter-of-fact about death and funerals. When his granddad was laid up with a slipped disc, complaining that it 'hurt like Hell' Jack reassured him that if he quickly said sorry for all the bad things he'd done, he would be sure to get into Heaven after all. His grandfather was fifty-six, and his general health was excellent. Jack saw him as

Childhood Development

very old, and as such he could be expected to die.

Jessica was ahead of Jack in life experiences: she had been to a funeral. It was that of her great-aunt, whom she had not known well, and since it had been difficult to find someone to look after Jessica, and anyway, she was so sensible these days, her parents took her along. She was interested in the whole short ceremony and remarked that it was like the ghost train when the coffin trundled through the curtains on its rollers.

The sadness of losing someone you've loved and the horrid permanence of death doesn't impinge fully on children, unless it is a parent whom they have lost. The Carter family of three children experienced a tragedy. Justin, the four-year-old, was killed by a Range Rover reversing. Her brother and sister of five and seven respectively lost no time in going through Justin's toys and dividing them up. It seemed shocking, but adults, when you come to think about it, are anxious to know what's in the will if they stand to gain. The difference is only word-deep.

Birth is the other essential of human existence. Unless they already have a brother or sister, children of this age are likely to suggest to their parents that they should have a baby. It is not so much the process of birth that fascinates them at seven, but the babies themselves. Ellie said she would think about it. 'Or if not,' said Jessica, 'I'd like to learn to play the piano.'

Eight years

Seven was a pensive age. Eight is boisterous, expansive. Your eight-year-old isn't given to inward brooding and is not so easily hurt. She – or he – has the confidence to tackle anything, though not always the judgement. Some of the sweet, imaginative, *Alice in Wonderland* aura of childhood is being replaced by a bustling, business-like air. There's the impression of an independent

School-time

someone who knows where she is going and is well on the way to being an adult.

Jessica dealt with her parents now as a person in her own right, whose views were as valid as theirs. In fact she was a know-all, and couldn't bear being told what to do. Ellie found that she responded better to hints and suggestions. Nor was she any longer under the sway of Miss Martin, her teacher, although she liked her – in a patronising way.

Jack, too, felt that he was practically on a level with the adults. As well as his same-age friends, he had Barry. Barry was big – eleven – and a useful ally if Jack was being bullied at school. Jack admired him enormously.

Healthwise, eight is a fine age. Infections are progressively fewer and thrown off more quickly, although Jack had an ear infection a couple of times. Eight-year-olds have more stamina than sevens, but on the downside they are still apt to be accident-prone. This comes from a combination of fearlessness and carelessness. It is not uncommon for an eight-year-old to break a bone.

Because, with her boundless energy and insatiable curiosity she is living at top speed, your child may be subject to signs of tension, such as headache, stomach-ache, fidgetiness or frequent trips to the loo to pass water. Jack had the irritating habit, of which he was hardly aware, of jiggling his legs whenever he was sitting down. It was as though his muscles were raring to go.

All this energy expenditure needed fuelling. Even Jack, never a wonderful eater, finished his plate steadily and with interest, while some of his friends were into third helpings – the bottomless pit syndrome. Jack could now cut his meat with a knife, if it wasn't too tough, but his friend Stevie couldn't. Ellie was afraid that Jessica would get fat from the amount she tucked away, so there was a food policy of more fruit and vegetables as fillers. This helped.

Childhood Development

Although they eat well, eight-year-olds don't like to waste much time on it: there is so much else they want to do. Jack and his friends would bolt their school dinner, then explode out into the playground to race about. The herd instinct affected the boys more than the girls. It gave them a sense of masculine identity, and when they were together they would shout derogatory comments at the girls, which they would never have done one-to-one.

Jessica had a best friend, Susie, who was in her class. They played together and shared endless, giggly secrets. This friendship lasted all the time they were at that school, unlike the frequent changes of earlier. She and Susie were also part of a small group, but they didn't have the same fierce gang loyalty as the boys. They were agreed, however, that boys were stupid.

Children of this age can co-operate and organise, for instance, a play together or in Jack's case a 'Guess the Weight of the Cake' stall at the school fête. They had ideas about what was fair, but could not yet operate the democratic principle of majority decisions. Instead, it was the one who was strongest or who had the loudest voice who chose.

Most eight-year-olds are collectors: an indication of intelligence and of career success later. Together with this comes a strong sense of property, especially for their own things. They are also interested in money, on a realistic basis. 'He's money-mad,' said Sarah, when Jack started putting a price on the various useful jobs around the home and he had sufficient self-control to save up for a siren for his bike. It made a highly satisfying sound, reminiscent of a police car.

Occasionally – and to parents, worryingly – an eight-year-old may feel that he actually needs some money. In much the same way as a starving man may feel that it is no crime to steal the bread he needs, an eight-year-old may take money. Children who take money from their mother's purse when they are younger, usually do it as a substitute for love they want. The eight-year-old needs it to buy something.

The relationship between mother and child at about eight is once again very intense. Like a toddler following his mother everywhere, Jack haunted Sarah's every move. It wasn't that her mere presence made him feel safe, as it used to do. Now he was after a 'meaningful' relationship – a psychological interaction and exchange of ideas. At this stage he wanted to tell her all about school, blow by blow, where before he had brushed aside any show of interest.

Jealousy was never far from the surface and Jack even looked askance at Dom, if he seemed to be monopolising Sarah's attention. Mothers are still the most favoured parents for most children of eight, but fathers are beginning to receive a better share of affection. Their company, one-to-one, is valued, and they are certainly the best at knock-about games.

Sex

Sex has become relevant by this age. Boys and girls at the same school are separating – spontaneously – and each sex views the other with curiosity and suspicion. The basic facts of reproduction are taught in schools in the UK, the USA and Australia. There is nothing erotic about this teaching, nor do the children want that. Smutty jokes and puns and the acquisition of four-letter words arise at this time. When Jessica first said 'Fuck off, I'm busy,' it came as a shock to Ellie, but more was to come. Children today cannot be expected to be the only people not to use the uglier Anglo-Saxon expressions.

By eight your child should know, not only about 'not talking to strangers' and steering clear of their cars, but that even with close family and friends, touching in the genital area is bad. Your child must learn to say 'No' loudly and to tell you of any such incidents. Some little girls of eight have an exciting, not unpleasant sensation if they are touched up, and these children are just as innocent but especially vulnerable. It is a tightrope walk for parents to make their children aware of dangers without imbuing them with a fear of all men, and a distorted view of sex. Little boys, when they are tense or fidgety at this age, often embarrass their mothers by fiddling with their genitals. Yet it is counter-productive to tell them sharply to stop it.

How parents make a baby and how it gets born are both questions that require proper answers now. Fortunately, your child is likely to make it easy for you by asking specific questions, which you can answer shortly and factually, one by one. Embarrassment won't come into it from the child's viewpoint. He is simply wanting authoritative information – and who better than a parent to provide it?

Little girls are usually more inquisitive than boys. After all, it is they who could one day grow a baby in their own tummy. As well, they need to know in good time about periods, since a substantial minority will have their first one at nine or ten.

Nine to ten years

The impression of Jack at eight that lingered in Sarah's mind was his eagerness for life. His watchwords: 'I can't wait to . . .' rang in her ears. It was Jessica's bubbling over with laughter at her own jokes and her enjoyment of the Mary Poppins story that summed it up for Ellie.

Nine to ten is precious. It is the last year of pure childishness. After this there is the rocky road that leads through adolescence to a future where parents and children are on a different footing. Already you may find that your child doesn't want you to baby him or her – at any rate not when anyone else is around. Nevertheless, he will frequently quote you as a top authority: 'My mother says . . .' Sometimes children of this age will completely ignore an adult who comes into the room. This isn't rudeness, merely that adults in general may seem irrelevant.

Jack was beginning to discard some of the toys that had, only recently, been favourites. He was into computer games, chemistry, his collection of fossils and a club with a secret password, consisting of four of his friends. Jessica couldn't quite bear to throw Rabbit out, decrepit though he had become, and she often played with her doll, Agatha, who had a full set of clothes and equipment. Agatha was often ill, went to visit the doctor, went to school or was naughty. Jessica collected little horses in china, plastic or wood, and she was planning to have her own pony when she was rich.

If TV hasn't been allowed to take over, nine–ten is a great age for reading. Jessica still enjoyed fairy tales, but most children have moved on to believable stories: classics like *Treasure Island* and *Tom Sawyer*, and endless dog, cat and horse stories. In the home there is a reasonable chance that your child will be responsible enough to look after his own pet, with some reminders. These are important, otherwise, if you feed the creature it will transfer its affections to you.

Looking after an animal means that hygiene matters. Unfortunately, children of this age, especially boys, often have an aversion to washing – unnecessary and a waste of time. You also have to chase them up about cleaning their teeth, although apples and raw carrots are a help, and keeping their hair tidy. Jessica, in contrast to Jack, was definitely concerned to have her hair looking nice.

Both sexes have an interest in clothes, and want to have a say when new clothes are bought. Footgear seems to be the most important – and expensive. Jessica could be relied upon to choose sensibly when she dressed in the morning, although she would wear the same outfit day after day, if she liked it. She didn't notice it getting grubby. Jack, like his father, preferred his oldest clothes, but fortunately he was growing too tall for his tattiest old favourites.

Looking after clothes simply doesn't come into the nine–ten-year-old's book. Jack regularly left his clothes where they lay when he stepped out of them. This is not unusual. Jessica at least picked them up off the floor and put them in a crumpled bundle on a chair.

You don't have to rack your brains, thinking of things for your child to do, now. At this age he can motivate himself and plan ahead, and his ideas are realistic and reasonable. Given the opportunity, nine- to ten-year-olds relish the sheer joy of physical exercise. Boys are bitten by the football bug, while girls diversify with tennis, netball, hockey, swimming and gym according to individual taste.

On the health front this is an age of minimal trouble. Any tendency to asthma or hay fever improves around now, and the minor bodily ills like tummy-aches, headaches and snuffly colds diminish. The appetite settles from voracious to good, with a continuing preference for plain foods, without sauces and spice. Jack was forthright about the foods he didn't like. 'I hate spinach, yuck,' he said. Other foods that children of this age often dislike include all fish except fish fingers, stew, liver and cabbage, while there are no complaints about baked beans, burgers, chips and ice-cream.

Some children go off breakfast – adult example counts here. For growing, high-energy spenders the first meal of the day matters, even if we can cope without.

Nine- and ten-year-olds have the makings of really nice people. They want to fit in. They also want their parents to conform, especially when they appear at a school function. Instead of feeling pleased, Jack was embarrassed when he came first in his class for science. He felt singled out, when he would rather have been one of the crowd.

Moral sense develops at this age. Cheating and telling lies (about anything important) are fiercely disapproved of, and depending on your input, your child's conscience grows: even when no one is looking. Kindness towards younger and weaker people or anyone who is sad or has been hurt, begins to show now, as well as applying to oneself the principles of truth and honesty.

Your child may be genuinely concerned about social and world problems and it is patronising not to discuss these seriously, if your youngster is interested. On the other hand, there is not much worry about death or God at this stage. They are taken for granted as requiring no special action at present. All in all, when your child just gets into double figures – at ten – he or she is likely to be happy, well-balanced and prepared for the future. She has grown up a long way, and you, too, will have kept step and developed into a wiser, more mature adult.

Helping your child's development

Above all, you have a schoolchild on your hands, and you have a tricky path to follow. You want to support your child, and also to support his teacher. You want to show the school your interest and involvement without being considered an over-anxious pest. It is difficult to help your youngster with the basics of reading and sums, because the teacher may be using a different approach from the one you know. It is worth asking at a parent–teacher evening – better than making a special trip – what you can do at home that might be useful.

It is always educational as well as pleasurable to read

Childhood Development

to your child, and when he or she has learned the rudiments, to 'hear' her reading. And of course, when your child is learning to play a musical instrument, from a recorder to the piano, he will practise much better if you are listening and encouraging.

School-work must be treated as of similar importance to his father's job – or yours – and however inconvenient it may be, it is worth a bag of gold to your little one if you go to speech days, school sports, carol concerts and anything else the school lays on for parents. As you sit on the excruciatingly uncomfortable chair for hours, remember that this is what motivates children to try their hardest and teachers to remain keen. It can be wonderfully interesting to hear an objective assessment of your youngster – how he or she behaves when you aren't there, whether he's a good mixer or she shows any special talent or interest.

It is the latter which figures at this stage. Sir Joshua Reynolds was mad keen on painting as a boy, although he was by no means the best in his artistic family. It was his zeal and persistence that lifted him head and shoulders above the others in the end and made him the most sought-after portrait painter of his time.

Character, too, is beginning to shine out. It is at this age that the priceless gift of charisma starts showing itself, a kind of creativity in personal relations. There are no exams in this subject, although it has more influence than any other on your child's success in life.

Sarah was worried at the amount of time Jack spent in aimless fooling around with his friends. This wasn't as pointless and useless as it seemed. He was soaking up feelings in exchange with the others.

Father's role

At least fathers know that they have a role at this age.

School-time

Mothers are everyday useful and necessary, while fathers have a degree of rarity value – mothers are seldom long-distance lorry drivers and rarely choose jobs that involve frequent conferences in Switzerland. Trips with Dad are all special excursions, and his views, less frequently heard, carry extra weight. Maintaining discipline is often loaded onto the father. In no way need or should it be physical.

From seven onwards your child is well able to understand when his father explains why something is wrong or harmful to other people. As parents you have the power to turn the whole world dark just by your disapproval.

It can be confusing for fathers nowadays. We are halfway through a cultural revolution. Fathers are taking a bigger part in bringing up their children, from nappy-changing to going to the school to discuss 'A' Level choices. It is at nine to ten that a comfortable, companionable rapport is properly established between father and child. The relationship with fathers runs more smoothly than with mothers, with fewer emotional ups and downs – so long as the father respects his child's growing maturity.

Sometimes there is a father–son ganging up against mother, sisters, the whole female world. This slots in with the anti-the-other-sex bias of children of this age, but is not helpful to development. Fathers and daughters get on very well without this factor coming into it.

From seven to ten children can be critical about their parents – any father who smokes these days is likely to be nagged by his child. Jack thought Dom drank too much and said so: a pint of beer struck him as an enormous volume. Jessica loved doing jobs with her father, for instance making a bookshelf with bricks and two planks. She felt that he was terrifically clever at his work, and had half-decided to be an engineer too when she grew up. Her pride in him showed in the many sentences beginning: 'My daddy can . . .'

Grandparents' corner

You may have been hurt and shocked by your seven-year-old grandchild's being so rude and argumentative – for no reason. It is tempting to tell your daughter or daughter-in-law that she needs to be firm, and your son or son-in-law that he isn't pulling his weight in the matter. Worst of all, you may feel like intervening when the youngster is behaving badly to his mother.

It is better to bite your lip for the next couple of years, while your grandchild grows out of this phase. The relationship is too precious to risk souring it now. The wisest grandparent sticks to sharing some activities with the child – reading to him, playing a board game, planting bulbs. When he is alone with you, for instance visiting you, ten to one he will be his ordinary friendly self. The special patience and understanding that grandparents possess works its magic best in private.

In family politics grandparents have no authority and can make no decisions. Authoritarian grandparents don't work, but they can be wonderful as wise and experienced consultants and pourers of oil on troubled feelings. Since the responsibility isn't theirs, they can be calmer, more relaxed in their approach. The sense of family running through the generations is of benefit to all. It gives an emotional security which may be put to the test in family crises.

Of course, in a one-parent family, the grandmother may be a vital cog in how it works, and the grandfather a first-class father substitute. Even so, the feelings and indeed rights, of the mother deserve the most sensitive recognition and care.

9

The Threshold:
eleven to twelve years

Ten years old was unique. Your child was poised at the mid-point of her young life. A decade of childhood lay behind her, a decade of adolescence to come. The years of dependency for her and detailed, practical responsibility for you are over. Ahead, through years eleven, twelve and onwards, your child will progressively detach herself from your care and guidance until she can make her own decisions and cope – more or less – with life on her own.

Your role is like that of the piano accompanist to a singer: constantly, sympathetically adjusting to the pace and mood of your child's development, providing support but not taking the leading part. It takes the greatest sensitivity to leave go, yet to reassure your youngster of your ongoing love and interest, mixed now with a sprinkling of respect.

Eleven years

If ten was a charming age, when everything seemed easy and peacefully constructive, year eleven will come as a shock. It is a turbulent, exciting year, leading who knows where, like the take-off of the first spacecraft. You may have imagined that the most dramatic change must be from helpless babe to confident, competent schoolchild. Not a bit of it. The development just beginning involves a total physical transformation and

Childhood Development

psychological and intellectual development that can leave you behind, floundering.

Why the years eleven and twelve are so important is because this is when puberty begins for many children. Even more than with his or her development so far, your child will run to his own personal schedule. A perfectly normal child can be a year or two or three ahead of or behind the average. Incidentally, the one who matures late may well go farthest in the end. My son, Seb, was quite small for his age and mad on horses. He decided to be a jockey. His plan was wrecked by a late, long growth spurt which made him much too tall. Now he is an airline pilot.

Adolescence is the period of all-over changes – mind and body – at the end of which your child rates as an adult. Puberty is the sum total of the physical and physiological changes which enable him to be a parent like you, in due time. For several years before puberty begins there is a build-up of hormones from the pituitary gland in the brain. These act on the sex glands, the ovaries and testicles, to produce their hormones in turn, and a whole train of events is set off.

Children until this stage are a unisex shape. Boys and girls can take parts of either sex in a school play (Jessica was one of the three kings). But from now there is no pretending that the two sexes are only different because of the way we treat them. While the timing can be variable, the programme of puberty is standard, with the two sexes diverging.

Girls are usually ahead of boys, and already, at eleven, Jessica was going into her growth spurt. This would peak at twelve to thirteen and taper off after fourteen if she continued at the average rate. She was shooting up and had reached ninety per cent of what her height would be at twenty-one – in ten years' time. Her weight, on the other hand, was only fifty per cent of the adult figure. Only a quarter of the boys at school

The Threshold

had started their growth spurt, and most had reached no more than eighty per cent of their final height at eleven.

It was obvious that Jessica's bones were growing fast. It started with her hands and feet: Ellie thought she would have to buy new shoes for her every week. Forearms and shin-bones came next, then thighs and upper arms. Of course her head and neck and trunk grew too, but her limbs became longer in proportion. With boys this is even more marked. For Jessica there was a specifically female change: her hips became wider. Together with her bones, her muscles were also developing. For a year or two she, as a girl, was taller and stronger than most boys of the same age.

There were also more subtle changes. The tiny breast buds, which had been just discernible since she was nine, had now become little cone-shaped bulges. All over her body there was a softening and rounding of her contours, from a layer of fat under the skin. Together with her broader hips, Jessica was acquiring a feminine shape. A hint of down in the pubic region was changing to a sparse growth of longer, straight hairs.

Among her friends at school there was enormous diversity. At one extreme there were a bunch who were well-advanced and quite solid-looking. One or two of these had already started their periods – ahead of the most favoured time of twelve and three quarters, give or take six months. The timing of menarche depends on what runs in the family and also on nutrition: a weight of 7st (47kg) often seems to activate the switch-on. Other girls remained small and slim and childlike: their time would come (see puberty chart, p 269).

Jack at eleven was very little different physically from the year before. His growth spurt hadn't started, but his great friend, Barry, who was thirteen now, seemed a giant by comparison. His limbs were growing, with awkward feet and hands on the ends, his shoulders broadening, his chest, and heart and lungs developing – and his voice-box was getting bigger, so his voice was breaking. A few boys' voices go funny as early as eleven, and their first pubic hair may show before the growth spurt begins. But not for Jack (see puberty chart, p 269).

The unaccustomed flood of sex and growth hormones coursing – invisibly – through body and brain, and the bewildering physical changes starting up are matched by the beginnings of an emotional and psychological revolution. The agreeable balance of your ten-year-old, happy with his child's place in the family, has gone. A different, difficult-to-understand person is taking over in his stead. It is a re-run – only more so – of that change-over from the peaceful good sense of the five-year-old to the rude, awkward six-year-old stage.

Self-assertion develops at eleven. We all agree that this is a good trait in adults, but in your eleven-year-old it comes over as a generally impudent attitude, chequered with outbursts of extreme rudeness. Jessica was unaware of the effect of her giving her views so forthrightly. 'What have I done?' she would ask indignantly when Ellie was cross at some insulting remark to a visitor. Then she would flounce upstairs and bang her door – several times.

Jack had always had a propensity to argue, and this now reached obsessional proportions. Neither Sarah, Dom nor any other adult could make an observation without Jack's turning it into an argument. He did the same with his friends, but they, like him, enjoyed it. Even when he wasn't disagreeing, Jack was talking: the plus side of this was his increased sociability. The delights of having an eleven-year-old about the house are their bubbling spontaneity and frequent bursts of laughter – never mind the tendency to grumpiness in the mornings.

The Threshold

'She's so *alive*,' remarked Jessica's grandmother, a tactful soul. Indeed it seemed, at first sight, as though Jessica was never still. She wriggled in her chair, rocked it back and forth, stretched her arms and legs, fiddled with her shoes and, at the drop of a hat, got up to look at something across the room. Then suddenly she would be tired. Fatigue comes on more often at eleven than ten, perhaps because of the energy used up in growing.

Eleven-year-olds are also more susceptible to coughs and colds, and their temperature control is often faulty. Jack was always complaining of being either boiling hot or freezing. As you would expect, since that is the time for growing and repairing, sleep is an urgent necessity at this age. Once an eleven-year-old is asleep he is dead to the world: noises and lights make no impact.

Jack had an alarm clock. He was proud of it, but fifty per cent of the time it didn't wake him. He went to bed – grumbling – at about 9.30. Most of his friends did the same, except at weekends. Quite often he didn't want to get up in the morning, but this was often because he had been reading – by torch-light – under the bedclothes until past midnight.

As well as sleep, your eleven-year-old has a pressing need for nourishment. His or her appetite is huge – a matter for self-congratulation for most boys, but causing embarrassment among some of the girls. Jessica and her friends were always hungry, but they did discuss dieting. Because of their developing concern with social, ethical and environmental issues, some children decide to be vegetarian at this age. A few refuse to eat eggs because it means taking nourishment that was meant for a chick. There is no moral veto on crisps, coke or chocolate – regrettably.

As well as a well-developed appetite for food, your eleven-year-old has an insatiable hunger for new experiences. Because he feels himself growing up apace,

Childhood Development

he is becoming increasingly interested in what adults say and do. Jack rigged up a tape-recorder under the sofa to check on his parents' conversation after he had gone to bed. In fact, they had been talking about money – one of Jack's major interests at this time. When an honorary aunt asked him what sort of lady he would like to marry when he grew up, he replied: 'I may not bother at all, but if I do, she's got to be rich.' He managed to accumulate a considerable sum by blatantly angling for cash hand-outs and carefulness with what he'd got to the point of scroogery.

Neither Jack nor Jessica had the time, patience or inclination to keep their rooms and their possessions in any other order than chaos. Now and again Jessica would stuff a few garments away into a drawer and make it shut. She was interested in clothes – to buy and put on – and sporadically in her hair, teeth and fingernails.

Jack couldn't care less about any of it yet, apart from sports gear. He 'hated' anything that might be regarded as work in the home, but he did his school-work, to be the same as the others. Some of his friends had decided, realistically this time, what career they wanted to follow. Steve, for instance was set on being a doctor and was busy practising on anyone who had cut or bruised themselves. He hasn't changed from this. Most of the youngsters were still in a state of flux – one moment wanting to be a spy, the next a concert pianist or a racing driver.

The ripples of their ever-changing moods, and the odd peaks of intense emotion which come out of the blue, make eleven-year-olds difficult to live with. They are often rebellious, taking everything as a challenge, yet they often desperately want physical affection and hugs from their parents: so long as they don't do it in public or without a tacit invitation.

Friendships with others of their own age are

important. Here again boys and girls tend to differ. Jack had his best friend, Steve, and they both belonged to a big anti-girl group. Jessica had four good friends, none very much more favoured than the others. The main development in the way both sexes view their friends at about eleven is that they choose them not just as playmates who enjoy the same games, but for character traits such as kindness, generosity, 'makes me laugh', or being a good sport.

To be accepted by the peer group now has the highest priority. Adults' opinions don't matter so much and parents have lost their haloes. This means that you cannot so easily persuade or bargain with your eleven-year-old to see things your way. Even teachers are subject to the most disrespectful criticism. Jessica was scathing about Miss Parsons's abysmal dress sense, and her music teacher's halitosis.

Jokes about bottoms, bowels and – increasingly – sex, were current at school, especially among the boys. This was partly because at this age children are more aware of their own changing bodies, and the practical aspects of sexual intercourse interest them. Jack and his cronies thought the whole process 'amazing', while Jessica told her confidantes that it sounded rather nasty.

Twelve years

Twelve is a honey of an age. In contrast to the turbulence of being eleven, your twelve-year-old has recovered his balance. He is less insistent about getting his way and is once more open to reason. He wants everyone to like him, grown-ups included. Of course, this isn't an overnight change but you can notice the trend.

Physical progress. Physically, twelve marks a crucial stage for boys. Although there can be startling disparities in the timing between perfectly normal boys,

Childhood Development

a large proportion are beginning to show the changes of puberty – and to catch up with the girls. While only a quarter of boys were into their growth spurt at eleven, now the majority are. The peak age is fourteen, and it is even more dramatic than the girls'. A boy may grow 4ins (10cm) taller during the year. At twelve, however, the process is only just starting up.

The first sign that Jack noticed was that his penis and testicles were getting bigger, and a few long, soft hairs had appeared in the pubic region. Over the next year or two these would become coarser, curly and increasingly profuse. Jack had read, with a mixture of fascination and horror, that the testicles grow to fifteen times their original size: 1g at ages two to ten years, reaching 15g by seventeen.

Jack's friend, Steve, went through a fat phase at this time, and for over a year he was among the thirty per cent of boys who develop noticeable breast swelling. Each sex produces a certain amount of the sex hormone of the other. Boys, like girls, add to their fat store during early puberty; but while the proportion of fat in girls increases to twenty-two per cent of body weight between eleven and seventeen, for boys the early increase goes into reverse by the end: down to ten or twelve per cent.

While girls, to their disgust, are getting broader hips plus a layer of fat on their thighs, boys are developing broader shoulders and proportionately longer legs and may reach a gangly stage. Later on their hips actually become narrower in proportion. Another bony change is in the face. In boys, especially, the brow becomes more prominent, and in both sexes the jawbone enlarges to accommodate more teeth. This makes the young face look more oval than round, and in the in-between stage, heart-breakingly vulnerable.

This is partly due to the new, big teeth coming through at this stage. The canines – the vampire teeth

The Threshold

– appear at any time from nine to twelve, followed a year or so later by the molars, at ten to thirteen. That leaves only the second row of molars, the wisdom teeth, which don't usually crop up until past childhood. Sometimes the new teeth coming through look crooked or appear behind the milk teeth. Usually they right themselves, without any dental assistance, but help is at hand if necessary. (See tooth charts p 271.)

Another sign of growing up that develops a little later than the first pubic hair in both sexes, is underarm hair. New style sweat glands develop in the same area, which produce sweat with a characteristic smell: the *raison d'être* of the great deodorant industry. Any youngster liable to have freckles will have a crop now: you may remember another freckly stage at about six. Ellie had to explain to Jessica that the new freckles did not make her look childish, but were a sign of growing up. After all, at twelve, she was practically as tall as her mother, and anyway ninety-five per cent of her own adult height.

If Jessica had been in a muddle about who or what she was last year, now it was clear that she was a young woman in the making. She told Ellie that she could no longer put up with the humiliation – she used such words these days – of the clothes that Ellie chose for her, or, horror of horrors, actually made. Jessica's own taste ran to skin-tight tops, which was unfortunate in such a fast grower, wide elasticated belts which strangled her middle and skirts so short that even her fairly liberal-minded school banned them.

Jessica was glad to have a shape, but some of her friends were going about hunched up to conceal their budding breasts. 'It means I can't run away to sea, if things get too bad at school,' wailed Emily. She had tried to control the situation with a crêpe bandage, but it kept slipping down. Jessica wasn't interested in boys: the fact that most of them were smaller than she was

Childhood Development

at this stage was off-putting. Nevertheless, she knew that this would change some time soon.

Courageous parents now arrange mixed parties, as more grown-up and they have to be held at night. Even if you go into another room, it is vital that you are at hand throughout. Otherwise, however well they start off, parties for this age group easily deteriorate. Some of the less mature boys tend to gang up and become unmanageably lively and rude. On the other hand, such hiding-in-the-dark games as Hide and Seek, Sardines and Murder must be included – for the oddly exciting chances of contact with someone of the other sex. No one would admit this.

Little boys have erections from time to time from babyhood, but Jack was interested, then embarrassed to find they were happening frequently these days. Any excitement, for instance rough and tumble play or football, could set one off. He didn't have any 'wet dreams' – emissions of seminal fluid in the night – yet, but Dom and also Barry had told him about them. The first time usually crops up about a year after the testicles have begun getting larger. There are important practical details about what to do with any damp sheets or pyjamas. It is good to know that these matters are natural and normal. Dom also explained to Jack about girls' periods; this saved a lot of sniggering confusion.

'Don't treat me as if I were a baby,' was a frequent complaint from Jack, but it was difficult for Sarah to strike the right balance. Twelve-year-olds are not adults in miniature. While they are surprisingly mature on some occasions, on others they are very childish. They are struggling for self-sufficiency and longing to be looked after – simultaneously. Jack was typical. He would exhaust himself during one of his bursts of enthusiasm, and then suddenly become very tired, with a headache, a stomach-ache or a sore throat. This was when he became very young again.

The Threshold

One indication of the drive for independence is a total lack of interest in family outings. Jessica at twelve preferred the company of her same-age friends, whatever they were doing. It was a particular pleasure to spend the night at a friend's house, or vice versa. There was a limitless amount to talk about, long after they had gone to bed. There was gossip, serious problems of religions and starving people, and giggly jokes with double meanings.

Being eleven or twelve is synonymous with being hungry. There is a genuine need for between-meal snacks – coke, milk, biscuits and fruit – and most youngsters of this age can make themselves something more solid: like sausages and baked beans on toast. Doorsteps of bread thickly layered with butter and jam fill in the odd chinks. Jack and Steve made a special drink: coffee. It consisted of coffee and drinking chocolate boiled up in milk. Toffoe was the tea-based variant.

For children who enjoy reading – some are too busy – mystery, adventure and sporting stories are top favourites, and some adult books. Romantic stuff only appeals to a few girls, but a lot of boys are into sci-fi. Jessica had enjoyed reading *Cranford* at school. She felt a bond of sympathy with Miss Matty, who rolled a ball under her bed before getting into it, to make sure that no one was hiding underneath. It wasn't frightening books or television programmes that scared Jessica, but odd creaks and noises at night and in the dark. She still occasionally dreamed about bad men.

TV is popular with twelve-year-olds, but computer games have taken over in some households, especially with the boys. An earlier technological invention entertains girls in particular – the telephone. Jessica would call Emily as soon as she came in from school, although they had been together all day. You could never get through to Bill or Ellie in the evening.

Sport is the ruling passion for some twelve-year-olds,

Childhood Development

especially boys, and the basis of their friendships. It wasn't for Jack. He didn't excel at any particular sport, so he lost interest. Instead, he loved making models, was a useful carpenter and enjoyed his collection of CDs. They didn't provide him with exercise, though. Jessica liked tennis and she wanted to learn fencing, but team games didn't appeal to her. She decorated her bedroom with only a little help, and she liked camping – even when it was just one night in a friend's garden.

Twelve is an age to enjoy – for parents and child. There is an atmosphere of sunny good humour, before the dreaded period of teenage moods sets in. Apart from a little jealousy of brothers or sisters, this is an age of tolerance, even towards mothers. Jessica realised that Ellie couldn't help being so hopelessly out-of-date in everything she said and did. Jack, too, felt quite friendly towards Dom and Sarah, despite their deficiencies.

Nevertheless, twelve-year-olds can have problems. For some there are worries from school: the work, friends and bullying. At home, apart from the irritation of thoroughly spoilt younger siblings, there can be serious concern about the parents' relationship. By this age, everyone has friends whose families have been struck by divorce: the smashing of the very foundations of a child's existence. Ordinary disagreements between the parents can be misinterpreted by an anxious child as the beginning of a break-up. There is also the haunting fear that if they themselves don't behave perfectly, one or other parent will go away – and it will be their fault.

Jack put Sarah through an exhaustive questionnaire, to check whether she was contemplating leaving. In the course of a row (after the washing machine had flooded) she had said, with more feeling than usual, that she was fed up with being left to do everything

The Threshold

while the pair of them – Dom and Jack – didn't lift a finger.

Some parents are shocked if a son, who knows right from wrong perfectly well, cheats at a game, or a daughter takes something belonging to another child. These are aberrations in youngsters who are still in the middle of building their personal set of values, and who may have worries pressing on their minds. This sort of behaviour is a passing phase to do with growing up, unless the youngster has serious problems.

Twelve is still a child – just. Next year he or she will be a teenager or in officialese: 'a young person'. Over the last dozen years you have fed, protected, guided and above all, loved your child. Soon he must venture into a world where the traps of sex and drink and drugs lie in his path, and he has the stress of exams that really matter, and decisions he must live with about how he will support himself. A sign of down-to-earth maturity is that not so many teenagers as ten-year-olds aim to be vets.

Meanwhile, there is a great deal for you to do.

Helping your child's development

Your child's urgent needs at eleven to twelve are clear-cut:
Plenty of good, nourishing and filling food: he or she will have an adult capacity and require three proper meals and three snacks in between, the last one near bedtime. By twelve he will stick to these regular times, rather than the uncontrolled eating of eleven.
Plenty of sleep: going to bed is less of a battle at twelve than eleven, and sleep when it comes is not so heavy. However, if your twelve-year-old goes to bed too long after his last meal, he may wake up from hunger.
Exercise: some children lose all interest in school games

Childhood Development

at this age, but exercise is still necessary for their health. Golf, squash, tennis, skating, running and swimming are more individualistic possibilities.

Privacy: this includes physically, except with same-sex friends, for bathing or changing clothes; and emotionally. Youngsters of eleven and twelve need to be able to get away from other people. Ideally each one should have a room of his own which is sacrosanct.

Security: a toddler would be scared if he had the freedom to wander in a garden the size of Hyde Park. Your near-teenager needs to have definite boundaries to his behaviour, set by you. These should not, of course, be needlessly restrictive, but your child will feel that you don't care about him if you don't make any rules.

Opportunities to air his views and have them treated with respect: on politics, religion, ethics, sex and lifestyles. It is good to ask his opinion on any practical matter, too, so long as you are not likely to discard it out of hand.

Check that girls know just what to expect and what to do about their *periods* now; boys probably don't need to know about emissions before they are thirteen.

Reminders about the rare but unpleasant *paedophile tendencies of some adults*. Boys of about twelve are particularly attractive to these men. It is tricky to strike a balance between being alarmist or over-complacent in giving advice.

There is also the big question – which school? The really vital years in education start now. You will probably have had hopes and plans for some time, based on your own experience. Now you have some highly relevant information to guide you: your child's interests and abilities and style of working will all have revealed themselves by this time. The choice of secondary school must fit these, together with the current teacher's advice and your child's own wishes. The latter may depend on where a friend is going or other relatively transient grounds.

The other factors are to do with feasibility: what is available, is the journey possible, and is it affordable? Your political views on the one hand or snob values on the other, should not influence you in deciding what is truly best for your youngster.

Father's role

The relationship with Dad is developing. When she was ten or eleven Jessica believed that Bill was good at everything, knew everything and was rich. She liked to think that she took after him much more than after Ellie, and she enjoyed trips with him, without Ellie. She felt more in harmony with Bill than Ellie. Girls are often quite horrible to their mothers for a year or so at this age.

Jack felt that Dom was 'awfully strict', because like many fathers, he was considered the final court of appeal in matters of discipline – and, quite rightly, he always backed up Sarah's judgements. Since he did not give his views so often, Jack took more notice of what Dom said – on any subject – compared with his mother.

By the time they were twelve, Jack and Jessica were both on happy terms with their fathers, in different ways. Jessica had lost some of her uncritical admiration for Bill and felt more comfortable with him. She told him, only half-jokingly, that he was too fat and would die of a heart attack but she still liked to think that she looked like him. Jack, on the other hand, was less critical of Dom than before, but he still mentioned that he had a short temper. Jack also thought he was mean to Sarah and didn't spend enough time with the family. It is fairly common for boys of Jack's age to feel protective towards their mothers.

Childhood Development

Several of Jack's and Jessica's friends complained about disciplinarian fathers, but nearly all of them, of both sexes, wanted to resemble their fathers rather than their mothers. This was in spite of thinking the latter were nicer. Some parents were severely condemned for smoking.

Grandparents' corner

Eleven-year-olds are naturally rude and argumentative. Don't feel hurt if you are in the firing line, and don't blame the poor parents. It's your grandchild's age and it doesn't last. In fact, eleven-year-olds are secretly very proud of their families and they like the idea of belonging to them. They enjoy whole family activities, grandparents included, especially trips to somewhere special like the river, the sea, the zoo, a concert or a theme park. Outings with grandparents on their own are popular too – a picnic is always welcomed.

By the time your grandchild is twelve, he or she will be better-mannered. On the down side, he is no longer keen to go out with you or his parents. He prefers his friends, and it is not so bad if you offer to take one or two of them on any trip you are suggesting. Nevertheless, you are greatly valued as an alternative resource, a sure supplier of affection and sympathy without much risk of criticism. This is appreciated especially when fathers are cross, school is horrible, life isn't fair and there's no one who understands.

10

Brothers and Sisters

Brothers and sisters impinge on a child's life from all angles. Most adults who were only children feel they were deprived, and children from four upwards often ask for a brother or sister – to be the same as their friends. They may not be so keen when the situation actually arises. Laura, aged six, the youngest but one in a family of four, complained to her mother: 'Why did you have the others? Why didn't you just have me?'

It is often when the first child is about two to two and a half that the second baby arrives; it is the recommended age gap from the mother's point of view, physically.

Alison didn't notice her mother's pregnant bulge until she was told the interesting news a few weeks before the expected date. It becomes too boring if a young child knows months in advance. Alison was important in helping to get things ready for *her* baby brother or sister.

Sheila and Tom thought that when the new baby was born and needing a lot of attention, it would be a convenient time for Alison to start nursery school and also graduate to a proper bed. The nursery school teacher put them right, when they went to put Alison's name down. This plan would mean too many major changes all at once for Alison to adjust to. Either she would have to be established in her new regime some weeks before the baby's arrival, or it should be postponed until well after the event.

It had to be the latter, so Alison didn't miss any of the excitement. A special aunty came in to help look after her towards the end of Sheila's pregnancy and afterwards. Alison had a new baby doll with all the trappings on the very day her brother was born. She took it with her when she went to the hospital with Granny. Sheila had been forewarned of the necessity for tact at this momentous meeting of sister and brother. Sheila's arms were outstretched to hug Alison, who was not much more than a baby herself, and the new baby was lying in his crib.

When Alison craned over the edge for her first look at him, she discovered a present from him to her at the foot of the cot. It was tiny bear.

Alison seemed delighted with little Robbie, but, of course, she knew that was what was expected. Some jealousy is normal and inevitable, since there is no doubt that a new baby steals some of his mother's attention from the ex-baby. Alison needed extra supplies of love and praise and reassurance. It was companionable that she could nurse her doll in parallel with Sheila and Robbie, even attempting breast-feeding. Alison and Sheila agreed that babies are so weak and helpless that you just have to do everything for them.

Andrew was two and a half, too. He didn't take to his new brother so well. After his suggestion – 'Send him back' – was shushed, Andrew changed tack. 'Nice baba,' he would murmur sweetly, kindly patting the infant's head, but his mother found Andrew's tooth marks on the baby's hand when he was crying. A sly pinch, or at worst, a pillow accidentally getting over the baby's face are other reactions of hurt and jealousy.

Other toddlers show their anxiety lest the newcomer will oust them from their important place in the family by reverting to bed-wetting, constant demands to be picked up, desperate thumb-sucking, tantrums or babyish behaviour. One little girl went back to crawling and making baby noises.

Impatience only makes matters worse. The slow cure is lots of love and cuddles, and private time away from the baby.

Three years

By the time they were three years old both Alison and Andrew were not as interested in the family baby, and a little less jealous. They had friends and playmates of their own. On the other hand, three-year-olds are not very popular with older brothers and sisters. I remember my daughter Mandy at this age nearly driving her brothers spare by walking through their intricate railway set-up on the floor – on purpose. And when they pushed her away she cried... She continued to be a nuisance to them when she was four. They called her The Goat.

Four years

Alison at four was becoming fed up with Robbie. He was no use to play with but kept taking her toys. She was often rough and cross with him, especially when Sheila wasn't there.

Five years

By the time he was five Andrew had become used to his young brother Ben, and in a lordly, grown-up way was kind and protective to him. He tried to teach him to play properly. They got on quite well most of the time, but you couldn't bank on it. They were better out-of-doors than too much on top of each other inside. It was usually indoors that Andrew would start teasing the toddler and making him cry by taking his toys and holding them up just out of reach.

Six years

Six years old is an awkward age for most children. They can be rude, assertive and uncooperative with adults, and bossy, even bullying to young siblings. Alison had been such a nice five-year-old big sister, but now she seemed to like nothing better than seeing Robbie get into trouble. He often did and Alison was smug. It was she who meanly informed Sheila when Robbie was painting a racing car on the sitting room wallpaper – but she hadn't told him not to when he started. Robbie had admired a mural at his nursery school.

Six-year-olds even quarrel with older brothers and sisters whom they used to look up to. Again, outdoor play is less fraught than when brothers and sisters are forced to be in close proximity.

Seven years

At seven there is bickering and teasing and little spurts of jealousy – towards younger ones: 'You never let me do that when I was little!' And towards older ones: 'Why can she stay up and see it? It isn't fair.'

Eight years

When Andrew and Alison were eight they were basically well-disposed to the younger ones, confident in their own superiority. Andrew and Ben often had what looked like life and death battles, wrestling on the floor. No one got hurt.

Brothers and Sisters

Nine years

Nine-year-olds usually admire their big brothers and sisters, boast about them and try to copy them, but they are apt to be ashamed of the younger fry when they are silly and show off in front of their friends.

Ten years

When he was ten, importantly in double figures (next step 100), Andrew increasingly found Ben a pest. Ben liked playing with Andrew, who was strong and clever and had good ideas. It wasn't reciprocal. Instead of being welcome to join in, Ben met with physical rejection in the form of pushing, kicking and hitting; but he still wanted to play with Andrew. Andrew had fights with his friends, too, at this age; and girls were not much better.

Eleven years

By eleven physical fights are being superseded to some extent by verbal battles. Both Andrew and Alison had very adequate vocabularies for trouncing their young brothers. Alison did not hesitate – even when she was in a good mood – to criticise the many faults she saw in young Robbie. The worst crime was that he was 'always getting at my things'. He had no respect for her property. In the end, Alison locked him out of her room, including when she had friends in to play, and Robbie was shut out by himself. Of course there were times when she relented and they could enjoy each other's company.

Eleven-year-olds quite like babies – there is no competition and they don't interfere – and they can almost worship very old brothers and sisters, those in the late teens.

Twelve years

Twelve years old is halfway to being grown-up. There's a certain unenthusiastic acceptance of younger brothers and sisters from now on – with family loyalty springing up if any outsider bullies or hurts them.

'He can be such a pest,' was how Andrew wearily summed up his relationship with Ben. They had endless arguments: endless because each of them was determined to have the last word.

Alison pinpointed the classic unfairness of family life: 'If Robbie hits me, I'm not supposed to hit him back.' Of course it isn't fair. Life isn't fair. That's why it is such a valuable experience to have brothers and sisters. Jack and Jessica, as onlies, didn't have a chance to develop fully the skills of assertiveness, compromise, responsibility for the weak – and sharing.

If you have a brother or sister there is always someone on your side when the grown-ups are unreasonable; and there are hundreds more games of imagination when there is someone else to play with, even if they are younger.

11

Hiccups in Development

'Is my baby all right?'

This is every mother's first thought when she has battled through labour or endured the drama of a Caesarean birth. Each newborn baby is an individual, different from any other, yet, miraculously, most of them are perfect, down to each tiny, shell-like fingernail. Nevertheless, sometimes small errors or anomalies can arise in the great complex plan of development.

Birthmarks

Since babies are so important they are weighed and measured and examined minutely all over. The smallest blemish will not pass unnoticed. Birthmarks, some of which don't appear right away, are not physically harmful and most of them disappear by themselves, over time.

Stork's beak marks – or angel kisses

These are very common, affecting at least forty per cent of babies. They appear as flat red patches on the eyelids, forehead or nape of the neck. They require no treatment and vanish within six months, except for those at the back of the neck which anyway become hidden by the hair. They are not pressure marks but something to do with the immaturity of the skin.

Childhood Development

Strawberry marks

Strawberry marks are soft and red with an irregular surface. They may be present at birth, but usually develop over the first few months, on the head or body. Twelve in a hundred white babies have at least one strawberry mark by their first birthday, and from then on they do not grow any bigger. Ninety per cent of them disappear without trace over the next six to seven years. If there is one in an awkward place it can be lasered away before that.

Port wine stain

This is the rarest type of birthmark. It is a dark purplish-red and doesn't fade. If it is in a prominent place on the face it may spoil the child's appearance or embarrass him later. Camouflage with a special cover-up cream is very effective.

Mongolian blue spots

These have nothing to do with Mongolia. They are bluish areas which look like bruises which occur naturally, usually on the back, in the skin of several races: Eskimos, Greeks and Italians and any of the Eastern or African peoples. They become almost invisible as the skin darkens, after babyhood. They are not truly birthmarks.

Two other skin conditions in the new baby are:

Milk rash or milia

These consists of tiny white spots under the skin, especially on the nose. They are normal, have nothing to do with milk, and your baby grows out of them.

Hiccups in Development

Blue hands and feet (but not blue lips)

This is normal in very young babies.

Jaundice

One in ten healthy newborn babies develops a yellow tinge to her skin and the whites of her eyes over the first two or three days. This is because the liver is not yet mature enough to deal efficiently with the worn-out red blood corpuscles which require disposal. The situation usually rights itself during the next week, but there is a harmless treatment with ultraviolet light – phototherapy – which speeds things up. As you might expect, premature babies are particularly likely to get jaundice: the treatment is the same.

Rhesus factor incompatibility between the blood of the mother and that of the baby used to cause serious jaundice, but now preventative measures are applied during the pregnancy.

Umbilical hernia (outie)

Sometimes when the stump of the umbilical cord comes away it leaves a bigger than usual gap in the muscles where the cord of twisted blood vessels from placenta to baby went through. This causes a bulge at the navel, which gets bigger when the baby cries. It doesn't hurt him and it doesn't matter, since it is not abnormal. The muscles will close the gap naturally during later development and no artificial manoeuvre helps.

Childhood Development

Inguinal hernia

This is a bulge in the groin and scrotum in some baby boys; it may seem to disappear when the child lies down. This kind of hernia is caused by the passageway by which the testicle came down from its original site inside the abdomen remaining open. This allows a loop of intestine to slip down. It is a very minor developmental fault, but since the intestine could get twisted or caught, it is best put right as soon as possible by a small operation.

Cleft lip

This is a slip in development which looks alarming. The top lip and palate are formed in two halves which join before birth – normally. Occasionally the join isn't completed at the right time and you get the cleft lip appearance. Plastic surgery will ensure that the error is repaired long before the little one goes to school, leaving an almost invisible scar. The snag is that you have to wait until the baby is three months old before the operation is performed, since this gives the best results.

The palate may also be divided and in this case the baby must have a plate fitted to the roof of his mouth to help the two halves to come together. Incidentally, it makes feeding easier. The final palate repair is done when the youngster is between a year and eighteen months old.

Club foot

Usually both feet are affected: they turn in at the ankle so that the child would be walking on the sides of his feet – if nothing was done. It is all due to a cramped

Hiccups in Development

position of the feet in the womb, and the sooner treatment is started the more effective. It consists in the application of splints and plasters to persuade the feet to grow the right way.

Congenital dislocation of the hip (CDH)

This anomaly in which the thigh-bone tends to slip out of its socket at the hip has a hereditary basis in twenty per cent of cases, while in others it is associated with a breech birth – arriving into the world bottom first. It is particularly common in Northern Italy, Lapland and Japan but crops up in the UK once in 200 births. It will be diagnosed during the baby's first physical examination and checked regularly later. Treatment consists in splinting for two to three months, and when this is started in the first week the outlook is excellent for normal development thereafter.

Size

Size is a feature that is measured on Day One. The normal range for weight is 5½–9½lbs (2500–4200g) – a little less for Asian babies – and for length 20ins (50cm) give or take 1in (2cm). Babies weighing 3½lbs (1500g) or less need special care.

Small babies

Small babies come in two packs:
- born early, at thirty-seven weeks of pregnancy or before
- small-for-dates: born full-term but little and light

Those born prematurely nearly catch up during their first two years, while small-for-dates babes tend to develop into small, but not unhealthy, children by the time they start school and later.

Slow growers

There is an enormous individual variation, but most babies tend to put on 10lbs in their first year, 7lbs in the second, and five in the third and then to slow down until the great growth spurt at puberty. There are numerous possible reasons for growing slowly:
– far the likeliest is genetic: it runs in the family
– small-for-dates start, in some cases
– feeding difficulties (see p 225)
– emotional problems: a baby or child who feels unloved or unwanted will not thrive
– overactive thyroid gland, also underactive
– a range of congenital disorders with other, more obvious symptoms, eg Down's syndrome, heart and kidney problems etc.

Big babies

The commonest reasons are:
– family trends (the most likely)
– mother with diabetes

Big babies tend to gain weight more slowly than small-sizers and may be only a few pounds heavier by school-time. Those who remain well above average size and weight are likely to be overfed. Bottle-fed babies and others who start on solid foods, especially cereals, before they are four months, are the usual victims. (See growth charts pp 279–84.)

Fat children

As with their parents, excess fat in children is a disorder of prosperous countries, although not of the richest

Hiccups in Development

people in them. Extra-protective mothers may make their young children fat, often because of 'building them up' after an illness. Older children cannot be made to eat, although a habit can be started of fat and sugar-laden foods. Lack of exercise is both a cause and a result of surplus weight. It takes more effort for a fat child to run about and he is not likely to have the pleasure of shining at any sport, except, possibly, swimming. Fat throws a strain on the growing back and knee joints and can affect posture.

The long and short of it

Shortness goes with hereditary factors and generally small size, and is in rare cases associated with CDH or various chronic disorders. Tallness is also usually a matter of the genes, or part of general oversize from too-generous nourishment. There are a few hereditary conditions, for instance Klinefelter's syndrome and acromegaly: the excess height is the least important feature of these conditions.

Feeding difficulties

Feeding is key. It is essentially a matter of development: before birth your baby is tube-fed, through the umbilical cord from the placenta. When she is born she can already taste, smell, root for the nipple, open her mouth – and swallow. Feeding goes hand-in-hand with the development of that uniquely close relationship between mother and baby, with breast-feeding providing the maximum physical contact.

Surprisingly, a healthy breast-fed baby wakes more frequently than one who is bottle-fed and gains weight a little more slowly. Breast-feeds are smaller. Most mothers give their babies a Rolls Royce start with the perfectly balanced combination of nutrients and immunising properties of their own natural product. Only about a quarter continue after the first month, but breast or bottle, the essential ingredients are love and trust between mother and babe, in a magic circle.

As your little one is increasingly able to feed herself, by beaker, by fingers, then spoon and fork, her relationship with you alters. When she eats not just with you but with the family, then with other children at school, these other people have a huge influence on what she chooses to eat.

Difficulties in the early days

Problems may be a matter of temperament. 'Good', quiet babies gain less than the demanding type who are fed more often for the sake of peace. Your own attitude to food and diet, as a mother, is significant, too. If you have any hang-ups around calories and weight (your own) they can transmit to your baby or child.

Up to a third of mothers are worried about their child's lack of appetite, refusal of healthy foods like spinach, or obstreperous behaviour at mealtimes. Fussy feeding, involving more dislikes than likes, affects at least thirty per cent of youngsters at some time between the ages of three and eight years. Highly active, restless children are the worst. The less you cajole or threaten them the more easily the phase passes, as it always does unless your child is ill. In that case he or she won't have the wish or the energy to play.

Colic

Colic comprises excessively long and frequent bouts of fussing and crying. It can start up when the baby –

Hiccups in Development

more often a boy – is two to four weeks old, and continues for three or four months. It has traditionally been blamed on a kind of indigestion, hence its name, but it seems to be related to a stressful pregnancy for the mother, or a stressful relationship between the parents.

Failure to thrive

This amounts to a failure to put on weight at the expected rate, together with a lack of happy liveliness. It can happen at any time during childhood, but is most frequently noticed before the age of eighteen months. It is important if you, the mother, have any problems, that these are sorted out. After that, the baby's needs must be met. He should be cushioned with love and warmth, and stimulated by play – which adds up to time and attention from you.

It is never too soon to play. Even small babies enjoy games where you talk or sing to them, carry them round to show them the world, jiggle them on your lap, play piggies with their toes and trickle water on their tummies in the bath. If you are depressed or have 'flu or another illness that makes you feel bad, your baby cannot enjoy anything either, including his feeds.

Sleep

Sleep problems are commonplace in the first four years. It is normal for a very young baby to have alternating short snatches of sleep and periods of hungry wakefulness throughout the twenty-four hours. It is especially noticeable at night. Babies vary greatly and you may have an alert, awake type: the bonus is that he is likely to be a bright child later. The usual

Childhood Development

pattern is for a new baby to sleep for three- to four-hour stretches, after the first ten days or so, requiring a feed each time he wakes: amounting to six times in the twenty-four-hour period.

By three months there are three or four sleep periods, with longer wakefulness in the day. Nevertheless, during the whole of the first year it is normal and usual for a baby to wake in the night at least once, but up to three times. After their first birthday most little ones sleep through the night, plus an afternoon nap, totalling fourteen to sixteen hours of sleep in all. If the afternoon rest is too long or too late the baby won't be ready to go to sleep at night: and by the age of two or two and a half, a daytime nap is no longer needed – or possible (see sleep chart p 273).

A good many babies are awake nearly all day from about nine months – quite normally. Others, from eighteen months onwards, are always thoroughly awake from 5am, raring to start the day. This is a long-term situation. There is no cure and it isn't unhealthy. Most babies of six to twelve months protest when they are put down to sleep, hopefully for the night, and bigger children complain about their bedtimes routinely. There is no magic formula, but a consistent, regular routine helps. Nor can you safely leave a baby or young child to cry alone without checking that he isn't ill, uncomfortable, frightened or unhappy.

Nightmares

These are alarming dreams from which your child wakes up crying with fear. They happen occasionally at any age, but especially under nine and at times of extra stress: moving house, exams, or even a birthday party next day. The child can remember the nightmare, and needs you to hug him and reassure him that 'it was only a dream' and he is safe with you.

Hiccups in Development

Night terrors

Night terrors are different. They affect normal children between the ages of two and six, and always between fifteen and ninety minutes after they've gone to sleep. The child screams and sits bolt upright, wide eyes staring but not seeing, because he is still asleep. He cannot take in your words of comfort because he cannot hear them, so you must hold him close – continuing with the reassurance – until he comes back to reality. He won't know what it was that frightened him, but he needs to be thoroughly awake before going to sleep again. He usually drops off easily and doesn't remember anything about the episode in the morning.

Sleep-talking

As a rule merely a confused jumble – often affects children of between five to twelve when there are interesting or exciting events going on in their lives: being in a school play, going in an aircraft for the first time, seeing a lion... The child is asleep and dreaming. There is no need to do anything, since it is a normal occurrence.

Sleep-walking

Sleep-walking is less common than talking, but fifteen per cent of children do it at least once, usually between the ages of ten and fourteen. Like night terrors, sleep-walking is likeliest soon after falling asleep, when the child is deeply asleep, and the child is still sleeping during his excursion. All you should do is lead him gently back to bed, tuck him up, and check that he cannot walk out of the house and that there is nothing that could injure him, should he repeat the walk. Children hardly ever hurt themselves sleep-walking: it is only their conscious mind that is switched off.

Sleep-walking is usually associated with a period of worry, for instance about their parents' relationship, or exams which really matter.

Toilet-training

Most babies, but by no means all, begin to have some control over their water and motions at about eighteen months. Occasionally a child shows that he is aware of having passed water, then of actually passing it, as young as fifteen months. Once the child has shown that he is aware of what is happening, potty-training can begin: it is pointless before. Your child will probably be dry during the day at two to two and a half, and at night with occasional slips, from three to three and a half, but there are no hard and fast rules.

Bed-wetting (enuresis)

Some children go past their third birthday without any dry nights. This is usually due to slow maturing of the control mechanism: it often runs in families. More often, the child will have some dry nights. This is good for morale, since it indicates that dry nights are possible. Over ten per cent of youngsters are still bed-wetting at five to seven years. What is needed is time and patience – and a check that there is no medical cause.

When a child who had been dry starts having wet beds – called secondary enuresis – the likely cause is an emotional upset. Five-year-old Cathy was upset by her parents' split, and her daddy's going away. Medication with desmopressin or imipramine may help, while for older children there is the pad and buzzer apparatus. This alerts the child when he begins

Hiccups in Development

to pass water, and gradually he may learn to beat the buzzer. Some children respond to a system of gold stars pasted on a chart, to represent dry nights, but whatever the method, it can only work if anxiety about 'failure' is assuaged.

Bowel control

This is easier and in most cases is achieved at about two. In some children it can be delayed for as long as two more years. The usual cause is a running battle between mother and toddler and potty. After a medical check to exclude the unlikely possibility of a bowel disorder, limitless loving patience and a system of rewards is urgently needed, plus, perhaps, help from a child guidance centre.

Sometimes a child who had mastered the business of bowel control suddenly refuses to try. This can be because of having a hard, constipated motion – common after a feverish illness – which might be painful to pass. The answer, with your doctor's help and advice, is to lubricate the hard stool and clear the back passage, then to increase the fruit and vegetables in your child's diet. In the short term, softening laxatives help to rebuild the youngster's confidence.

Fits

Convulsions in which all the child's muscles jerk can occur when a child has had a difficult birth, or is developing long-term epilepsy. The common type of fit in a young child, usually in the one- to three-year range, is a *febrile convulsion*. A child of this age may run a temperature during a simple illness, like a cold. In those who are susceptible, and the tendency is likely to have been present in other members of the family, the

Childhood Development

immature brain is less stable than in an adult, and can be irritated by the fever. The brain in turn stimulates the nerves to the muscles and they set off the jerky movements.

While the child is fitting, a matter of a few seconds to a few minutes, lie him on his front with his face to one side. This saves any vomit running back and choking him, if he is sick. When he comes round or falls asleep, call the doctor. Then get the child to bed and cool him down. Tepid sponging is helpful if a child is very hot. This type of fit is not serious and does not lead on to epilepsy.

Delay in walking

The commonest age to start walking is one, but many wait until they are fifteen or sixteen months, while some young athletes are cruising round the furniture from nine months. If the rest of the child's development is keeping up, and particularly if he or she has an efficient way of getting around by crawl, there is no need to worry if walking is a little late (see the route plan chart, p 263). A physical check of hips and feet may be worthwhile at this stage.

Delay in talking

Speech is so important to your child's whole life that it is handy to know roughly what to expect:

One-syllable babbling, such as bababa or mumumum	9 months
Different syllables, not the same one always	11 months
Mama, Dada etc. as appropriate	14 months

A real word	18 months
Two-word sentence	2½ years
Understandable speech	4 years

Delay in speaking may be due to poor hearing and this is most likely in premature babies, after meningitis, with an ear infection or if there is early deafness in the family. There may be a curable cause, but if not there is absolutely vital training.

Dyslexia

Some children have enormous difficulty in learning to make sense of written and printed words, and the problem persists. This may be dyslexia, a disorder that is mildly hereditary and in no way connected with intelligence. An expert is needed to make a firm diagnosis of dyslexia, but any child who has severe reading difficulties needs extra help to master the skill. There are particular manoeuvres which help genuine dyslexics, and many highly successful people were dyslexic children. Most of them had a miserable time until their problem was recognised, being misjudged as lazy and not trying.

With all these relatively minor hiccups in development, it is your watchful concern, as a parent, that usually brings them to notice, and sets the ball rolling so that your child receives the best help available. And it is your practical effort that is likely to be the most important factor in his overcoming the problem.

A child with one of the major developmental difficulties would not survive without your devoted care, but the professional input is essential. Such problems as cerebral palsy, autism, Down's syndrome and other forms of mental handicap in your child have a profound effect on yours and your partner's whole way of life. Other people with children in the same situation provide the best and most understanding support, and the most useful information. Fortunately, there are associations for nearly every disability: see useful addresses p 285. There are books, too, on each of them, but the one ingredient that is paramount, whatever the treatment or management, is love.

12

What They Were Like:
famous people as children

However celebrated they become, all the great and the good were children once. Can you tell if your child will turn out to be a genius? You may be delighted with her funny, clever sayings or amazed at the grown-up things she can do. Or you may be worried and disheartened because other people's children seem to be forging ahead.

Your child may be studious and obedient and give you never a moment's worry, like John Ruskin, or an incorrigible tearaway and lazy to the marrow of his bones, like Winston Churchill. Some parents knew they had a remarkably talented child on their hands, for instance those of Mozart and of Lord Macaulay. Mozart's father did his best to cash in on the child prodigy, Macaulay's parents encouraged him but tried to keep his childhood as normal as possible.

Bad reports

A surprising number of parents of the famous had been worried and disappointed by their poor early progress.

Charles Darwin's teachers wrote him off as 'below the common standard in intellect', and although his father was paying the fees, he had difficulty in obtaining a university place. His father was disgusted with him: 'You will be a disgrace to yourself and all your family,' he said, and went on to complain of his messing up the house with his 'rubbish'. Charles had collections of pebbles, shells, plants and insects. Children who are avid collectors of anything often distinguish themselves. Churchill had over a thousand toy soldiers, in the end, while Edward Jenner – to whom we owe vaccination – collected fossils and dormouse nests.

Unfortunately, Charles Darwin's mother died when he was only eight: she might have been more tolerant and loving than his father. After her death, Charles developed a stutter for the rest of his life. It seems that he was truly a late developer – very late, since he was well into his twenties before he showed any sign of talent. Yet it was his painstaking work and brilliant reasoning which changed the status of God and made Darwin's name familiar to schoolchildren all over the world. His own youngest child had Down's syndrome: no family, however intellectually distinguished, is immune.

Winston Churchill: everyone knows the story of his entrance exam to Harrow. His paper consisted of the figure 1, in brackets, and two smudges. He remained bottom of his class throughout. At his junior school, previously, his teacher said, 'I used to think he was the naughtiest boy in the world.' He had been born prematurely and remained undersized, and found his contemporaries all bigger and cleverer and better at sport than he was.

'It is not pleasant to feel oneself so completely outclassed and left behind at the very beginning of the race' – his childhood was the most unhappy period of his life and his father was deeply disappointed.

Aneurin Bevan, the great socialist politician who launched the National Health Service, showed similarities to Churchill in his boyhood. He too hated school and did badly: he was moved down among younger boys, since he didn't keep up with his own age group.

What They Were Like

He too was a trouble to his teachers: one threatened to resign if Aneurin did not leave. His home, however, was the opposite of the formal grandeur of Blenheim. The Bevans shared warmth, poverty and a love of books.

His mother was the mainspring of the house, determined that nothing she could do for her children's future would be left undone. If Aneurin was lazy at school, he educated himself by incessant reading, often until dawn.

Beatrice Webb, the social reformer, was one of those whose parents underestimated her. Her father had never liked her and her mother said: 'Beatrice is the only one of my children who is below the general level of intelligence.' They were a wealthy, cultured family, and the other eight daughters were a pride and joy to their parents: they all made socially successful marriages later. Another trial to her parents was that Beatrice was always ailing, with coughs and colds and tummy-aches – perhaps the signs of a child who was unhappy and asking to be loved and looked after . . .

Even serious physical handicaps cannot quench the bubbling spring of life in a young child. All newborn babies look so helpless and fragile that it is difficult to imagine them as determined adults, making their mark in the world. It seems even more unlikely with a pint-sized prem – such as Isaac Newton, Charles Wesley, Anna Pavlova and the present Pope – and of course, Churchill. Both Picasso and Thomas Hardy were about to be discarded as stillbirths, when they were slapped into life.

These were delicate children – so was Alexander Pope, a hunchback who never grew taller than 4ft 6ins, and was always too weak to dress himself unaided. Yet he was an erudite and greatly respected poet. Lord Byron, another poet, had a deformed foot; Sir Walter Scott, the novelist, was crippled by polio when he was two, and the musician, Weber, could not walk until he was four, because of hip disease. The most remarkable of all was Helen Keller. She had brain fever at eighteen months which left her deaf and blind – before she had learned to talk. She became one of the best-educated women of her day and an author. Her parents did not give up when they were told that she was hopelessly brain-damaged, and her teacher worked tirelessly with the little girl for years.

Milestones

Milestones on the road of childhood development can be a useful guide and it is always reassuring when your little one passes them at the expected time. But like flowers, some children blossom later than others, but just as beautifully. You would think that a child who did not talk when all the other mothers' babies were prattling away would be sure to turn out to be intellectually dull. Albert Einstein's parents were worried when their son hadn't said a word by the time he was four. He did then learn slowly, but was still not very fluent at age nine. At sixteen he failed the entrance to Zurich Polytechnic, but an uncle taught him algebra and his mathematical genius was stimulated to lead to the theory of relativity.

Allessandro Volta, the pioneer in electricity whom we remember with volts and voltage, also said nothing until he was four. After that he never stopped talking, his parents found.

Reading

The British government is currently concerned because so many children at primary school have a

What They Were Like

'reading age' well below their chronological age. And reading is the key to all other knowledge. But poor progress in reading – fortunately – *need* not mean a slow mind. Jan Smuts could not read until he was twelve, while John Hunter, probably our greatest English surgeon, did not master it until he was seventeen. The two aunts who tried to teach the poet Yeats to read decided that he was mentally defective: but he wrote the most haunting verse later.

George Stephenson, who gave us the steam engine, could neither read nor write when he was eighteen – but this was due to never having been taught. He learned very quickly when he had the chance. George Bernard Shaw could write – wonderfully well – but he never learned to spell properly. He wrote phonetically, like a five-year-old. He was a trial to his teachers and his parents.

Difficult children

Churchill and Bevan had been ordinary naughty boys, but Shaw was in a league on his own. He resented being sent to school, and felt it a rejection: 'My inurement in that damnable boy prison effected its real purpose of preventing my being a nuisance to my mother for at least half the day.' His school, unlike many in that era, did not mete out cruel punishments: silence and sitting still were the two sanctions. George B. complained even of this: 'the punishment was not cruel enough to effect its purpose – so I learned nothing.' His teacher called him 'The Devil Incarnate' after he had started a competition in which the winner came bottom of the class!

Other children were difficult in a different way. Oscar Wilde hated school and had no friends: he hated sport, wouldn't climb trees or play any adventurous games, or indeed anything that involved exercise. He liked flowers. Florence Nightingale was much the same. She had got it into her head that she looked odd in some way, and as a seven-year-old would hide if there were visitors, especially other children. Agatha Christie was another loner, spending hours in long, solitary walks, making up stories which all ended in tragedy.

Young Charles Darwin was a story-teller of another kind. He was always inventing accounts of the clever and daring acts he had performed – to impress his parents. They were not deceived. Nor did they respond to the underlying longing for affection.

Clever children

While some children destined for a brilliant career show few signs of this in their early years, others are infant prodigies. Jonathan Swift, Lord Macaulay, Dr Johnson, Voltaire and the poet Coleridge could all read the Bible at three, and Picasso could draw before he could speak. Mozart could play the clavichord at three and was composing music by five, while Goethe at seven knew seven languages, including the tricky ones, Greek and Hebrew. Sigmund Freud was permanently top of the form, although he preferred to recall from his childhood the primal scene – his parents having sex and his neurotic response.

Growing up close to nature stimulated the scientific curiosity of such men as Edward Jenner, and nourished the imagination of the writers Thomas Hardy, the Brontë sisters, Agatha Christie and today's novelist, Maeve Binchy. She recalls the hills and the sea near Dublin, a gentle, bookish father and a fiercely protective mother who filled the house with other people's children, so that hers had no reason to stray.

It was a happy family, although Maeve was fed up

What They Were Like

when they couldn't exchange her new baby sister for a rabbit. The only shouting quarrel her parents had was overheard by the children, who immediately decided that divorce was inevitable. They had even planned which of them should live with each parent – until the evening came and the row was dissolved into laughter. Because of her supportive family it didn't worry Maeve that she was tall and fat and no good at games, but quite clever – all the elements to make her unpopular at school.

The one snag of Maeve's happy home was that she was still living there, contentedly, when she was thirty – and both her parents died. She'd had no practice at fending for herself, and little idea of what she wanted to do ultimately. Her childhood ambition had been to be a judge, with wig and gown, without, of course, the preliminary years of study and work at the bar.

Edna O'Brien's Irish childhood was not idyllic. Her father loved the horses, greyhounds and cards and when his gambling hit a bad streak and he was in his cups, she was terrified of him. Her mother was intensely houseproud and kept the home like a doll's house, perfect to the smallest detail. Religion was a major influence, with hell and purgatory always in view. There were no books in the house because Edna's mother suspected they might lead to sin and her father only read the *Irish Field*. Edna wrote stories and her first novel when she was nine – of course these were all destroyed.

John Ruskin: if Edna O'Brien's upbringing was made bleak by religion, John Ruskin's was a thousand times worse. His mother was a good woman, a dedicated evangelical puritan who believed all pleasure to be sinful. That meant toys were out. Even when a kindly aunt brought him a Punch and Judy they were immediately locked away, never to be seen again. At first his only plaything was a bunch of keys although

Childhood Development

later he was allowed a ball and a cart.

The little boy amused himself tracing the pattern of the carpet, the graining of the floorboards – or a wasp on the windowpane. No book but the Bible was read on Sundays, and there were no such wild pleasures as writing letters. Sunday dinner was cold meat. Before he was three John could recite the whole of Psalm 119. Since his mother educated him herself he had no contact with other children, and since his parents kept themselves to themselves he saw few adults either.

Nevertheless, he looked back with gratitude on the 'priceless gift of peace'. No one in the Ruskin household ever spoke sharply or even gave an angry glance, but John was always whipped – for the good of his soul – if he failed to obey instantly, cried or tumbled. He never did wrong – or right – and he never learned to love or be loved. When, long years later, he married, he was unable to consummate the marriage. As an author he was successful and respected; as a human being he was an utter failure. His mother meant well.

Happy homes

It is perfectly possible to have a happy childhood and achieve greatness.

Linnaeus, the Swedish botanist who worked out the two-part Latin names for all our plants, remembers growing up in a country rectory in an atmosphere of: 'complete affection, simple habits and sincere piety'.

Jane Austen was also brought up as a rector's daughter and described her childhood as 'serene and loving'. Her parents guided their children by example and by their gentle personalities rather than with rules and precepts. They had many friends and entertained frequently in a setting of classical learning.

Franklin Roosevelt was an only child who was

What They Were Like

surrounded by love but never pampered.

Gandhi's father did not scold him or punish him but was sad when his son used bad words and stole some money. Gandhi was married at thirteen, but both partners stayed with their own parents.

Robert Louis Stevenson's charmed early life was entirely due to his mother's sunny personality. She made light of all discomforts, made any change seem like a holiday and found interest and enjoyment in everything, though her husband was by nature morose.

Lord Baden-Powell of the scout movement also had a wonder-woman mother. Left a widow with nine children when Robert was three, she taught all of them reading, writing and arithmetic as well as the principles of honour and duty, perseverance and self-reliance. There was such trust in the house that the children had a communal cash box from which they helped themselves to their pocket money, leaving a note of the amount. Since such well-known figures of the day as Thackeray, Ruskin and Thomas Huxley were frequent visitors, the children's interest was stimulated in both science and literature.

The family cannot have been short of money.

Poverty

Poverty of itself and even the lack of books and learning in the home has not held back some of the highest achievers.

Hans Andersen was the son of a poor cobbler, and was himself an idle dreamer – it seemed. Nevertheless he struck success at twenty-four with his first book: *A Journey on Foot*, and never looked back.

Aneurin Bevan's poor home, where it was a struggle to find the money for food, was happy and his father loved his few books.

Childhood Development

George Stephenson was born into the direst poverty and instead of going to school worked as a cowherd as a boy. His family needed the money.

David Livingstone, the explorer, was put to work in a cotton factory from six in the morning until eight at night, from the age of ten. He studied after work.

Lord Nuffield was also the main breadwinner for his family from the age of fifteen: his father had become ill. At fourteen he had saved up for an old bicycle with solid tyres: he took it to pieces to study the mechanics.

Keir Hardie became his family's breadwinner from an even earlier age – seven.

William Booth of the Salvation Army was the youngest son in a desperately poor family of seventeen children.

Abraham Lincoln and *Benjamin Franklin* both came from poor homes, but this did not prevent them from making their remarkable contributions to society.

Every baby is a wonder, so weak and small, yet containing that marvellous well-spring of life and spirit that through the unfolding miracle of development can lead – who knows where? Maybe to the sort of achievements that bring fame, perhaps to a life full of love and happiness. Parents, even those who have seemed most harsh, 'want the best' for their child. Most of us hope they will be able to achieve their full potential – and be happy. From these histories of some notable people when they were children, it seems impossible to predict what hidden qualities they had and where they would lead.

The best kind of home and family for a child to grow in body and understanding would include:
- a loving mother who expresses her love in practical ways
- a father who is involved
- the stimulus of adult friends visiting and their conversation

What They Were Like

- opportunities to read widely, with some good books in the home
- introduction to the ways of the countryside and other living, growing things
- sharing the joy of beauty in all forms: nature, architecture, art, poetry and music
- enough money for necessities

Appendices

Toys and Play

Play is pleasure. It is also important because it is a young child's work. Through it he learns and practises everything he or she needs to know to be a grown-up. Yet you don't have to teach your child to play. She does it naturally, because she enjoys it. The learning part is only a side-effect to her.

Play helps every aspect of your child's development:
- physical, for example, riding a trike
- creative, for instance, with paints or play-dough
- intellectual, from picture lotto to chess
- social, with playmates of any age, from a two-year-old to Granny
- imaginative, with dolls, dressing up or miniature cars
- emotional, acting away fears of monsters and lions or practising caring for a sick Teddy

Since play is your child's work he deserves 'good working conditions' – that is somewhere safe to play – and reliable equipment – the toys. Anything a child uses to play with becomes a toy, and at baby and toddler stage your household tools and utensils often serve the purpose. You will also be buying, and sometimes making, toys to give to your little one. For maximum interest and delight you will choose those to suit your child's stage of development, and sometimes to help it in a particular way.

General points
- safety is paramount: watch out for sharp points and

Toys and Play

edges, loose parts like insecurely fixed eyes and pieces a young child might swallow (until three and a half they put everything in their mouths), of batteries he could get out, unstable sit-and-ride and climbing toys. *Note*: look for the Lion Mark which shows the toy meets the British Safety Standards, or CE, meaning European safety standards.
- big is not always best: a bear your toddler can carry around is a better companion than a huge one that has to sit in a chair.
- don't choose a toy aimed at an older age unless you are quite sure he can use it on his own: it will bore and frustrate rather than stimulate him.

Toys by age

Age is a poor guide to choosing a toy, but it is the best we have. We adults vary enormously: one thirty-year-old may be a whizz with computers, another is into cordon bleu cooking – or tennis. So it is with our children, but at first they cannot tell us where their interests will lie.

First six months

- colourful, tinkling mobiles
- toys suspended within reach of his hands – to bat
- rattles light enough to grasp, with different sounds, colours and shapes
- a small, soft, light, companion toy: an animal or a rag doll

Playing with baby means carrying him, rocking him, holding him high, telling him about the world round him, singing, and playing baby games: peek-a-boo, This Little Piggy, Round and Round the Garden, Incy Wincy Spider and, when he can sit up, Pat-a-cake.

Childhood Development

Six to twelve months (sitting up)

- ball with a bell inside
- cloth-covered foam bricks to grab – and drop
- nesting and stacking beakers
- small stuffed toys
- little wooden car with a peg person who comes out
- baby-bouncer: adjust so her feet just touch the floor
- wobbly balls and roll-back toys: you have to help
- baby-walker, towards the end of this period: you have to supervise

One year

- push-along walker toys, such as a wagon, a doll's pram, an animal on wheels
- cloth and plastic animals and dolls
- interesting big balls and roller toys
- bath toys: plastic fish and ducks, boat, mug to pour with
- bricks to load the wagon

One and a half years

- pull-along toys, more push-alongs
- domestic equipment: pots and pans, doll's bed with bedclothes, dustpan and brush, hammer and pegs
- musical instruments: xylophone, tambourine, drum
- toy cars
- telephone
- posting box

Two years

- wooden screwdriver and screws
- hammer and pegboard
- doll's clothes and equipment

- miniature cars and garage
- sand toys
- huge beads to thread
- basic trike with wide-based wheels
- simple jigsaws
- picture books
- wheelbarrow and gardening set
- thick crayons
- blackboard

Three years

- dressing-up clothes, nurse's, doctor's, policeman's uniform (popular for several years to follow)
- basic Lego
- Wendy house or makeshift
- picture lotto, Snap or Happy Families cards; needs your help to play with another child
- play-dough
- round-ended scissors

PLUS all the toys from earlier

Four years

- glove puppets
- doll's house, farm, zoo, soldiers
- bike with stabilisers or big trike to pedal
- construction sets with designs to follow
- battery and wind-up toys
- simple story books
- painting and drawing materials
- climbing frame, slide (nursery school or park playground may provide big outdoor toys: supervision essential)

PLUS toys from earlier

Childhood Development

Five years

- skipping rope
- scooter, scooter-skate, pogo-stick
- cutting out and pasting equipment
- carpentry set with real, small tools
- train and rails, to add to
- Snakes and Ladders and other simple dice games

Six years

- models to make that require glue
- real cooking equipment and materials: supervise
- dominoes and draughts
- detective or naturalist set
- jigsaws

Seven years

- two-wheel bike
- model aeroplanes, boats, trains
- bat and ball for games
- remote control cars, boats
- make-up set (real)

PLUS earlier toys

Eight years

- more difficult board games
- Scalextrix, electric train sets
- hand-held computer games
- hand-craft sets, eg weaving
- microscope (simple)
- toy theatre
- conjuring and magic sets

PLUS earlier toys

Toys and Play

Nine years

- computer games
- chess, backgammon
- Scrabble, Cluedo, Monopoly, Trivial Pursuits
- typewriter
- camera

PLUS some earlier equipment

Ten years and over

Toys are out, special interests are in. From now on you will be told what to choose, or at any rate the area of interest. At around eleven your child may be particularly insistent on having it *now* – whatever it is that 'everyone else' has or is doing. She – or he – becomes more realistic in the following years.

Interests and activities (all requiring state-of-the-art equipment)

Outdoor

- all sports, including spectator sport (many girls lose interest soon, especially for team games)
- horse-riding, especially girls
- swimming
- cycling
- skating (usually indoors)

Indoor

- television, computers, music, reading
- collecting: discs, coins, stamps, china objects and various collectibles, shells, fossils etc
- painting, drawing, writing stories
- playing a musical instrument
- chemistry and other science
- making things: sewing, cooking, carpentry

Childhood Development

Toys to encourage particular aspects of development

Most of these are geared towards the first five years.

To strengthen muscles

- trike, bike, rocking toys, swing
- balls and bats
- water toys, snorkel

To practise co-ordination

- stacking and posting toys
- coloured paper, paste and scissors
- screwdriver and screws (wooden)
- Lego and other construction sets

To encourage speech

- toy telephone, preferably two, with a collaborator
- glove or finger puppets
- dolly tea-set
- dressing-up clothes, uniforms for Let's Pretend

To stimulate imagination

- dolls, Action Man, dolls' houses
- little worlds: farm, zoo, garage and cars, soldiers
- dressing-up gear, disguises
- toy theatre
- wigwam or play house

For discrimination

- jigsaws
- posting/sorting boxes
- card games, dominoes

Toys and Play

For creativity and self-expression

- crayons, water colours, and bright wash-off paint in pots
- play-dough (messy but calming)
- musical instruments: xylophone, drum, recorder

There is a huge selection of definitely educational toys, designed to help with telling the time, numbers, pre-reading, science, history, geography etc.

Books and Reading

Books are a GOOD THING.

Toys are a delight and a help to your child's development, but books are essential. They are the key to all knowledge, nourishment for the growing mind – and a magic carpet to fantasy land. Reading has two great advantages over television and computer screens. You can do it anywhere, indoors or out, and it involves some effort on the part of the reader. In addition, reading always runs at the pace that suits the individual, and you can stop and start or go back a few pages, at will.

The best stimulus to make your child want to delve into the treasure trove of books for himself is to see you reading and enjoying it, and for books and trips to the library to be as much a part of every day as coffee.

While many children have mastered the basics by the time they are seven or eight, learning to read, like everything to do with development, varies widely from one child to another. Of course, the competence of the teacher and her methods are one factor. The phonic approach – C–A–T – is the most effective long-term, while Look and Say gives encouraging immediate results. The other, more important component is when your child's brain is ready to read. This is not a matter of intelligence. Slow readers who certainly made good include Louis Pasteur, Henry Ford, William Thackeray and G. B. Shaw – among a host of others.

Books and Reading

Your role lies in encouraging your child's interest, and in:

Supplying the raw materials

Under fifteen months

This is the pre-book stage, when your little one is busy learning to talk and acquiring the building blocks of reading – words.

Baby books
These are basically brightly-coloured picture books which are indestructible because they will be handled, not read.
- *bath books* which float. This is not the best way to teach your child to look after books
- *cloth books* which Baby can clutch. These are not like real books either
- *cardboard and plastic books* are the best introduction, enjoyed as part of a comfortable, cuddly session on your knee – until he gets restless

From fifteen months to two years

Now your toddler is on the trail towards reading.
Fifteen months: he shows his interest by grabbing the book, patting the pictures and 'helping' to scrabble the pages over.
Eighteen months: now the pictures mean something to her: if you ask her 'Where's the car?' – or the dog – she will point to it with conscious cleverness. She turns over two or three pages together.
Two years: now he will say the names of the animals or objects pictured himself, and sometimes, as a tremendous joke, pretend to pick up for instance a cake, from the picture. He can turn the pages one by one,

Childhood Development

and is careful about it, because now he links the pictures with the story and wants the exact sequence to be repeated each time. He knows some of the words and phrases by heart, and will fuss if you change them or try to skip a page or two.

Beginning books
Mike Inkpen: *Wibbly Pig*, one of a series
Judith Kerr: *Mog's Kittens* series
David McKee: *Elmer's Colours* series
Alan Snow: *Woof*
There are also Ladybird and Campbells books with very simple pictures aimed at teaching useful household words and colours, for example.

Two to four years

Classics to introduce now:
Beatrix Potter series
National Trust Book of Nursery Rhymes
A. A. Milne's stories and poems
Alison Uttley's *Little Grey Rabbit* series
Other books:
Janet and Allan Ahlberg: *The Baby's Catalogue*
  Peepo
  Each Peach Pear Plum
Martin Waddell: *Owl Babies*
  The Pig in the Pond
  (good at bedtime)
Eric Hill: *Spot* series
Eileen Browne: *Where's That Bus?*
Catherine and Laurence Anholt: *Here Come the Babies* (good for a toddler with a new baby in the family)
Eric Carle: *The Very Hungry Caterpillar*
Jan Pienkowski: *Meg and Mog* series
Sarah Hayes: *This is the Bear*
Jes Alborough: *It's the Bear*

Books and Reading

Babette Cole: *Dr Dog*
Sara McBratney: *Guess How Much I Love You*
David McKee: *Elmer the Famous Patchwork Elephant*

From about three onwards your child is interested in real stories with a (simple) plot, like *The Very Hungry Caterpillar*, a best-seller for twenty years. He will finish sentences of the story for you, and may be able to tell you – if you ask – what happens next.

Four to six years

Roald Dahl: *The Enormous Crodocile*
             Minpins
Janet and Allan Ahlberg: *Starting School*
Roger Hargreaves: *Mr Men* and *Little Miss* series
Jill Murphy: *All in One Piece*
Judith Kerr: *Mog the Forgetful Cat*
Ian Beck: *Emily and the Golden Acorn*
Margaret Mahy: *The Three-legged Cat*
John Burningham: *Mr Gumpy's Outing*
Rod Campbell: *Dear Zoo*

Old favourites
Michael Bond: *Paddington Bear* series
John Cunliffe: *Postman Pat* series
Reverend Awdry: *Thomas the Tank Engine* series
De Brunhoff: *Babar*
Katherine Hale: *Orlando* series
Maurice Sendak: *Where the Wild Things Are*

Six to eight years

Tony Bradman: *Dilly the Dinosaur* series
Henrietta Brandford: *Dimanche Diller*
Joyce Brisley: *Milly Molly Mandy* (very old favourite)
Jeff Brown: *Flat Stanley*
Dorothy Edwards: *My Naughty Little Sister* (old favourite)

Childhood Development

Ann Jungman: *Vlad the Drac* series
Jill Murphy: *The Worst Witch*
Dick King-Smith: *The Hodgeheg*
Joyce Dunbar: *Mouse and Mole*
Ann Forsyth: *Tall Tale Tom*
Robin Pulver: *Mrs Toggle and the Dinosaur*
Humphrey Carpenter: *Mr Majeika*
Ursula Moray Williams: *Gobbolino the Witch's Cat*
Pat Hutchins: *The House That Sailed Away*
Jill Tomlinson: *The Owl Who Was Afraid of the Dark*
Penny Dale: *Bet You Can't*
Allan Ahlberg: *Miss Dose the Doctor's Daughter*
Magdalen Nabb: *Josie Smith and Eileen* (prize winner)

Your child will love your reading to her, but she will also want to show you that she can read, too. Sharing the reading will encourage her to tackle more difficult books. She will like to have her own shelf of favourite stories and books.

Eight to twelve

Sylvia Waugh: *Mennyms*
               Mennyms in the Wilderness
Grace Hallworth: *Cric Crac: West Indian Stories*
Anne Fine: *Goggle Eyes*
          Flour Babies (prize winner)
L. Fitzhugh: *Harrier the Spy*
Philip Ridley: *Meteorite Spoon*
Frank Rodgers: *The Ship-Shape Shop*
Jennifer Northway: *Get Lost, Laura!*
Mwenye Hadithi: *Greedy Zebra*
Gillian Cross: *The Great Elephant Chase*
Alan Garner: *Elidor*
Russell Stannard: *The Time and Space of Uncle Albert*
Robert Westall: *Machine Gunners*
Brian Jaques: *Redwall* series
Hilary McKay: *Exiles and Exiles at Home* (prize winner)

Books and Reading

E. B. White: *Charlotte's Web*
Jean Richardson: *Tall Inside*

Anything by Roald Dahl strikes a chord with this age group, and the Kingfisher series of treasuries of short stories by well-known contemporary writers: Funny Stories, Bedtime Stories, Animal Stories etc

Keen and advanced readers of twelve and over

Paula Danzinger: *Earth to Matthew*
S. E. Hinton: *The Outsiders*
Sue Townsend: *The Secret Diary of Adrian Mole Aged 13¾*
Berlie Doherty: *Dear Nobody* (prize winner)
Judy Blume: *Superfudge*
Robert O'Brien: *Z for Zachariah*
Robert Swindells: *Stone Cold* (prize winner)
Lois Duncan: *Don't Look Behind You*
Cynthia Voigt: *On Fortune's Wheel*
Paul Zindel: *Pigman*
Robert Leeson: *Coming Home*
Eleanor Allen: *The Day Matt Sold Great-Grandma*
Gillian Cross: *Rent-a-Genius*
Margaret Mahy: *Memory*

The Point series, published by Scholastic, bring out new books all the time: Point Horror, Point Sci-fi, Point Crime, Point Romance etc. They are aimed mainly at teenagers.

Not-so-keen readers of eight to fourteen years

Reading is important, but no one reads easily without practice. The trick is to catch your child's interest with exciting or amusing stories, and for these to be sufficiently easy to read, so that effort is rewarded by success.

Childhood Development

Old and more recent Classics

Laurie Ingalls Wilder: *The Little House on the Prairie* series
Franklin Dixon: *The Hardy Boys*
Louisa M. Alcott: *Little Women, Good Wives*
Lynne Reid Banks: *The Indian in the Cupboard*
Enid Blyton: *The Famous Five* series
Carolyn Keene: *Nancy Drew* series
Willard Price: *Amazon Adventure* (and others)
Mary Norton: *The Borrowers*
Rudyard Kipling: *Just So Stories*
Joan Aiken: *The Wolves of Willoughby Chase* (and others)
Jack London: *White Fang*
C. S. Lewis: *Chronicles of Narnia*
E. Nesbit: *The Railway Children*
Michelle Margorian: *Good Night Mr Tom*
Arthur Ransome: *Swallows and Amazons*
Mark Twain: *The Adventures of Tom Sawyer*
Ian Serralier: *The Silver Sword*
Noel Streatfield: *Ballet Shoes*
Rosemary Sutcliffe: *The Eagle of the Ninth*
Philippa Pierce: *Tom's Midnight Garden*
Helen Cresswell: *Mondial and Bagthorpes* series
Lewis Carrol: *Alice in Wonderland, Alice Through the Looking Glass*
R. L. Stevenson: *Treasure Island*
J. M. Barrie: *Peter Pan and Wendy*
Hans Christian Andersen: *Stories* and *Fairy Tales*

There are also some collections:
Walker Book of Fairy Tales
Walker Book of Poetry

Books with pictures

Ann Turnbull/Lisa Flather: *The Last Wolf*
Tony Blundell: *Beware of Boys*

Books and Reading

Babette Cole: *Princess Smartypants*
Margaret Mahy: *The Rattlebang Picnic*
Theresa Radcliffe: *Shadow the Deer*
Graeme Base: *The Eleventh Hour*
Michael Rosen: *Moving*
Chief Seattle/Susan Jeffers: *Brother Eagle Sister Sky*
Jon Scieszka: *The Frog Prince Continued*
Michael Salmon: *Count Munch*

Short stories

Humphrey Carpenter: *Mr Majeika's Postbag*
Malorie Blackman: *Girl Wonder and the Terrific Twins*

The Puffin Book of Funny Stories

Terry Jones/Michael Foreman: *Fantastic Stories*
Margaret Joy: *See You at the Match*
Catherine Storr: *Last Stories of Polly and the Wolf*

Easy novels

Alan Davidson: *Catfoot and the Case of the Big Woofy Dog*
Jon Scieszka: *The Time Warp Trio* series
Dick King-Smith: *Dodos Are Forever*
Ken Oppel: *A Bad Case of Ghosts*
Jill Murphy: *The Worst Witch All at Sea*
Nina Bawden: *The Real Plato Jones*
Susan Cooper: *The Boggart*
Anne Fine: *Step by Wicked Step*
Andrew Norris: *Matt's Millions*
Bernard Ashley: *Seeing Off Uncle Jack*
Hutchinson Treasury of Children's Literature
Perham: *King Arthur and the Legends of Camelot*

These suggestions are by no means complete. Share with your child all the books you enjoyed as well as those that have become popular since you grew up.

Your public library

This can be a real help. There is often a story hour for the younger children and the children's librarian will do all she can to encourage your child to enjoy books. A visit to the library for both adult and youngster is a worthwhile routine, and can turn into a treasure hunt.

Route Plan Chart

No two children develop in exactly the same way or at exactly the same pace, but here are some of the landmarks to look out for on the journey.

Starting post

Weight: 5½–8½lbs (2500–3800g)
Length: 18–22ins (45–55cm)
Cries without tears
Coughs, sneezes, yawns, sucks, swallows
Seeks for the nipple
Prefers sweet taste – like human milk

One month

Little, throaty mewing sounds – as well as crying
Notices sounds, like a tinkling bell
Fixes eyes briefly on the face bending over him or her
Is soothed by being picked up and held snugly
Grips your finger if you put it in his palm
Fists closed, thumbs tucked in

Six weeks

Recognises mother: smiles with meaning
Coos, gurgles
Turns head and eyes to look and listen

Childhood Development

Startled by loud noise; may cry
Soothed by mother's voice
Nearly puts tongue out

Twelve weeks

Lifts head and chest when on her tummy
Plays with and looks at her hands: opens and closes them
Makes a sweep towards objects that interest him
Babbles and chuckles
Cries or looks sad if you go away

Twenty weeks

Loves to be propped up towards sitting
Smiles at mirror
Holds bottle of milk or juice to drink
Holds rattle or toy given to him
Looks for toy when he has dropped
'Says' da, ma, ba and lll

Six months

Excited when he sees you; friendly to everyone
Lifts head and arms to be picked up
Likes playing Peep-bo
Likes being bounced on your lap, standing or sitting
Tests everything in his mouth
Dribbles: may have two middle bottom teeth
Says mama, dada, nana, baba – sometimes with meaning

One year

Sits up by herself
Crawls

Route Plan Chart

Pulls herself onto her feet; can stagger along holding your hand
Drinks from a mug, with help
Understands familiar words like Daddy, Teddy, pussy
Points at what he wants
Beginning to be shy of strangers

Eighteen months

Walks with feet well apart; unsteady near-run
Feeds herself messily with a spoon
Manages mug by herself
Knows six to twenty words, including nose, eyes, mouth, hand
Balances three blocks on top of each other
Likes looking at a picture book with you
Will play by himself, preferably near you

Two years

Goes up and down stairs, two feet on each step, holding on
Round and round scribble with crayon in her fist
Kicks a ball with a straight, stiff leg
Can build a tower of six bricks
May have tantrums when he cannot make himself understood
Takes shoes and socks off; tries to put them on
Pretends to drive car, make tea, sweep up
Two- or three-word sentences; often says 'mine'

Three years

Goes upstairs with alternate feet, not down yet
Rides trike skilfully
Threads very big beads
Makes a 'train' with up to nine bricks

Childhood Development

Eats with spoon and fork
Holds pencil the right way; copies a cross and a circle
Clean and dry – may not be at night yet

Four years

Knows times of day
Understands if you say you are coming back
Can look forward to treats
Can dress herself
Uses a knife at meals
Chatterbox: tells you jokes and stories
s, f, th, sh and r may be difficult to pronounce

Five years

Likes playing ball games, but can't catch very well
Likes painting, drawing and dressing up
Shows off skills like hopping, head-over-heels, sliding
Counts up to twenty
Gives the people in her drawings noses, mouths, eyes and ears, and buttons on their clothes
Can say several nursery rhymes

Six years

Likes climbing – trees, frames, rocks
Confident and cheeky
Learns fast, beginning to read: needs help
Front teeth getting wobbly
Asking for a two-wheeler

Seven years

Better-behaved: wants to be liked by grown-ups
May have a run of colds and sore throats
Busy, interested in everything

Route Plan Chart

Writing with big, uneven letters
Reads by himself a little: likes to do it with you
Thinks adults are strong and clever – but not for long

Eight years

'I can't wait' and 'In a minute' are favourite phrases
Likes playing in same-sex group
Useful help with washing-up, cooking, pulling duvet up
Usually truthful
Interested in money and spending it

Nine years

Less childish: fairy tales are out
Not so keen to help: may sulk
May have tummy-aches or leg pains when stressed
Cheeky in a group; boys often exclude girls
Likes museums and other adult outings
Girls may develop breast buds

Ten years

Sense of fairness: open to reason
Loves secrets
Special talents, for instance for music, writing stories or science begin to emerge
Hero-worship and loyalty, for instance to school, develop
May read for information as well as pleasure

Eleven to twelve years

Puberty starts up: girls ahead of boys
Team games and competitive events popular
More friendships, still some gangs – especially boys

Childhood Development

Some start taking school-work seriously; others not at all
MUST know about sex, drugs, dangers in life
Draws away from parents: a lot to think about

Puberty Chart

Girls (8–18 years)
Breast development – bud: 9–13 years
                              – cone shape: 11–15 years
                              – nipple area differentiated: 13+
Pubic hair   – down: 10–13 years
                              – hairs, getting darker: 11–15 years
First period: 11–14½, but maybe anything from 9–18 years
Growth spurt: 11–14, peaking at 12 years
Underarm hair and sweat glands
Broadening of hips and extra fat over thighs, breasts, hips and bottom
Growth usually stops at 16 years

Boys (11–23 years)

Testicles and penis grow bigger: 11–13 years
Pubic hair   – down: 11–13 years
                              – hairs: 12–14 years
Growth spurt: 12–17, peaking at 14 years
Erections: 12+ years
Wet dreams: 13+ years
Voice – breaks: 12+ years
       – deepens: 14–15 years
Underarm hair and sweat glands; hair on upper lip
Shoulders broaden

Childhood Development

Growth usually stops around 18 years

Both sexes develop more freckles (if any) at 12+ years

The timing and the order of all these changes is subject to individual variation, depending on which areas are most sensitive to the hormones that control puberty development.

Tooth Chart

MILK TEETH

When they come and when they go: the order is nearly always the same, but the timing varies with each child. These are averages:

COMING THROUGH

	Upper Jaw	Lower Jaw
Middle front teeth	6–8 months	5–7 months
Side front teeth	8–11 months	7–10 months
Canines (Dracula teeth)	16–20 months	16–20 months
First molars (grinders)	10–16 months	10–16 months
Second molars (back)	20–30 months	20–30 months

FALLING OUT (Tooth Fairy Time)

Middle front teeth	7–8 years	6–7 years
Side front teeth	8–9 years	7–8 years
Canines	11–12 years	9–11 years
First molars	10–11 years	10–12 years
Second molars	10–11 years	11–13 years

PERMANENT TEETH

For these, too, the timing of when they come through varies from child to child.

Childhood Development

UPPER and LOWER JAWS

6-year molars	6 years
Four front teeth (smilers)	7–8 years
Premolars (near the front)	10–11 years
Canines	9–12 years
Second molars	10–13 years
Wisdom teeth	12–25 years (or later)

TOOTH CARE

Cleaning – start as soon as there are any teeth to clean
- baby stage with gauze
- 2 years with toothbrush
- 7 years can do it alone (but reminders needed)

Dentist – visit in second year, when it is all fun

Exercise – teeth need this, from hard and chewy foods

Avoid – sticky sweets: never at bedtime
- ice lollies
- fizzy drinks, especially coke
- sweetened pacifiers, miniature bottles, and any bottle left with a toddler to suck at will

Sleep Chart

Since some adults need a good eight and a half hours' sleep and others only five, it is not surprising that babies and children also vary widely in their amount of sleep. What follows is a rough guide to what children might do.

0–3 months: sleeping and waking alternate throughout the twenty-four hours, plus dozy twilight states in between.
Maximum stretch of uninterrupted sleep: 3–5 hours.

3 months: time to establish a definite bedtime routine in the evening, for instance:
   bath
   nightclothes
   say goodnight to people, pets
   evening feed in bedroom
   lullaby or little talk
   tuck up and leave
   (don't wait for Baby to sleep)

4 months: awake much more of the day.
Maximum stretch of sleep: 6 hours or more.

6 months: awake all day except for two naps, morning and early afternoon, but a very changeable pattern.

1 year: some babies are awake all day and asleep all night; some still like two naps, some only one, and may

Childhood Development

play in their cots rather than sleep. Go along with what your baby prefers.

15 months: only one nap or play-nap from now, after the midday meal, with plenty of stimulating playtime to follow.
Bedtime: 6–8pm. Usually no complaining.

18 months: Nap or play-nap after lunch, 1½ hours.
Bedtime: 6–8pm – fusses when you leave the room but soon settles.
Wakes 6–8am. Sleeps 12 hours.

2 years: play-nap after lunch, not more than 1½ hours if he sleeps then.
Bedtime: 6–7pm, but may actually go to sleep at any time between 6 and 10pm, depending on daytime sleep. Sleeps 12 hours and wakes accordingly.

2½ years: insistent on full bedtime ritual.

3 years: may still go along with play-rest after lunch, but not for much longer. Often dry all night.

4 years: no daytime nap or rest.
Bedtime: 7pm – tries to put it off. Half-hour with picture book or crayonning before going to sleep. Usually dry all night and does not need potting.
Wakes 7–8am, but some regularly wake at 5am. Play until getting up time.

5 years: life is exciting – may wake with a bad dream.
Bedtime: 7–8pm. Wakes 7–8am.

6 years:
Bedtime: 7.30–8pm. Wakes 5–8am.
Gets up by herself. Can dress herself but needs reminding.

7 years: still likes to be read to.
Bedtime: 7.30–8pm. Gets to sleep quickly, usually.

Sleep Chart

8 years: many excuses for not going to bed.
Bedtime: 8–8.30pm, perhaps 9pm at weekends.
Wakes: 7–7.30am. Gets up and gets dressed by himself.

9 years: knows his bedtime.
Bedtime: 8–9pm – may read or listen to the radio too long before going to sleep: check.
Sleeps about 10 hours.

10 years:
Bedtime: 8.30–9pm – later at weekends.
Sleeps 9½–10½ hours, boys longer than girls.

11 years:
Bedtime: usually around 9pm, but may be 7.30–10pm. Takes half an hour to go to sleep. Sleeps about 9½ hours.

12 years: parents no longer have evenings to themselves.
Bedtime: 9.30 but may be 8.30–10.30pm.
Sleeps 9–9½ hours.

REMEMBER – no child is the average.

Immunisation Schedule

When Due	*Which immunisations*	*Type*
2 months		
	Hib*	one injection
	Diphtheria, Whooping cough, Tetanus } – DTP	one injection
	Polio	by mouth
3 months		
	Hib*	one injection
	Diphtheria, Whooping cough, Tetanus } – DTP	one injection
	Polio	by mouth
4 months		
	Hib*	one injection
	Diphtheria, Whooping cough, Tetanus } – DTP	one injection
	Polio	by mouth

Immunisation Schedule

12–15 months	Measles Mumps Rubella } – MMR	one injection
3–5 years starting school	Diphtheria Tetanus }	booster injection
	Polio	booster by mouth
13 years	Tuberculosis – BCG	one injection
Leaving school	Diphtheria Tetanus }	one injection
	Polio	booster by mouth

*Hib protects against the Hib form of meningitis (Haemophilus influenzae type b)

Notes on Immunisation

Immunisation is one big reason why you as a parent of the twentieth or twenty-first century can expect your baby to sail through childhood safe from the killer infections that decimated Victorian families. Immunisation works by alerting the body in advance so that its defences will zap the enemy bacteria and viruses it may meet. This is done by introducing a vaccine – a harmless preparation of the germs or their chemicals – which stimulate the production of antibodies: special defenders against specific attackers. We adults use vaccines to protect ourselves against, for instance, typhoid when we travel abroad. The children's immunisation programme covers illnesses which affect children everywhere – unless they are immunised.

These are:
Diphtheria
Tetanus
Whooping cough (pertussis)
Polio (poliomyelitis)
Measles
Mumps
German measles (rubella)
TB (tuberculosis)
Hib (one type only of meningitis)

Side-effects

Sometimes babies react to the dose of vaccine during the first twenty-four hours with fretfulness and slight fever. A half-teaspoonful dose (2.5ml) of baby paracetamol syrup (Calpol) is soothing. Sometimes there is redness and swelling at the site of the injection: this reaction is not important and will fade in due course.

After the whooping cough vaccine one child in 10,000 may have a feverish convulsion and should continue with the tetanus and diphtheria only for the following injections.

One child in 1000 may have a similar feverish convulsion after the measles vaccine: this is far more likely with an attack of the illness itself. With the great success of the 1994 measles and rubella campaign, measles is well on the way to being eradicated from the UK altogether. It is, of course, rife in some other countries.

0-1 yr
GIRLS GROWTH CHART

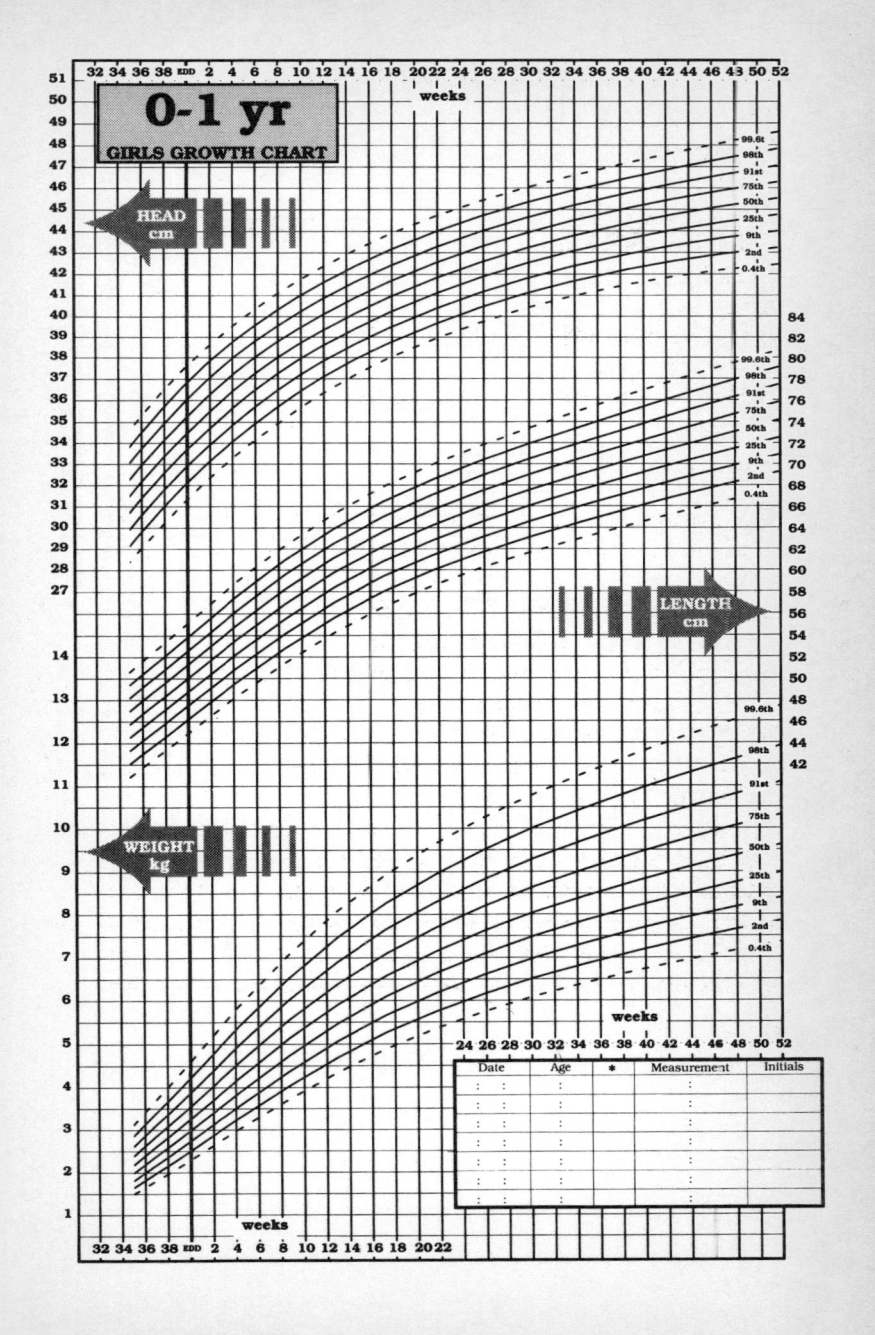

HEAD cm

LENGTH cm

WEIGHT kg

Date	Age	*	Measurement	Initials
:	:	:	:	
:	:	:	:	
:	:	:	:	
:	:	:	:	
:	:	:	:	
:	:	:	:	
:	:	:	:	

1-5 yrs
GIRLS GROWTH CHART

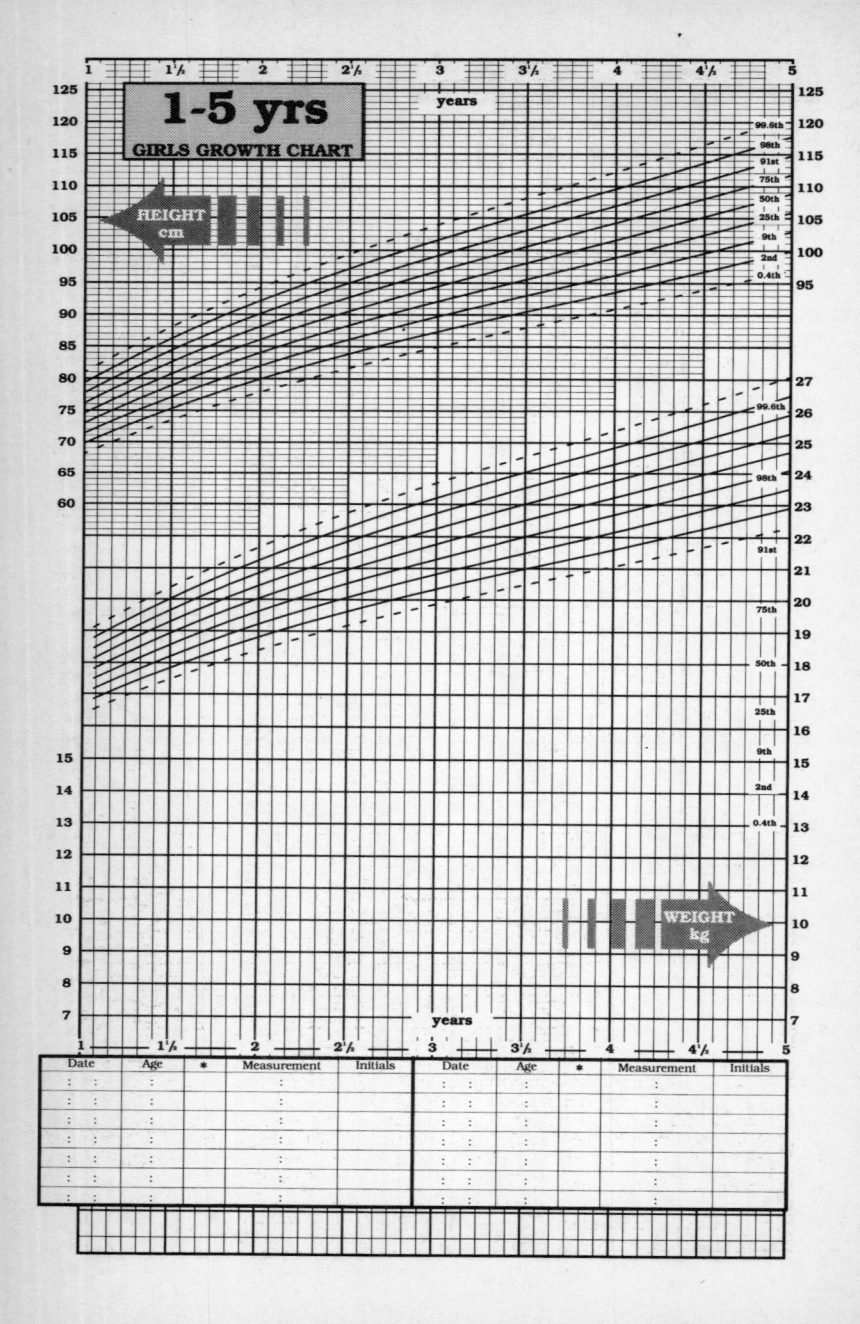

* Measurement: H = Height, W = Weight D.O.B. ......:......:......									
Date	Age	*	Measurement	Initials	Date	Age	*	Measurement	Initials
: :	:	:	:		: :	:	:	:	
: :	:	:	:		: :	:	:	:	
: :	:	:	:		: :	:	:	:	
: :	:	:	:		: :	:	:	:	
: :	:	:	:		: :	:	:	:	
: :	:	:	:		: :	:	:	:	
: :	:	:	:		: :	:	:	:	

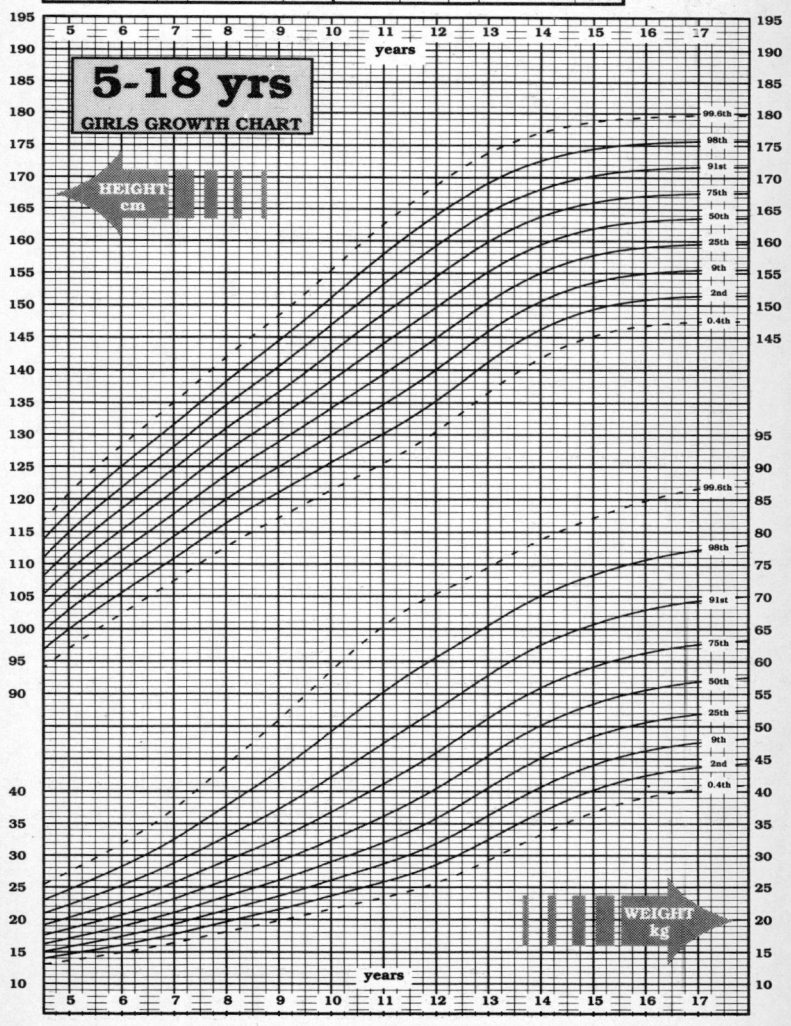

5-18 yrs
GIRLS GROWTH CHART

HEIGHT cm

WEIGHT kg

99.6th, 98th, 91st, 75th, 50th, 25th, 9th, 2nd, 0.4th

0-1 yr
BOYS GROWTH CHART

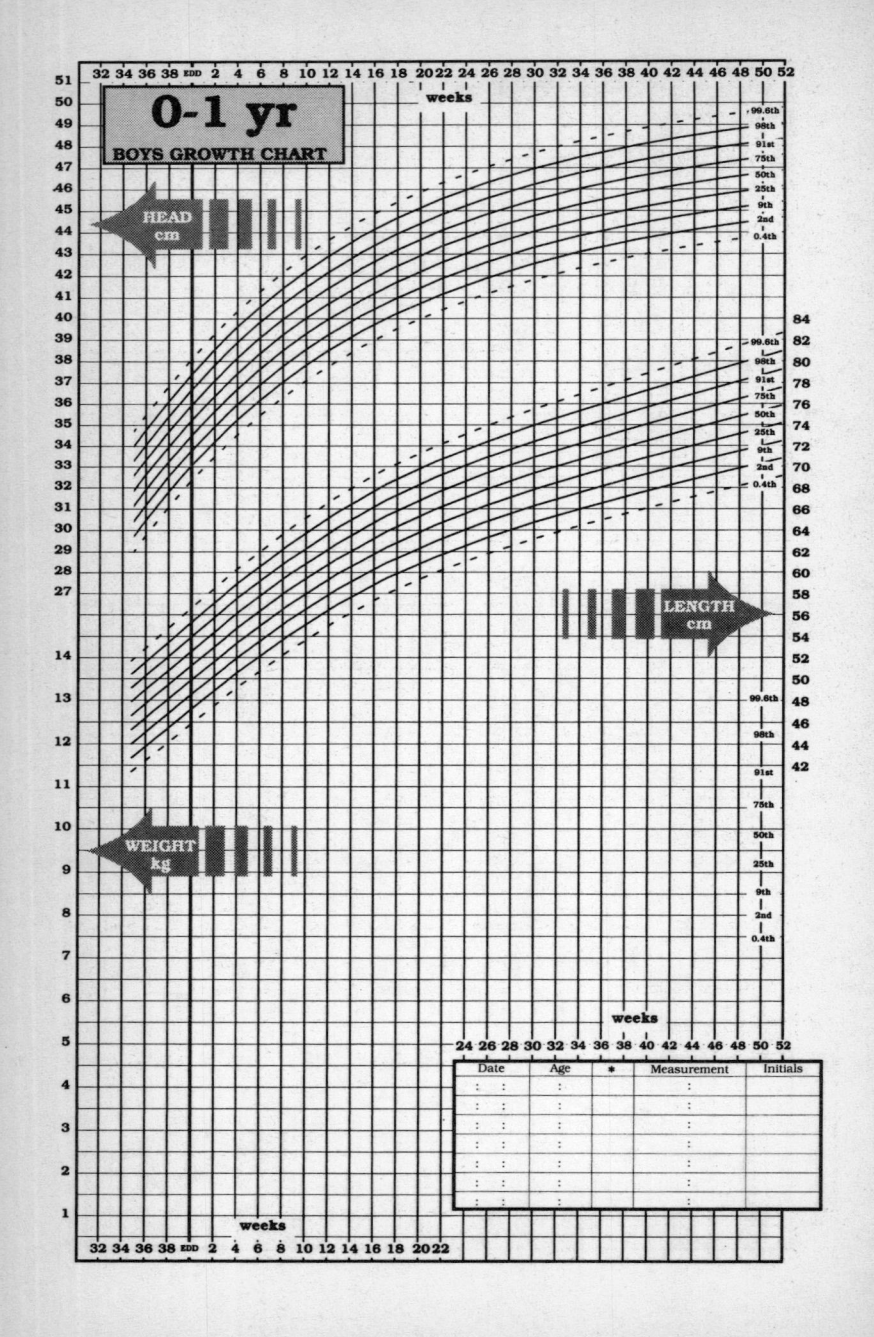

Date	Age	*	Measurement	Initials
: :	:	:	:	
: :	:	:	:	
: :	:	:	:	
: :	:	:	:	
: :	:	:	:	
: :	:	:	:	

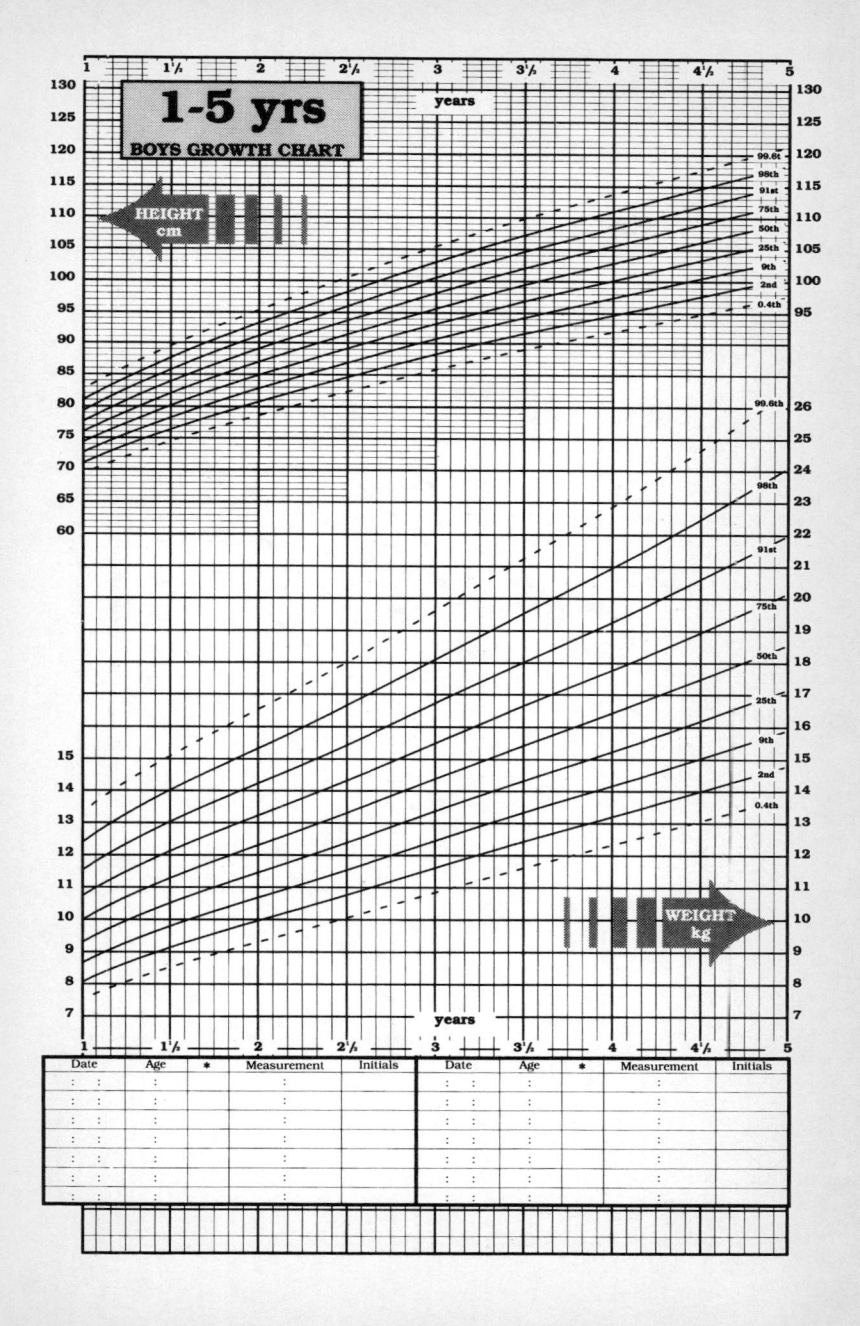

1-5 yrs
BOYS GROWTH CHART

HEIGHT cm

WEIGHT kg

years

Percentiles: 99.6th, 98th, 91st, 75th, 50th, 25th, 9th, 2nd, 0.4th

Date	Age	*	Measurement	Initials	Date	Age	*	Measurement	Initials
: :	:	:	:		: :	:	:	:	
: :	:	:	:		: :	:	:	:	
: :	:	:	:		: :	:	:	:	
: :	:	:	:		: :	:	:	:	
: :	:	:	:		: :	:	:	:	
: :	:	:	:		: :	:	:	:	

* **Measurement: H** = Height, **W** = Weight D.O.B. ....:......									
Date	Age	*	Measurement	Initials	Date	Age	*	Measurement	Initials
: :	:		:		: :	:		:	
: :	:		:		: :	:		:	
: :	:		:		: :	:		:	
: :	:		:		: :	:		:	
: :	:		:		: :	:		:	
: :	:		:		: :	:		:	

5-18 yrs
BOYS GROWTH CHART

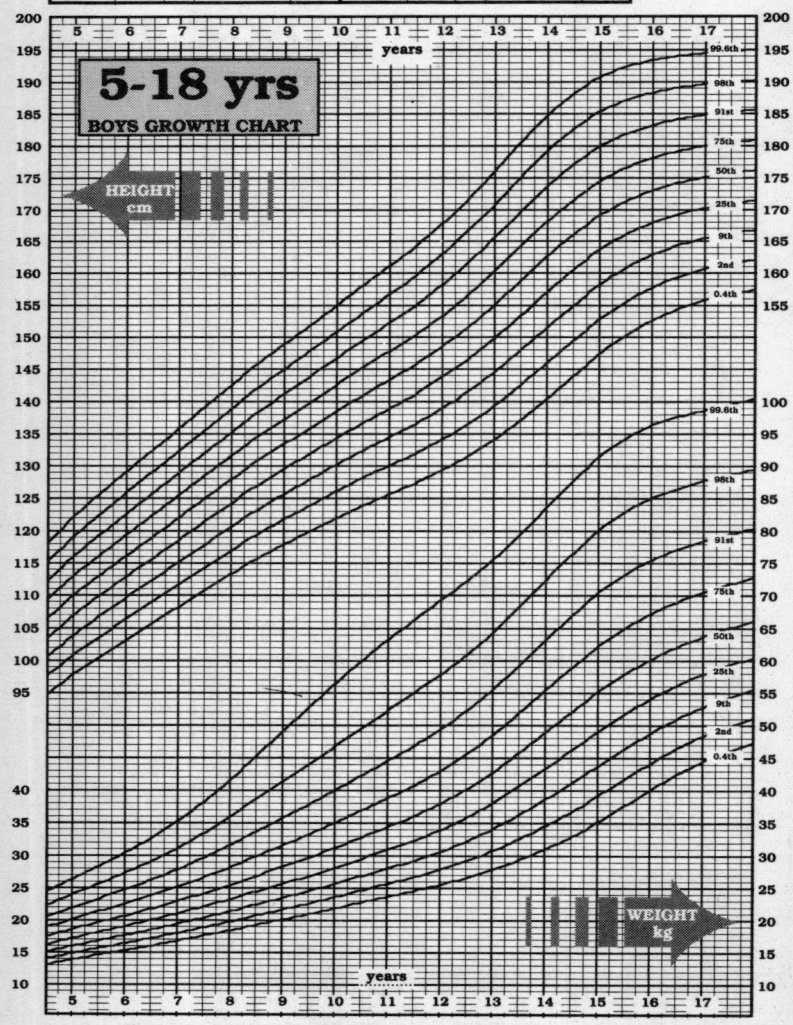

HEIGHT cm

WEIGHT kg

Height centiles: 99.6th, 98th, 91st, 75th, 50th, 25th, 9th, 2nd, 0.4th
Weight centiles: 99.6th, 98th, 91st, 75th, 50th, 25th, 9th, 2nd, 0.4th

Useful Addresses

Action Against Allergy
22/24 High Street
Hampton Hill
Middlesex TW12 1PD
0181 947 5082

Active Birth Centre
18 Laurier Road
London NW5 1SD
0171 267 3006

Allergy Support Service
62 Marshals Drive
St Albans
Herts AL1 4RF
01727 58705

AFASIC (Association for All
  Speech Impaired Children)
347 Central Markets
Smithfield
London EC1A 9NH
0171 236 3632

Association of Breastfeeding
  Mothers
26 Holmshaw Close
Sydenham Green
London SE26 4TH
0181 778 4769

Association for Improvements
  in Maternity Services
  (AIMS)
163 Liverpool Road
London N1 0RF
0171 278 5628

Asthma Society
300 Upper Street
London N1 2XX
0171 226 2260

Baby Life Support Systems
  (BLISS)
44 Museum Street
London WC1A 1LY

British Agencies for Adoption
  and Fostering
11 Southwark Street
London SE1 1RQ
0171 407 8800

British Diabetic Association
10 Queen Anne Street
London W1M 0BD
0171 323 1531

British Epilepsy Association
40 Hanover Square
Leeds LS3 1BE
01532 439 393

Childhood Development

British Paediatric Association
5 St Andrew's Place
Regent's Park
London NW1 4LB
0171 486 6151

British Pregnancy Advisory
  Service
7 Belgrave Road
London SW1
0171 233 5685

Child Growth Foundation
2 Mayfield Avenue
London W4 1PW
Copies of the growth charts
  (p 297-84) may be
  purchased from:
Harlow Printing
Maxwell Street
South Shields NE33 4PU
0191455 4286

Cleft Lip and Palate
  Association (CLAPA)
The Hospital for Sick Children
Great Ormond Street
London WC1N 3JH

Coeliac Society of the United
  Kingdom
PO Box 220
High Wycombe
Bucks HP11 2HY
01494 37278

CRY-SIS
27 Old Gloucester Street
London WC1
0171 404 5011

Cystic Fibrosis Research Trust
5 Blyth Road
Bromley
Kent BR1 3RS
0181 464 7211

Down's Syndrome Association
12 Clapham Common South
  Side
London SW4 7AA
0171 720 0008

Family Planning Association
27 Mortimer Street
London W1N 7RJ
0171 636 7866

Gingerbread Association for
  One-Parent Families
35 Wellington Street
London WC2E 7BN
0171 240 0953

Haemophilia Society
123 Westminster Bridge Road
London SE1 7HR
0171 928 2020

Hyperactive Children's
  Support Group
59 Meadowside
Angmering
West Sussex BN16 4BW

Invalid Children's Aid
  Association
126 Buckingham Palace Road
London SW1W 9SB
0171 730 9891

Lady Hoare Trust for
  Physically Disabled
  Children
North Street
Midhurst
West Sussex GU29 9DJ

La Leche League
  (Breastfeeding)
Box BM 3424
London WC1N 3XX
0171 404 5011

Useful Addresses

Maternity Alliance
15 Britannia Street
London WC1X 9JP
0171 837 1265

Mencap
117 Golden Lane
London EC1Y 0RT
0171 253 9433

Mind
22 Harley Street
London W1N 2ED
0171 637 0741

Miscarriage Association
PO Box 24
Ossett
West Yorks

Muscular Dystrophy Group of Great Britain
35 Macaulay Road
London SW4 0QP
0171 720 8055

National Association for Deaf/Blind and Rubella Children
311 Grays Inn Road
London WC1X 8PT
0171 278 1005

National Association for Gifted Children
1 South Audley Street
London W1Y 6JS
0171 499 1188

National Association for Maternal and Child Welfare
1 South Audley Street
London W1Y 6JS
0171 491 2772

National Association for the Welfare of Children in Hospital
29 Euston Road
London NW1 2SD
0171 833 2041

National Council for One-Parent Families
255 Kentish Town Road
London NW5 2LX
0171 267 1361

National Deaf Children's Society
15 Dufferin Street
London EC1
0171 250 0123

National Eczema Society
Tavistock House North
Tavistock Square
London WC1H 9SR
0171 388 4097

National Society for Autistic Children
276 Willesden Lane
London NW2 5RB
0181 451 1114

National Society for Mentally Handicapped Children
123 Golden Lane
London EC1Y 0RT
0171 253 9433

Parents Anonymous London (PAL)
6 Manor Gardens
Holloway Road
London N7 6LA
0171 263 8918

Childhood Development

Pre-School Playgroups
  Association
61 King's Cross Road
London WC1X 9LL
0171 833 0991

Relate (Marriage Guidance
  etc.)
76A New Cavendish Street
London W1
0171 580 1087

Royal National Institute for
  the Blind (RNIB)
224 Great Portland Street
London W1N 6AA
0171 388 1266

Royal National Institute for
  the Deaf (RNID)
105 Gower Street
London WC1E 6BR
0171 387 8033

SCOPE (The Spastics Society)
Shackleton Square
Priestly Way
Crawley
West Sussex RH10 2GZ
01293 522 655

Twin and Multiple Births
  Association (TAMBA)
PO Box 30
Little Sutton
0151 348 0020

AUSTRALIA

Association for Children with
  Learning Difficulties
12–14 Pindari Road
NSW 2210

Auspeld (Specific Learning
  Difficulties)
129 Greenwich Road
Greenwich
NSW 2065

Australian Association for the
  Welfare of Child Health
PO Box 113
Westmead
NSW 2145

Australian Capital Territory
  Children's Services
PO Box 24
Spence
ACT 2615

Australian Early Childhood
  Association
Woomeran Avenue
Darlinghurst
NSW 2010

Autistic Association
41 Cook Street
Forestville
NSW 2087

Child Protection and Family
  Crisis Unit
PO Box 83
Darlinghurst
NSW 2010

Children's Growth
  Foundation Ltd
PO Box 459
Maroubra
NSW 2035
02 315 7547

Useful Addresses

Down's Syndrome Association
31 O'Connell Street
North Parramatta
NSW 2151

Dyslexia Foundation
Irlen Clinic Children's Centre
University of Sydney
NSW 2006

Family Support Centre
632 Stronach Avenue
East Maitland
NSW 2323

Gifted and Talented Children's
 Association
PO Box 1086
Strathfield
NSW 2135

Juvenile Diabetes Foundation
of Australia
PO Box 1500
Chatswood
NSW 2057

Kanitane Mothercraft Society
Cnr Horsley Drive and
 Mitchell Street
Canamar
NSW 2163

Kindergarten Union
 Children's Services
129 York Street
Sydney
NSW 2000

Lady Gowrie Child Centres
– in all districts

National Epilepsy Association
 of Australia Inc.
PO Box 224
Parramatta
NSW 2150
02 891 6118

Parents' Centres Australia
4185 Hammers Road
Old Toongabbie
NSW 2146

Royal Society for the Welfare
 of Mothers and Babies
2 Shaw Street
Petersham
NSW 2049

USA

Allergy and Asthma Network/
 Mothers of Asthmatics
3554 Chain Bridge Road Ste
 200
Fairfax
VA 27032709

American Montessori Society
150 5th Avenue Ste 203
New York
NY 10011-4384

Association for Children with
 Down's Syndrome
2616 Martin Ave
Belmore
NY 11710

Childhood Development

Association for Help of the
Retarded Child
200 Park St Ste 1201
New York
NY 10003

Autism Society of America
7910 Woodmont Ave Ste 650
Bethesda
MD 20814

Children in Hospital
3000 Longwood Ave
Boston
MA 02115

Council for Exceptional
Children
1920 Association Drive
Reston
VA 22091-1589

Cystic Fibrosis Foundation
6931 Arlington Road NO 200
Bethesda
MD 20814

Federation for Children with
Special Needs
95 Berkley St Ste 104
Boston
MA 01266

Forward Face (cleft palate)
317 E. 34th St
New York
NY 10016

Juvenile Diabetes Association
432 Park Ave
New York
NY 10016 8013

Mothers at Home
8310 A Old Courthouse Road
Vienna
VA 22182

Mothers' Network (under fives)
70 W 36th St Ste 900
New York
NY 10018

National Headstart
Association
20 N. Union St Ste 320
Alexandria
VA 22314

Orton Dyslexia Association
Chester Building Ste 382
860 La Salle Road
Baltimore
MD 21286-2044

Parents Anonymous
675 W Foothill Bvd Ste 220
Clairmont
CA 91711-3416

Parents' Network
6236 Utah Ave NW
Washington
DC 20015

Spina Bifida Association of
America
4590 Macarthur Bvd NW Ste
250
Washington
DC 20007-4226

United States Cerebral Palsy
Association
1522 K St NW Ste 1112
Washington
DC 20005

Index

Active Birth classes 34–5, 40–1
acupuncture in childbirth 41
adoption 59–60
alcohol in pregnancy 8–9
anaesthetics in childbirth 42
ante-natal
  care 16–17
  classes 34–5
  tests 19
appetite 178, 201, 226
arguments 200
art 164–5
asthma and hay fever 192

babies (up to one year)
    first week 55
    first few weeks 237
    second week 55
    two to three weeks 55–6
    four weeks 56–8
    first six weeks 37–67
    six weeks 58
    eight weeks 70, 155
    ten weeks 70–1
    twelve weeks 71–2
    eight months 85–6, 156, 166
    nine months 86
    three months 155
    four months 72–3
    five months 73–5
    six months 68–9, 83
    seven months 83–5
    ten months 86–89, 156
  big 224
  body language 58–9

clothing 25
communicating 58
development
  finger control 88, 91
  helping 60–1, 79–81
  interest and stimulus 95
  nervous system 87
  reliable love 95, 227
  secure environment 94
  space to play 95
equipment 25–6
family resemblance 49–50
first few weeks
  crying 52–3
  development
    caring 60–1
    feeding 61–4
    hiccups 219–27
    playing 64–5, 227
  difficulties 226
  feeling and touch 50
  hearing 50
  personality 59
  poor progress 235–8
  reflexes 54–5
  sight 50
  sleeping 53–4, 57
  smiling 58
  sneezing, coughing, hiccuping and yawning 53
  sucking and swallowing 51, 57
  tasting and smelling 51
mid-day nap 104–5, 139
mobility 90
ownership 92

premature 223–4, 237
small 223–4
baby bouncers 74
baby-sitting 67, 88
baby-walkers 108
ball sense 144
bargaining 123
bath-time 91
birth
    Apgar test 44–6
    baby's angle 43
    first breath 44
    giving 37–43, *see also* labour
    impact on baby 46–7
    second-day medical 47–8
    water births 42
birthday parties 139–40, 169
birthmarks 219–20
bottle-feeding 62, 101
bow-legs 49
boys, erections 206
breast-feeding 61, 225–6
breath holding 118
brothers and sisters 186, 213–18

Caesarean births 41, 219
Cardiff Count 26
Care for the Family, study of fathers 127
character formation 194
characteristics of your child 170–1
children, ages
    (one to three years old) *see* toddlers
    (four to twelve years old)
    four years old 131–42, 167
        eating 139
        friends 139–40
        imagination 137–8
        language 133–5, 167
        numbers 135–7
        physical progress 131–3
        sleep 139
    five years 142–9, 168
        development, helping 145–8
        lying and stealing 148–9, 167
        physical progress 143–5
        school-starters 174
    six year olds 172, 174–8
        decision making 175
        physical progress 174–6
    seven year olds
        physical progress 181–2
        reading, writing and numbers 182–6
    eight year olds 186–90
        health 187
        sex 189–90
    nine to ten year olds 190–7
    ten year olds 190–7, 200
    eleven year olds 197–204, 207, 209–12
    twelve year olds 204, 206–9
        father's role 211
        grandparents 212
        physical progress 203–9
clever children 240–2
development
    helping 124–6, 145–8, 193–4, 209–22
    hiccups 219–34
    late 236
    milestones 238
difficult children 239–40
fat 151, 187, 224–5
opinions 210
Christingles 161
Christmas 161–2
cleft lip 222
clothes 191–2
club foot 222–3
colic 56, 72, 90, 226–7
communicating 58, 150, 155
computers 180, 207
    and fax machines 150

Index

Congenital dislocation of the hip (CDH) 223, 225, 238
contraception 7, 14
cot-deaths 57, 90
coughs and colds 201
crawling 86
criticism of parents 195–6
CTG (cardiotography) 26

darkness 138
deafness and blindness 238
developmental difficulties, major 233–4
diabetes test 25
divorce 208
DNA (deoxyribonucleicacid) 5–6, 19
Down's syndrome 24, 224, 234, 236
drawing and writing 93, 109, 132–3, 144, 183
dreams 177, 184, 228–9
dressing 91, 121, 123, 138
drinking, from a cup 77, 101, 112, 226
drugs in pregnancy 9
Dyslexia 175, 233–4

eating 117, 139
EDD (expected dates of delivery) 28
education, where it leads 170
emotional development 84–5, 93
epidural anaesthesia in childbirth 41
epilepsy 231–2
exercise 150–1, 180, 192, 208–10, 225

faces, discovering 85–6
failure to thrive 227
famous people as children 235–45
Father Christmas 137, 185
fathers 35–6, 127, 219
at birth 42–3
newborn baby 65–6
six weeks to six months 81
six to twelve months 103–4
toddlers 126–7
pre-school years 149–51
school-time 194–6
twelve year olds 211
fatigue 201
febrile convulsions 231
feeding 123
bottle-feeding 62, 224–6
breast feeding 61, 225–6
clock or demand 62–4
difficulties 225–6
knives and forks 147
mixed 75–7
spoon feeding 75, 108–9, 112, 139, 226
feminine shape 199
finger foods 77, 102, 226
fits 231–2
Foetal Alcohol Syndrome 8
fontanelles and funny-shaped heads 48–9
food 192, 209
fractures 177–8
freckles 205
friends 202–3, 212, 215

gas and air in childbirth 41
german measles (rubella) 9–11, 16
Gesell Arnold 165
girls, periods 206, 210
grandparents 36, 105
newborn babies 66–7
six weeks to six months 82
six to twelve months 104–6
toddlers 127–9
three years olds 215
Pre-school years 151–2
four year olds 215
five years olds 215–16
school-time 194–6
six year olds 216
seven year olds 216
eight year olds 216
nine year olds 217
ten year olds 217
eleven year olds 217
twelve year olds 212, 218

growth 177, 180–1, 198–200, 204, 224

Hallowe'en 160
hand-eye co-ordination 109
hands and arms 110
height 153, 198, 205, 225
herd instinct 188
homes, happy 242–3
hospitalisation 147
humour, developing sense of 71, 155
hygiene 191
hypnosis in childbirth 41

imaginary friends 140, 148
imagination 137–8
imitations 113
immunisation 75, 78–9
independence 207
infections 9–11
inguinal hernia 222
intensive care units (ICU) 42

jaundice 48, 221
jealousy 189, 208, 214–15

Klinfelter's syndrome 225

Labour 38
    pain relief 40–2
    stages 38–40
    starting signals 38–8
language and literature 113, 120, 133–5, 157–8
laughter 72–3, 94, 153–69, 190
libraries 183
Linnaeus 242
listeria 10
love 154–6, 169
    life and laughter 72–3, 94, 153–69
lying and stealing 148–9, 167, 188–9

massage and aromatherapy 11
maternal serum screening tests 23–4

maturity, readiness for school 171
meals 100–3, 139, 182, 226
memory 137
milk rash or milia 48, 220–1
minerals 11
moral values 147, 165–9, 193
mothers, return to work 88–9
music 32, 90, 125, 163–4, 172, 194

nappies 25
National Childbirth Trust (NCT) classes 34, 40–1
natures' seasons
    spring 158–9
    summer 159–60
    autumn 160
    winter 160–3
nightmares 228–9
numbers 135–7, 146, 175, 182–6

one-parent families 196
Open University 179
Orthodontic treatment 181–2

paedophilia 210–1
painting 177, 183
parents
    job sharing 104
    outings 172
parties 139–40, 169, 206
peer groups 203
pethidine in childbirth 41
pets 191
physical
    activities 151
    changes 200
play 95–6, 145
    out-of-doors 215–16
Playgroups and Nursery Schools 96, 124–5, 128, 140–2, 149, 155
potty training 230
poverty 237, 243–5
pre-pregnancy preparation 6–7
pre-school years 130–52
    father's role 149–51

Index

Grandparents 151–2
pregnancy 5–36, 154
  babies
    First month 18–19
    six weeks 19
    ten weeks 20–1
    two months 20
    twelve to thirteen weeks 21–2
    sixteen to eighteen weeks 22
    twenty to twenty-two weeks 24–5
    twenty-eight weeks to seven months 26
    thirty-two weeks 24–5
    thirty-six to forty weeks 27–8
    last day - first day 29
  conversations with unborn baby 32–3
  diet 11–13, 30–1
  hearing babies heart 16
  helping development 30–4
  hospital packing 28–9
  mothers
    first month 19
    six weeks 19
    two months 20
    ten weeks 21
    twelve to thirteen weeks 22
    sixteen to eighteen weeks 22–4
    twenty to twenty-two weeks 25–6
    twenty-eight to seven months 26
    thirty-two weeks 27
    thirty-six to forty weeks 28–9
    last day - first day 30
  practicalities during 30–4
  risks 7–11
  sickness and nausea 15
  signs and symptoms 14–15
  surprise 13–14
  tests 15–16
  twinkle-in-the-eye stage 6

premature babies 223–4, 237
privacy 210
puberty 198, 204

questions 123, 134, 149

reading 146, 191, 207, 238–9
  aloud 127, 182, 193–4
  and writing 136, 175, 182–6
religious festivals 159
rhythms and singing games 61, 98, 114, 129, 157–8
right and wrong 148, 195, 209

safety 90
salmonella 10
saunas 11
school-time
  choosing right school 170–4
  father's role 194–6
  first reactions 173–4
  five to ten years 170–96
  Grandparents' role 194–6
  helping your child's development 172, 193–4
school-work 202
schools, secondary 210–11
security 210
sex
  hormones 200, 204
  jokes 203
sight and hearing 50, 238
  tests 86
sitting up 74, 89
size 223
sleep 201, 209, 227–8
  talking 229
  walking 229–30
smoking in pregnancy 7–8
snacks 207
sociability 200
social and world problems 193
spina bifida 12, 23
spoiling 152
sport 207–8, 225, *see also* exercise
stairs, managing 111, 115, 132

standing up 89
STD (sexually-transmitted diseases) 10
Stephenson, George 239, 244
stories 120, 177
swimming 143–4, 181, 225

talking 73–4, 92, 97–8, 119–20, 122, 126
  delays 232–3
  first words 86–7, 133
  to babies 65
  vocabulary 109
tantrums 107, 117–18, 138, 215
taste, developing a sense of 76
teenage moods 208
teeth
  care 99–10, 147, 191
  permanent 174–5, 181, 204–5
teething 77, 86, 99–100
telephones 207
television 162–3, 178–80, 207
telling the truth 167
TENS apparatus in childbirth 41
Thackeray, William Makepeace 243
thinking and feeling 31–4
throwing 108, 132
toddlers (one to three years) 107–29, 156
  one year 89–94
  fifteen months 107–10
  eighteen months 110–14
  two years 107, 114–19, 166, 229
  everyday skills 120
  three years 122–4, 155, 157, 167
  see also Playgroups and Nursery Schools
toilet training 110, 114, 121–5, 138
  bed-wetting (enuresis) 173, 215, 230–1
  bowel control 122, 231
Tooth Fairy 137, 174, 185
toxoplasmosis 10
toys 79–81, 125, 191
treats 123
trikes 144

ultrasound scans 16, 23
umbilical hernia (outie) 221

vaccinations 9, 78–9
vegetarians 12–13, 201
vitamins 12–13

walking 96–7, 107–8, 232
water births 42
whooping cough 78–9

X-rays 9

Yoga, for pregnant women 35